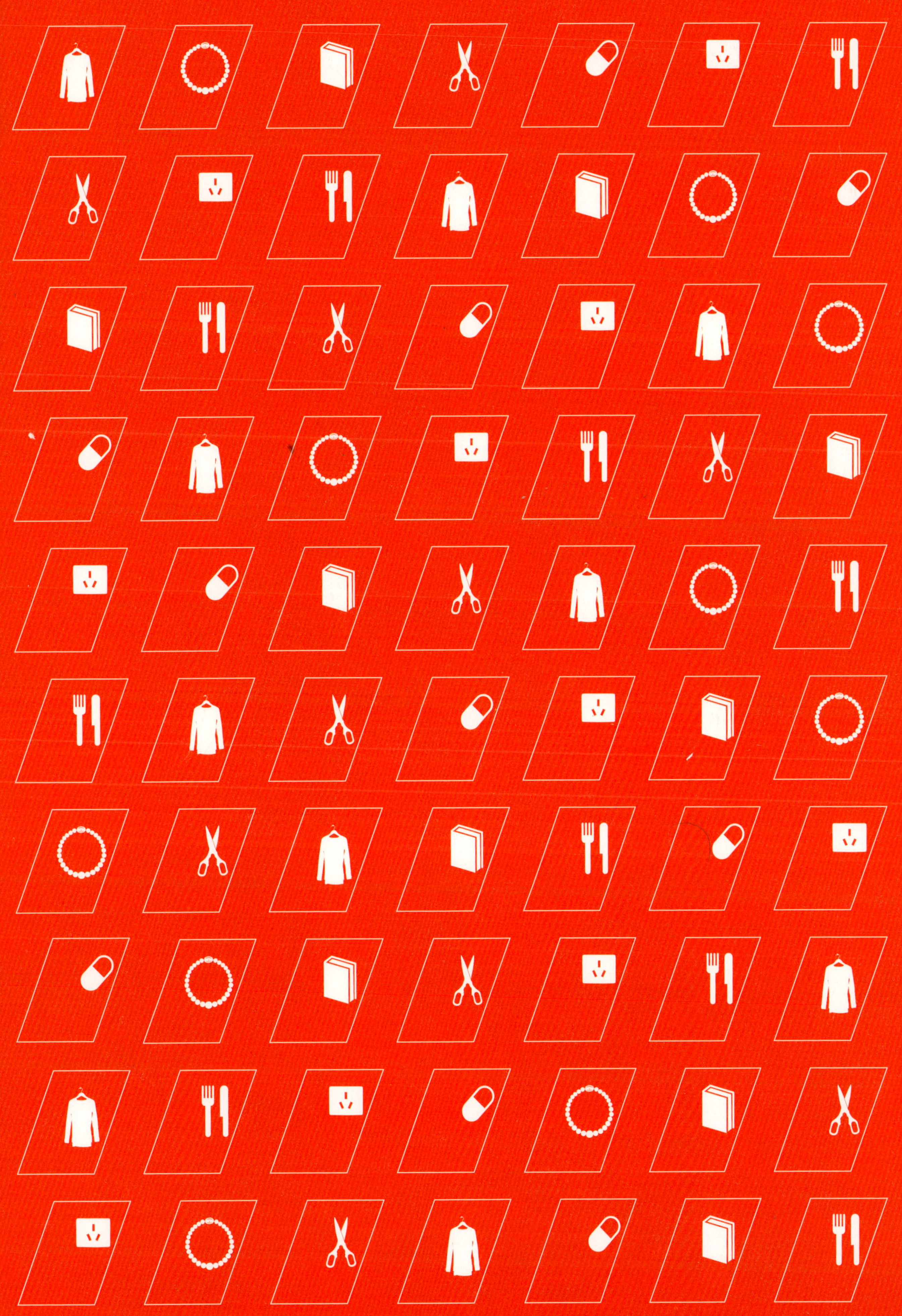

WELCOME
Global Excellent Store Dispiay Design
Copyright©by Sendpoints Publishing Co., Limited

Publisher: Lin Gengli
Editor in Chief: Lin Shijian
Executive Editor: Ellyse,Alice
Design Director: Lin Shijian
Executive Designer: Liu Minting

Address:
RoomC,15/ F Hua Chiao Commercial Centre, 678 Nathan Road, Mongkok,
KI, Hong Kong
Tel: (86)-20-89095121,34108463
Fax: (86)-20-89095206
Email: info@sendpoint.com.cn
Website: www.sendpoint.com.cn

Distributed by
Guangzhou Sendpoints Book Co., Ltd.
Sales Manager: Peng YangHui(China)   Limbo(International)

Guangzhou Tel: (86)-02-89095121
Beijing   Tel: (86)-10-84139071
Shanghai   Tel: (86)-21-63220892
Email: export@sendpoint.com.cn
Website: www.sendpoint.com.cn

ISBN: 978 - 988 - 19610 - 8 - 2

Printed and bound in China

Acknowledgements
I am very grateful to all of the people and companies who have participated in
this book. I would like to thank all of the designers and graphic studios who have
collaborated in this project.

WELCOME

GLOBAL BEST SELECTING STORE DISPLAY DESIGN

PREFACE

We can't live without shopping, shopping for clothes, shoes, bags, watches, books, toys, electrical appliances, glasses, foods, etc. We can find all kinds of shops in our city, in living quarters or in streets, such as large shopping malls, small size stores, excusive shops with character, and so on.

Except the value of goods, another major factor to attract customers is display design of shops. A successful shop display design will attract many customers and improve sales. As a result, we can see modern shop display designs are no longer limited to a place with counter and showcase simply. Designers will make use of more media and latest materials to create the visual display space for specific goods or the style and value of a brand.

With the development of technology, material and market, shop display design become more and more multiple, but the main three basic factors of a shop will not be changed; they are goods, customers and decorations.

First, display of goods. The primary purpose of shop display design is highlight the form and value of goods with appropriate design elements by understanding and seizing the value and character of goods, which let customers get in touch with goods simply, directly and clearly. The considerable elements of designs are the size, shape, color, quantity and style of goods.

Second, customers' behaviors. Generally, when customers walk into a shop, most of them will experience a series of psychological process which starts with "attention", so it requires designers offering plenty of ideas and various expressions to achieve the "attention" effect and stimulate consumer spending.

Third, decoration and application of space. For the same goods, people will always consider that the price of it will higher which is displayed in a better shop than the one in a worse shop. Without disturbing goods, application of every artificial decoration not only can present the style of the shop display design, but also stand out the character of goods. Also, a unique and attractive shop offers a good foundation to win the fierce market competition.

As a professional book for shop display design, "Welcome" is full of excellent shop display designs from all over the world. It will bring you into a variety of shops to spy into the design concept and inspiration of designers and let you know how to use art language, how to collaborate with the client who focuses on quality and design and how to create a design project which satisfies the client.

The shop display designs in this book present the trend of modern shop display design, some are creative store display with visual marketing, and some present their unique styles via structure and lighting. Every works in this book with drawings, full-color photographs and detailed project descriptions will let you know more about these outstanding works and offer you more valuable reading significance.

Thanks every designer and company so much for participating in this book, because of their works, we could offer readers an opportunity for studying, exchanging and sharing.

CONTENT

COSTUME SHOP
013~188

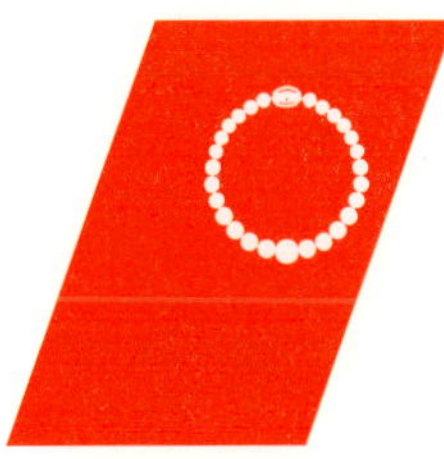

HAIR SHOP

DRUG SHOP

ELECTRICAL APPLIANCE SHOP

RESTAURANT

INDEX

COSTUME SHOP

Size?'s new store located on Bristol's Horsefair uses a concept which takes its inspiration from the locality. The store has an eclectic mix of materials and imagery to depict the heritage and modernity of Bristol. A focal point in the store is an 1824 painting of the fair itself, which is emblazoned across the back wall of the store, whilst around the store mannequins wearing carnival masks reflect the popular attraction of 'freak shows' of this time. Elsewhere we used graffiti style graphics to reflect the present day and the quirky character of the Size? sneaker brand.

A timeless black and white photograph was applied to the storefront, confirming its horsehair location, whilst inside store fixtures and fittings take a traditional wooden crate design with wood grain printed in different colours to provide a contemporary twist.

Company : *Checkland Kindleysides*
Designer : *Checkland Kindleysides*
Photographer : *Keith Parry*
Client : *Size?*
Country : *UK*

TRADE
SWEEPS
CITY
1968 FIRST
ST. PAULS CARNIVAL
SIXTIES
83 SOUND SYSTEM 'THE
IT'S SOUND CLASHES
1998 "WALLS
GRAFFITI JAM
2009 SIZE? OPENS
EUROPEAN
2007 LOCATION
SIZE

HASTLE
what
the horsefair

Marco & Mari in Beijing is a children fashion clothes shop, it is designed as a brand flagship store.

According to the style of the brand, the client demanded for European style designed. Based in this requirement, we chose arch which was determined by the Europe classical architecture as the theme, and mixed with the modern style decoration.

This brand new design idea was from clay art used by children and mellow sculpt looked like cotton candy. The plaster cover on the surface of the arch has closed grain, the texture gives the people a dessert-liked soft feeling.

Our design idea is to mix the power of arch and the loveliness of children clothes brand together.

The arch continuously spread around the store; carry on the symmetry structure of the classical architecture. The central area is for parents and children relax and rest. What the people see is like a pavilion stand in the courtyard. The rest area and main island furniture all repeat the arch and decoration like cotton candy, which is the idea we used to make the whole design style of the store unified.

Company : *Sako Architects*
Designer : *Sako Keiichiro*
Photographer : *Misae Hiromatsu*
Country : *Japan*

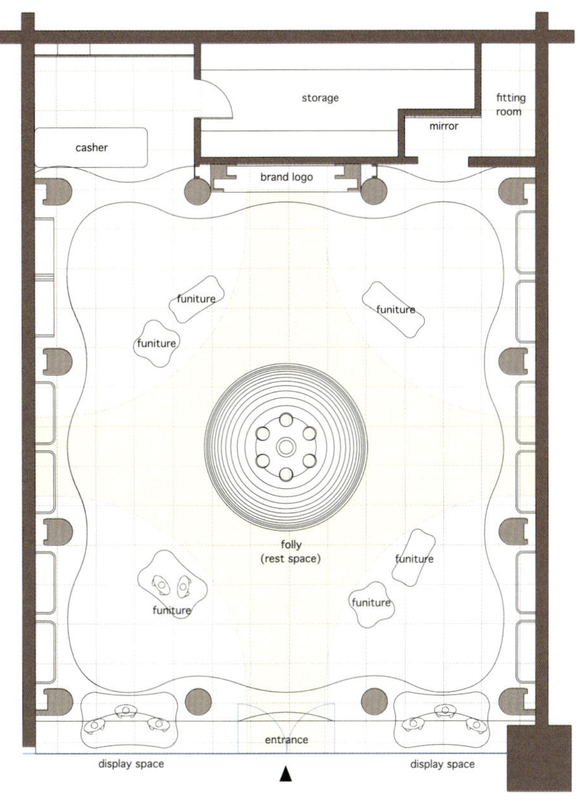

storage
fitting room
casher
mirror
brand logo
funiture
funiture
funiture
folly
(rest space)
funiture
funiture
funiture
display space
entrance
display space

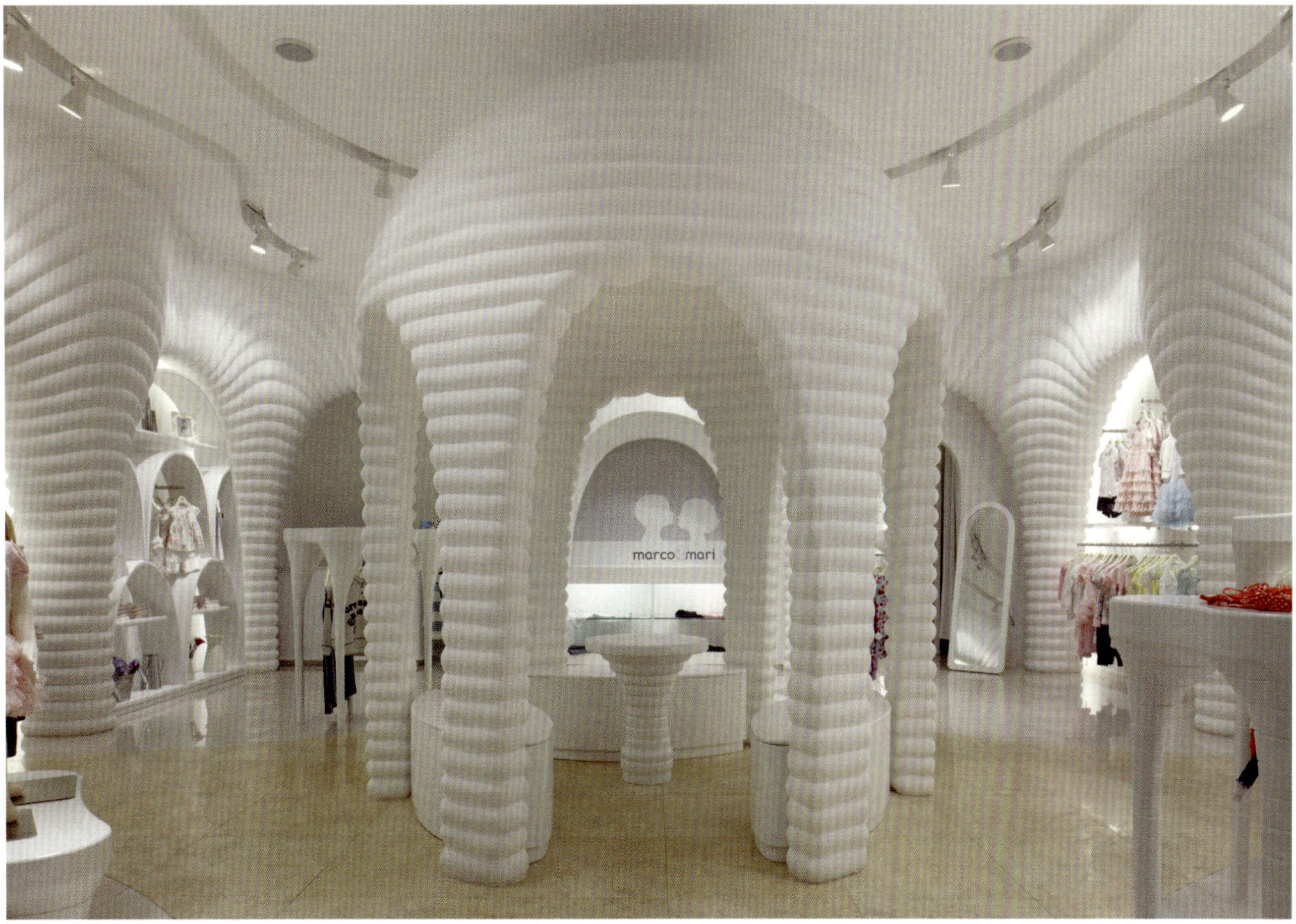

CONVERSE 1HUND (RED)

We worked with Converse on their (RED) campaign to communicate to consumers some of the collaborative charity work that they are involved with. Converse commissioned one hundred artists around the world to customise a pair of Chuck Taylor boots with the (RED) charity in mind.

Each time consumers buy a (RED) product, the company that makes the product donates a percentage of their profits to buy and distribute antiretroviral medicine for AIDS sufferers in Africa. We created a dramatic exhibition which conveyed how Converse's collaboration with artists connects creativity with change. Eye-catching product displays are set against artists' statements expressing their hopes for what the charity might achieve.

We commissioned an illustrator to create a piece of art to support the locality of the exhibition, with cues of St Paul's and the surrounding area. The installation, made entirely from masking tape, extended on to Carnaby Street as part of the exhibition launch event.

Launch material included an opening night invite and catalogue which detailed many of the hand-painted customised shoes along with details of the artists that created them.

Company : *Checkland Kindleysides*
Designer : *Checkland Kindleysides*
Photographer : *Checkland Kindleysides*
Client : *Converse*
Country : *UK*

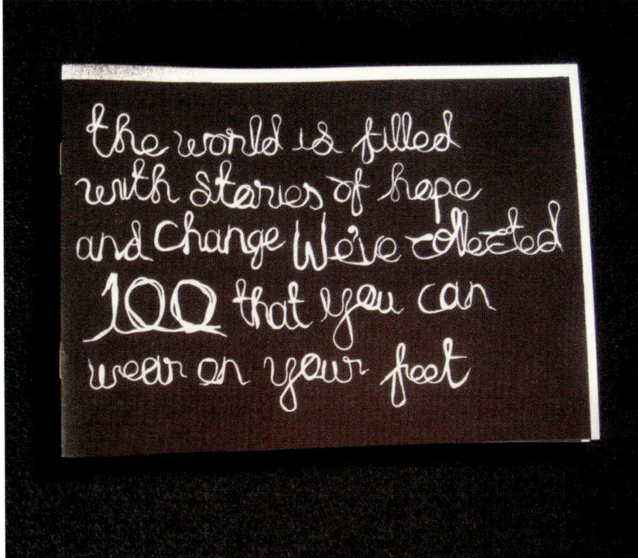

the world is filled
with stories of hope
and change We've collected
100 that you can
wear on your feet

stories of hope and change, and
100 that you can wear on your feet

Converse
ALL STAR
9
(CONVERSE) RED
100 shoes.
100 Artists.
100 visions
for a
better world

As part of the brief for their new store at Westfield London, Timberland challenged CK to bring the brand's iconic tree logo to life and show their environmental values in action. Taking cues from the Timberland logo and the dynamic tree-like roof supports which form the architecture of the centre, we created a lattice of reclaimed timber branches that stretch the full 25m length of the side elevation, the 11m storefront and the 8.5m height of the store, wrapping the store in the brand's iconic logo. The façade creates such a strong brand statement that the fret cut steel signage merely acts as endorsement that this is Timberland.

The structure creates interesting views into the store and the expanse of unusual shaped display windows allow almost every item of footwear to be showcased in a simple framework. While in the windows at the front of the store, displays are set against crafted, repurposed furniture and props.

The 3.5m doors, constructed out of salvaged planks, open wide to flank the entrance and welcome consumers into the store. At the front of the store glass and slate topped display tables showcase the latest footwear and clothing ranges from Timberland. Above, a reclaimed beam allows for intriguing merchandising and lowers the focus in this 4m high store.

The 238m² stores is navigated by gender, signposted with graphic imagery, with womens wear located on the left of the store and menswear to the right. To the centre of the store is the 'community totem' dedicated to telling how Timberland helps and supports community and environmental projects, such as reforestation (over 700,000 trees have been planted so far) and other community activities and projects like 'serv-a-palooza,' earthday. (Timberland's environmental community service day.)

Further along the 'store ingredients' detail the eco-friendly and reclaimed products used to build the store. More than 85% of the materials within the store have served other purposes in a previous life, with salvaged props and wood from reclaimed or sustainable sources used in flooring and merchandising furniture.

The store uses a variety of mid-floor fixtures at different heights including display tables made up of timber stacks with changeable tops as well as different sizes and heights of tables and reclaimed items of furniture, all of which can be mixed and matched and moved around the store to subtly change product displays.

Wooden (paralam) beams overhead draw consumers to the heart of the store and the main footwear display. This area incorporates two feature walls, to the right, clad in Timberland original boot leather, is the curved footwear wall, with the key footwear display, which uses a specially designed display bracket, allowing footwear to be merchandised at any angle, with large scale seasonal graphics depicting the great outdoors.

The 'shoe-lath' wall, which is made up of vintage shoe-laths, set against a hot rolled steel back panel allows for the relaxed and versatile visual merchandising of footwear, clothing and accessories.

As with other stores, local history has been referenced, at the Westfield store historic photography and graphics adorn the walls around the changing rooms, paying homage to the 1908 Olympic stadium that formerly stood on this site. While the walls of the spacious changing rooms are covered in large scale graphics, inviting customers to try on clothes surrounded by trees or snow covered mountains.

Bringing consumers back towards the front of the store is the cash desk with its raw handcrafted feel. The desk is carefully constructed out of layers of timber and leather off - cuts and is set against a backdrop of reclaimed doors.

"This store provides a perfect example of what we stand for as a brand. It reflects our heritage in craftsmanship; our relationship to the outdoors; as well as our environmental values in action. The store front and 'Market Place' interior design represents Timberland's iconic landmark in the retail world"
Ales Kernjak, Timberland, Head of Visual Communications.

Company : *Checkland Kindleysides*
Designer : *Checkland Kindleysides*
Photographer : *Keith Parry*
Client : *Timberland*
Country : *UK*

STOKE PAINTER
STEPH KENT
LEICESTER
HAD THESE
SHOES FOR
10 YEARS

LONDON·1908
DIPLOMA
OF MERIT

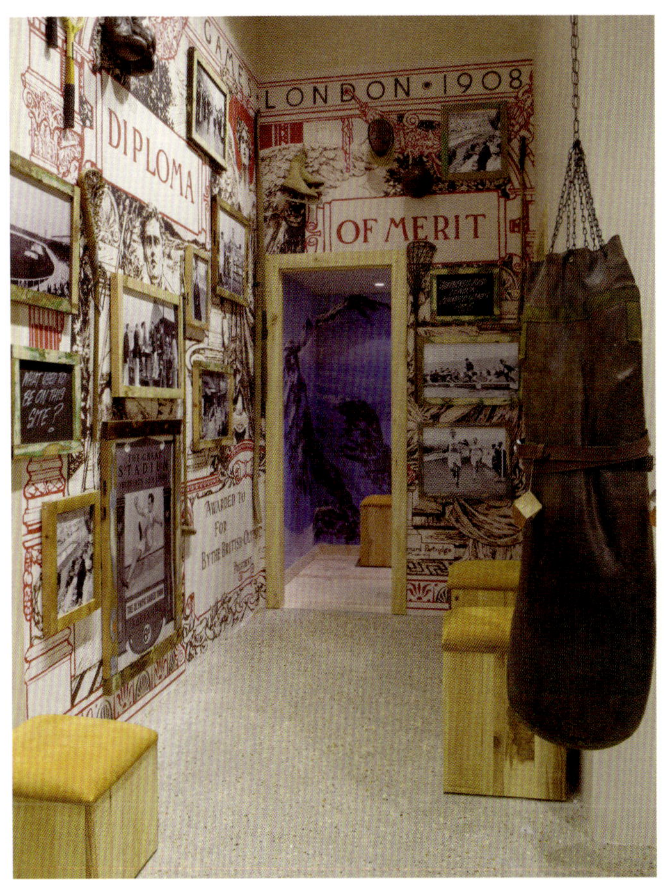

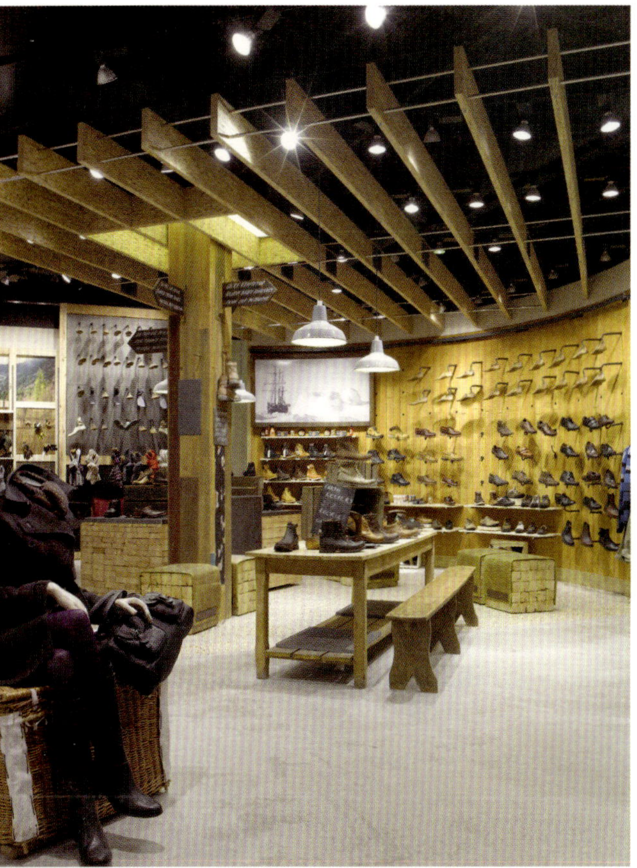

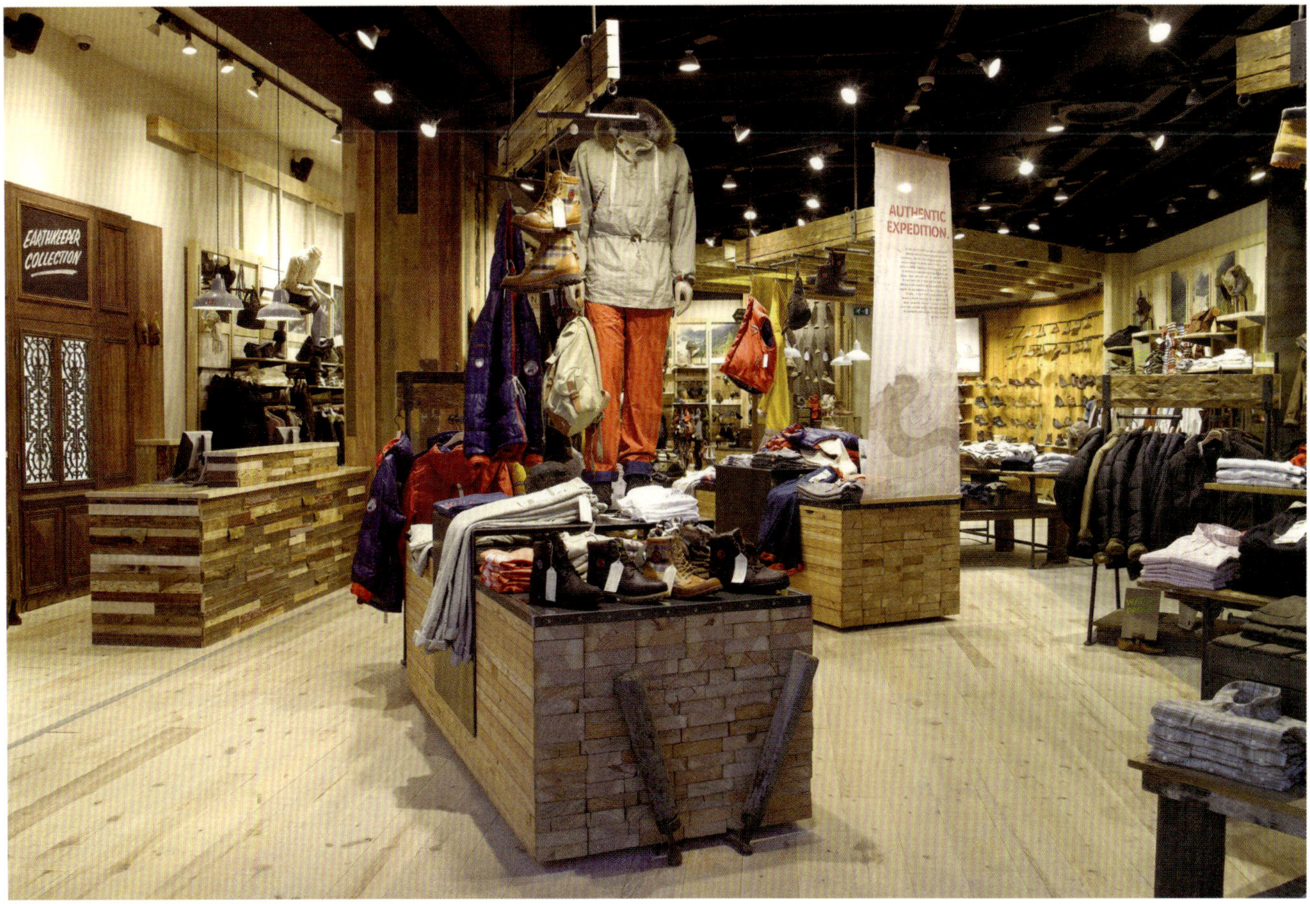
EARTHKEEPER COLLECTION
AUTHENTIC EXPEDITION.

STELLA MCCARTNEY POP-UP

Giles Miller's latest collaboration with Stella McCartney comes in the form of a bold and intriguing pop-up store for the Galleries Lafayette on Boulevard Hausmann in Paris.

The installation includes giant 3-dimensional cardboard letters ranging from 1.5 - 2 metres in height, as well as cubes with fluted patterns in their surfaces and gold-leafed faces.

The pop-up store was designed for the exclusive shopping centre in Paris, and having been shown for 3 weeks, it has now been flown back to the UK and installed in Selfridges on Oxford Street in London, where it will be on show for the next 2 weeks.

Giles Miller and Stella McCartney have collaborated on numerous visual merchandising projects since early 2009 when Giles created an entire wall from corrugated cardboard which incorporated Stella's signature horse pattern hand 'fluted' into the cardboard surfaces.

Other recent projects also include a cardboard martini glass which Giles has designed for luxury drinks brand Bombay Sapphire, and these glasses as well as his corrugated cardboard bar will be on show at the V&A's summer late event on 30th July.

Designer : *Giles Miller*
Photographer : *Richard Corcoran*
Client : *Stella McCartney*
Country : *France*

The Commission was to build a new showroom and office space for the fashion brand Cheap Monday. The client was moving from a cramped space where the staff was scattered out in different rooms so for the new office we wanted to create something a bit more open and fluid where the staff could interact more easily. The new office consists of 900 m² dispersed over two floors. A semi public upper floor which serves as a showroom and reception area and a more private lower floor where the design team sits. The space used to house a brewery so on the upper floor we simply stripped the walls from paint to reveal the existing tiled floors, walls and ceilings. Prior to designing the office we designed a shop in Copenhagen for Cheap Monday so the cloth and light fixtures in the showroom are the ones designed for the shop. On the lower floor we added elements instead of stripping down. Arranged along the facade are a couple of closed office rooms and placed in the middle of the room sits a conference room shaped as a pyramide. The sloping walls allow more light to enter the space and create the notion of an open landscape or terrain where you can sit and work or just take a stroll. Floors and walls are covered with grey needle punch carpet which creates a very good acoustique environment. A new ventilation system was introduced and was allowed to manifest itself in a bright yellow colour in the ceiling. It was also the single biggest cost in the budget. The building time was incredibly short 4-5 weeks.

Company : *Uglycute*
Designer : *Uglycute*
Photographer : *Mikael Olsson*
Country : *Sweden*

Dear Design, the team behind the project, has designed a light, open space to exhibit the brand's shoes. The main idea is to immerse visitors in the Arena (understood as a stadium), a space flooded with light framed by a hanging metal structure. Visitors enter the store from the street, from chaos to an organised space.

The Arena is shaped by the metal structure, a second skin that surrounds the existing container without touching it and also serves to exhibit the shoes.

The structure's fractal design is based on infinitely repeated Xs, the brand's symbol, down to the last detail: the supports, the backstitching on the skin on the bench and the counter, and the system of catches – always performing different functions.

Each hole in the structure allows for easy access to the exhibited product, highlighted by the use of white. This is the main element on this stage, where visitors are the leading actors.

The simplicity to this project lies in saving materials – only sheets of glossy white lacquered iron for the perimeter structure, Corian for the lettering, a Barrisol stretched ceiling for lighting, natural iron for the joinery, white polyurethane resin with glossy varnished finish for the floor, and white skin and iron sheets for the furniture.

Company : *Deardesign*
Designer : *Deardesign*
Client : *Munich*
Country : *Spain*

New York based architect and interior designer Rafael de Cárdenas has designed Nike Sportswear's STADIUM NYC, which coincides with the summer celebration of the FIFA World Cup. De Cárdenas collaborated with Nike to create a space where visitors can experience product, design, and innovation, combined with the worlds of film, photography, art and music.

In the retail space, pegboard, a utilitarian commodity, is highly worked to elaborate effect and immerses patrons in a field often overlooked as a defining pattern of commerce. De Cárdenas often employs everyday materials in his conceptual design propositions.

The main event space is designed to perform multiple functions. Polygonal modular cells dispersed throughout move and change like players on a field under a directional, pitch-like pattern of linear florescents. The arrangement of the cells according to event creates micro-spaces within the larger context to enable installation art, games, or other purposes.

Says de Cárdenas: "We began with a soccer field as a visual start and rotated, revolved and replicated it until we eventually came up with a unique pattern made of directional lines. We then applied this pattern to the floor to give it the dynamism of a sports/football field. The design allows people to move the triangular shapes and customize their own experience at stadium."

From architecture to the visual arts and event programming, STADIUM NYC will continue to look to various artistic partners to deliver creative expressions of soccer throughout the summer and into fall 2010.

Company : *Architecture At Large*
Photographer : *Allen Benedikt*
Country : *U.S.A*

Sigrun Woehr is the premier address for high-end footwear in the state of Baden-Württemberg. In 2003 we realised the Sigrun Woehr flagship store for our client in Stuttgart. We were now commissioned to develop an interior for the second Sigrun Woehr shop in Karlsruhe. This shop marks a new departure for Sigrun Woehr as she expands her range to include a new line of fashion and accessories. The new store was to be housed in a shop space in the city centre, which has a narrow floor plan stretching back almost 25m into the building. Our task was to create a spatial situation in which to present an exclusive range of goods, while at the same time enticing customers across the threshold.

The ceiling of the space was specially designed to make a strong initial impact. The ceiling is gradually lowered over the entire length of the shop towards the rear wall. This gives the room a more dynamic feel and creates a kind of section pull into the space. Three circular ceiling motifs executed in an elegant and fashionable palette of violet, fuchsia and pale pink tones create attractive focal points and draw the customer's gaze towards the far rear of the space.

A dark-stained, oak parquet floor, which creates a continuous, flowing expanse throughout the space, provides a powerful contrast to the ceiling. Solitary fittings are staged at intervals against this background, each accompanied by a colourful ceiling graphic above. Positioned in the centre of the room, each element forms the core of one of three zones into which the room is divided. Different geometric shapes were deliberately chosen for the individual elements. An amorphous central display unit in the entrance area gives a striking upbeat to the collection. Its unusual form also serves to draw curious customers into the space. The next area is introduced by the cash desk unit. Layered rectangles create a mobile effect and harbour space for glass presentation cabinets. The cash desk unit faces an ensemble of round tables. The varying heights, sizes, and surface materials of the tables – some are mirrored, others made from glass or steel – create a second attractive presentation area. The third area is denoted by two features in the centre of the room. Two supporting columns are concealed in the frame of a free-standing shelving unit containing presentation segments of varying dimensions, thanks to flexible, black separators. The shelving unit is grouped together with a polygon seating element, which also functions as a communication island.

The walls enclosing these three zones are executed in grey and beige. White presentation shelving and niches are either recessed in the walls or superimposed against a recessed wall. An optimal lighting scheme results in immaculate presentation of all the goods on display.

A separate department was created for the new, high-class fashion line in the far rear of the store. This separate area is introduced by two mannequins positioned in front of a backdrop of a concertinaed, smoky glass wall. The glass concertina visually divides the space and the smokiness of the glass acts as a translucent filter. A circle of mirror film designed as an incised lattice reflects the concentric circles of the ceilings cape. The area itself is dominated by a large, oval table that stands on a plush, pink carpet. The ceiling above the table is recessed and mirrored. Four textile lamps mounted on projecting arms emit from this opening and span the entire space. The enclosing walls of this area are covered in a champagne-coloured wallpaper with crocodile leather texture, creating a stylish backdrop to the ascetic, suspended, steel clothing rails.

The Sigrun Woehr Karlsruhe store successfully exploits a difficult floor plan using striking fittings and strong ceiling motifs to demarcate separate zones. The presentation of goods is accomplished by means of a dynamic wall design, supplemented by highlighted presentation areas and core elements in the centre of the room. The new fashion line is presented within a dedicated area that strikes a distinct visual note and yet is incorporated into the overall concept in a compelling and coherent manner.

Designers : *Peter Ippolito, Gunter Fleitz, Silke Hoffmann, Judy Hänel, Britta Kleweken*

Photographer : *Zooey Braun*

Clients : *Sigrun Woehr, Karlsruhe*

Country : *Germany*

The Hirshleifer's shoe store in Manhasset New York, completed in December 2009, is a subtle reference and an homage to the world of art and design history, mainly Italian and American.

It is indeed a space where references and memories happen in a metaphysical way and are not entirely visible at first sight, a place for a dialogue between two opposite texts: the first is minimalist, rigorous and precise, alluding to the art of several American figures such as Sol LeWitt, Carl Andre or Donald Judd in its physicality and spirituality; the second is a reference to the rich, sensual, decadent, unpredictable and free world of the Radical Design groups that changed the course of design in Italy from the late sixties to the eighties.

Sergio Mannino negotiates masterfully between the tendencies of each "text" - style – to create surprising effects that contain continuity within the contradictions.

Space and timing are experienced through a proscenium of subtle humor and strict precision.

The rigorous formalism of the minimalists (whose formal precision is also easily found in the obsessive care for the details typical of the Italian culture) is challenged by "folies", unexpected elements winking at you from some other world: a glass case sitting on a sofa (a reference to a 1967 piece by Italian Architect Gio Ponti); a neon sculpture gently curved but burning in white artificial light (another reference to the Italian art world of the sixties, this time, Lucio Fontana's Concetti Spaziali); a bloody red wall that sets the backdrop of the scene. As in a theater nothing in the store is real or natural: the floor has woodgrain but is made of ceramic tiles; the Fjord red stones by Moroso are soft and upholstered in fabric and leather; the biomorphic and the geometric shapes in the space are embedded in heavy, shiny lacquers or neon lighting, yet the result is noisy silence, indeed a statement.

Company : *Sergio Mannino Studio*
Designers : *Sergio Mannino, Garnet Spagrud,*
Francesco Bruni,
Francesca Scalettaris
Photographer : *Massimiliano Bolzonella*
Country : *U.S.A*

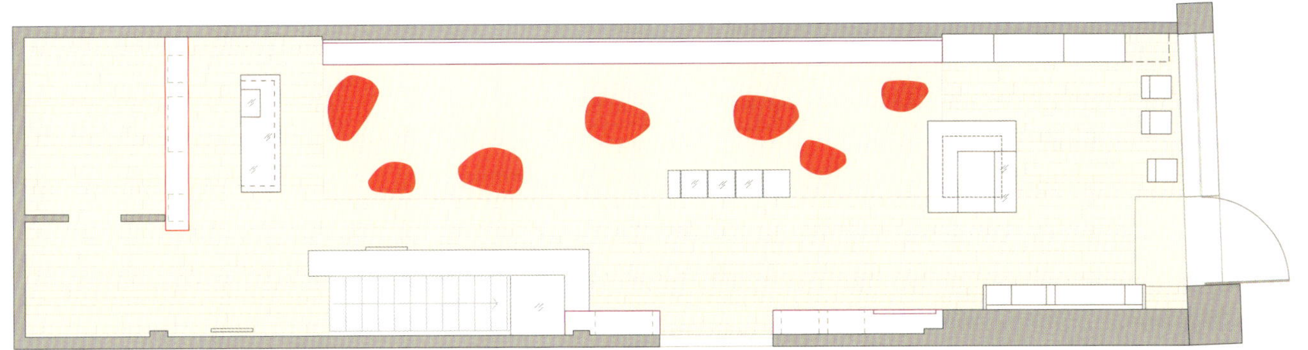

To interpret small spaces is able to result simple but of sure to combine the demands of a showroom it implies a notable it trains.

Studio Uno Design, a group formed by two Tuscan designers, has the worth to have realized a rational project but delicious and to the functional meantime for the solos 15 available metriquadris, based on the impassioned planning for the beautiful things.

MONTECARLO appears as a small bright pearl in the historical heart of the town.

Still before crossing the threshold of the shop it is perceived the wealth of the details, in fact, the small showcase assembles the whole stylistic essence that and contained to the inside.

The use of the paper from protected and of the mirrors to magnify the space with the chandeliers of diamonds shows that the small spaces can result well anymore also generous, if the objects are projected with care to satisfy every thing around it.

The final product transmits a notable cleaning of the forms enriched by details that they alternate him between the innocence of the white and the audacity of the finish gold and they go him to combine in a only homogeneous subject qaule the resin of the flooring.

The idea and the objects that surround us are the essential elements: light and reflexes are the synthesis that you/they constantly edge us.

Company : *Uno Design*
Designer : *Uno Design*
Country : *Italy*

MONTECARLO

RICHMOND

The vision for this store was to create an environment where customers could immerse themselves in the pioneering spirit of Levi's®. Located in the heart of Berlin, the store has a striking façade of arched windows, spanning the full three storey height of the store.

We wanted to create a space where Levi's® relationships with artists, musicians and film makers could be nurtured, generating a youthful mix of global and local creativity. It is this freshness and integrity that will make Levi's® Berlin a destination.

The ground and the first floors are small spaces for such a grand façade, but these open out to a spacious second floor.

A beautiful curved staircase was installed creating a central feature and journey between the floors. This is set against a graphic backdrop, displaying a timeline with imagery from its early roots to the present day.

On the ground floor is a gallery where the 'newness' and 'innovation' of Levi's® products can be displayed, along with the work of local artists, musicians and film makers. Levi's® Blue is then presented on the first floor, here simple white fixtures display the range with clarity, with feature garments in burnt orange punctuating the space.

On the second floor we created a series of rooms for customers to explore. Firstly a space dedicated to the most celebrated jean ever, Levi's® 501™, then a larger area for more mainstream lines. A denim 'vault' with three metre high vaults, presents the most collectable apparel sourced from the Levi's® markets around the world, making it a Mecca for denim aficionados. Assisting staff are like 'curators', with an expert knowledge of Levi's® helping customers discover more, and become passionate, even obsessive about the brand. 'Invited' customers are shown a secret doorway within one of the vaults which leads to a hidden room, with a leather floor and mahogany style cupboards, where the rarest of products are locked away… denim heaven.

The store expresses the different personalities of the brand, creating a strong definitive area for each, sympathetically brought together to create the ultimate expression of Levi's®.

Company : *Checkland Kindleysides*
Designer : *Checkland Kindleysides*
Photographer : *Daniel Grund*
Client : Levi's®
Country : *UK*

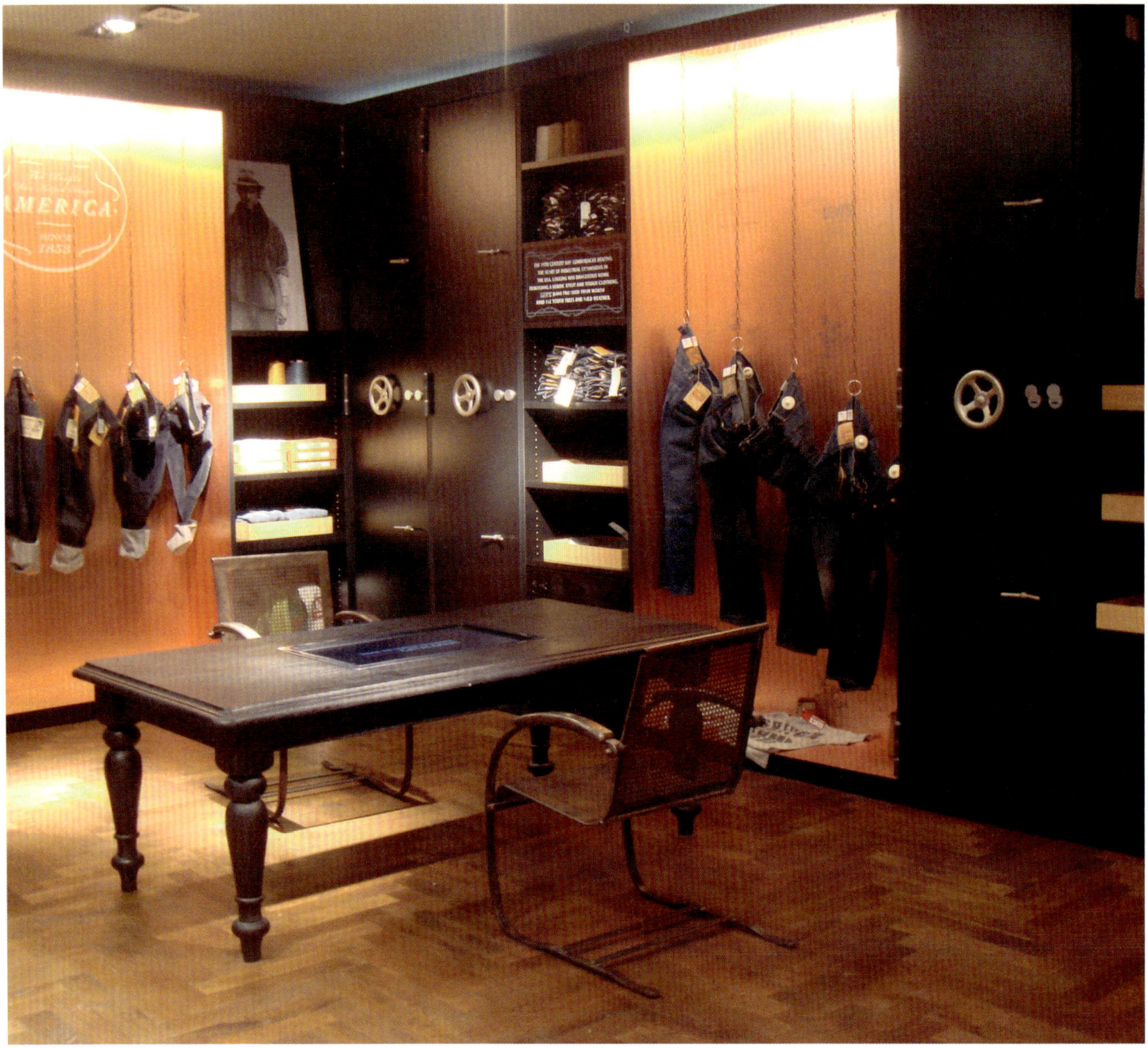

Levi's
Levi's
Levi's
Levi's

NEW FLAGSHIP STORE FOR LEVI'S® ON REGENT STREET

The store is designed as a journey through an artisan's working environment and starts as you step off the street into a 'courtyard', an area which is crafted to feel like an open, exhibition like space. With a whitewashed ceiling and reclaimed brick walls it provides a light and airy entrance to the store. This transition space is called 'Origin' and forms the opening 80sqm of the store. The space is reserved purely for curation of craft, and is designed to create a vibrant, engaging and creative experience of the world of Levi's®, 'Origin' will showcase everything from exclusive product collaborations to art exhibitions providing a level of intrigue and impact unique to fashion retailing. It serves to highlight new and innovative product whilst capturing the imagination and making a connection between youthful creativity and the workplace of the artisan, compelling visitors to explore further. Through two sets of huge factory doors, visitors enter the main body of the store where latest collections will be displayed. There is a clean and industrial look and feel, reflective of a workshop or factory. It's deliberately purposeful and real, meaningfully designed to be robust and with function. Furniture and fixtures are therefore designed to be simple, functional and flexible; this is a constantly changing and busy vibrant environment. It's where newness is brought to the fore and expressed. It's abundant with product, but also spacious and well defined.

The design of the central floor displays provide a contemporary execution of haberdasher's counter, yet the materials and method of construction: a metal framework, with a cream stove enamelled finish and Georgian wired glass panels, provide an industrial twist.

Company : *Checkland Kindleysides*
Designer : *Checkland Kindleysides*
Photographer : *Keith Parry*
Client : *Levi's®*
Country : *UK*

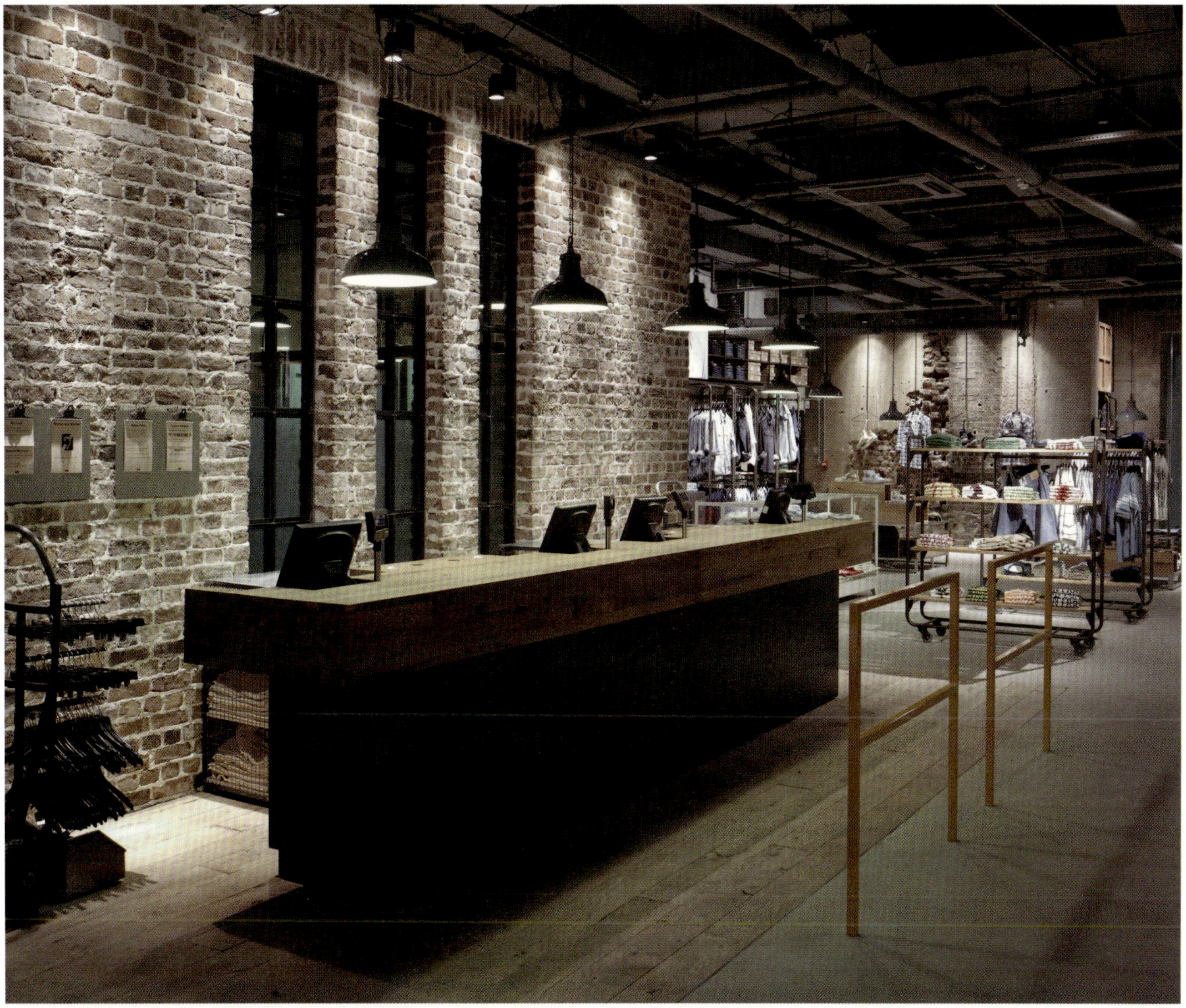

B
D
B1
C1
D1
B2
C2
D2
B3
D3
C3
B4
B5
D4
E4

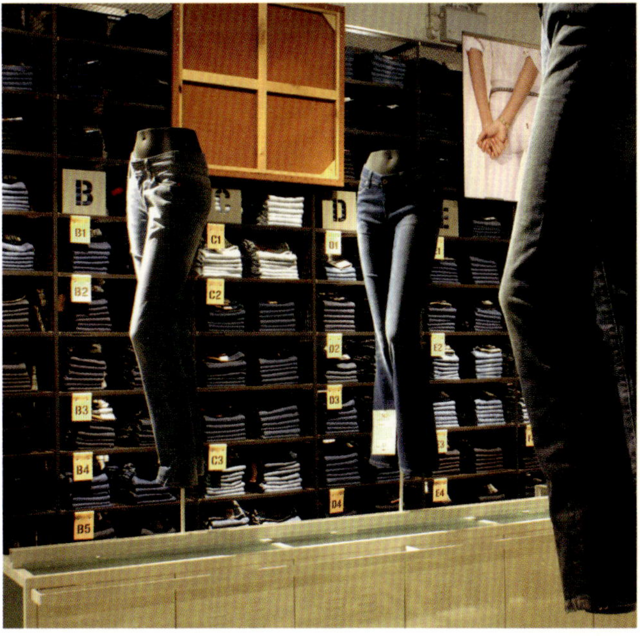

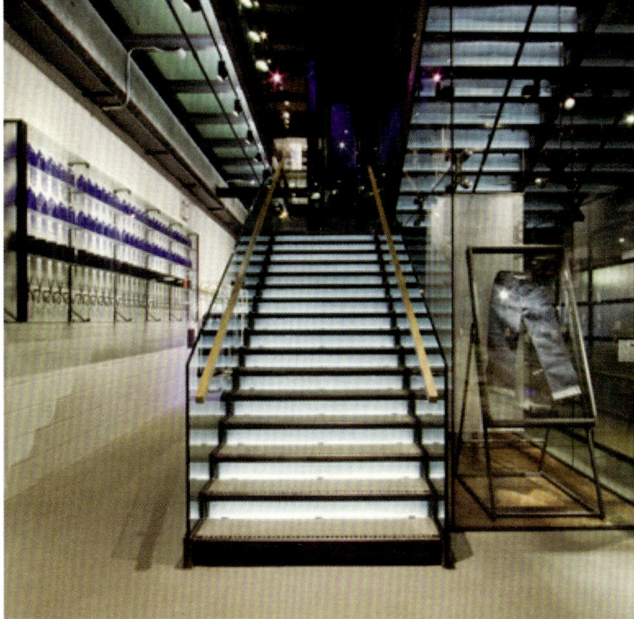

Creation of "Gigalove" brand, communication and the space of the first store.

The idea was to create a store in a commercial mall challenging the space limits and usual languages, imagining to work in a pre-existing environments with pre-existing elements.

The space is divided in 2 parts, main frontal one for the large sale counter, display area, tile wall, and fake "pre-existing" staircase and doors; the rear space defined by the different window (two layers of glass with acrylic cylinders inside) hosts a tall "bookshelf for products and 3 changing rooms, each of it covered in a different tartan fabric.

The passage area has a light ceiling with display hooks and 2 facing mirrored walls creating an infinity "elevator" effect.

The display system is mainly resolved with the creation of metal green "trolleys" pierced with different shapes holes including a heart shaped one. Different accessories can be hung to the trolleys (hanging tube, shelves, hooks…)

A long (8 m.) wall is covered with standard white tiles printed in tones of blue and representing symbols and themes linked to the city where the shop is located and becoming in any of the future shops the identifying and changing element.

The hexagonal sale counter and its suspended "hat" completely covered with mirror panels and works like a sort of kaleidoscope hosting 6 large music speakers.

The floor made in industrial wood stripes is aged and painted in a rough way and the floor to ceiling glass window solution typical of commercial galleries is avoided adopting 2 black metal fascias framing the view inside.

The acrylic cylinders window makes the inside invisible when passing by and it reveals the interior only through a 90 degrees point of view.

Different language layers and decorative expedients challenging the rules of mass distribution to offer wearing apparel for a teenagers audience.

Company : *Antonio Gardoni Studio*
Creative Director : *Antonio Gardoni*
Designer : *Antonio Gardoni*
Photographer : *Antonio Gardoni*
Client : *Eurosport*
Country : *Italy*

GIGALOVE
GIGALOVE

GIGALOVE
GIGAL

gigalove
ALLYOUN SGIGALOVE

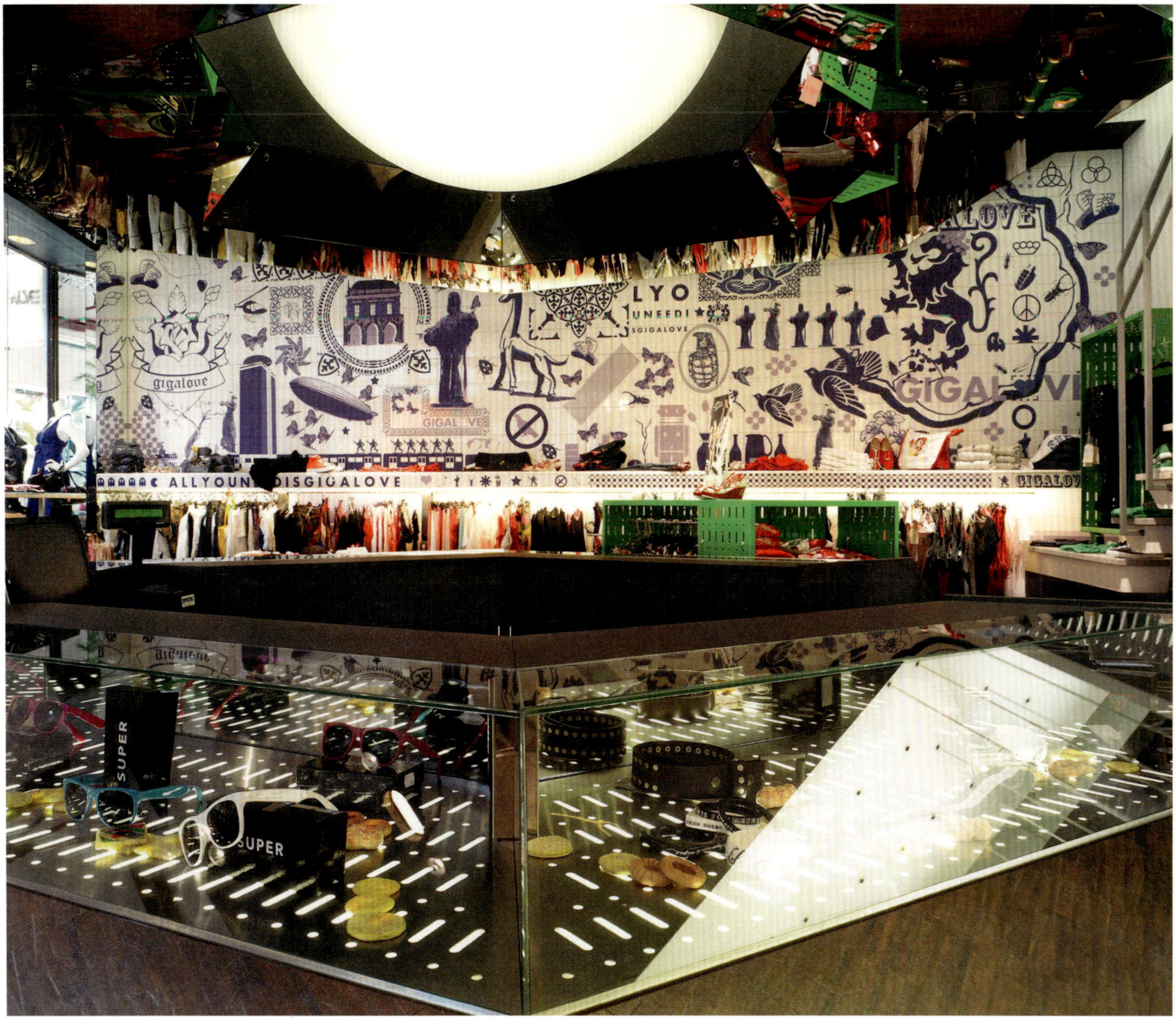

"Nothing is lost, nothing is created, everything is transformed."

The project's brief was to create a temporary store aimed to guest different typologies of products on a rotation base, in a way the purpose was to sell everything: clothes, accessories, home decorations, guitars, hats, books...The project's location was a large empty space in an outlet village on the skirting board of Brescia.

How to display the possible products without knowing their characteristics and identity was the main issue to be resolved and the whole final project is deeply shaped by this problem.

The absence of product's identity is transformed in a floor to ceiling surface painted in a common grey colour revealing trough many different opening systems a yellow pop interior.

Door's hinges, sliding guides, pivoting systems, counterweighted panel, accordion doors, roller blinds and drawers are only few of the tricks used to transform grey into light to reveal countless and flexible display opportunities.

The introduction of video and led panels is done to support the continuously changeable in-store communication, together with a series of fluorescent tubes that can be switched on and off to create writing.

A series of trolleys with different dimensions and possible accessories (hanging tubes / shelves) can be used to occupy the central space and when not in use they can be stored in the small back stockroom.

Outside a large movie-screen signage is the support to inform about the temporary hosted commercial activity and in a side window a board with repositionable numbers becomes the "countdown" for the days missing to the closedown.

"Goods" is a project that plays with common, almost banal elements and with the typical stereotypes of the retail's world, creating a precarious and slightly disturbing space.

Company : *Antonio Gardoni Studio*
Creative Director : *Antonio Gardoni*
Designer : *Antonio Gardoni*
Photographer : *Antonio Gardoni*
Client : *Ascom*
Country : *Italy*

The latest V2K store design is one of a kind. Located in the centre of Istanbul's classiest shopping district, a striking angular entrance welcomes visitors to browse designer pieces by top brands from all over the world. A large angular column reaches up and passes a mezzanine floor, creating an impressive space at the entrance to the store, while a gridlike wall of lightbulbs down the side of the store provides a powerful banner for slogans which can be modified as desired.

Company : *Autoban*
Photographer : *Ali Bekman*
Country : *Turkey*

VAKKO NISANTASI

Vakko's flagship store stands to represent the true identity of the country's finest luxury brand. Autoban rose to the challenge by choosing luxurious materials and customised seating throughout the five floors of the store. Inspired by the swirling Vakko logo, a lamp with a similarly curved lampshade was produced specially for the project, while sleek and simple embedded patterns were introduced along the internal surfaces, adding to the luxurious element of the overall experience.

Company : *Autoban*
Photographer : *Ali Bekman*
Country : *Turkey*

DOUBLE OO'09"The double curve" - The shop spaces formed with two curves. One big curve expands obliquely into the inside considering the view from a street in front and the movement line and another gentle curve of the ceiling link in three dimensions. First, I analyzed the given environment
(the arrangement of the construction to the front street and the site). Then, I thought that the space construction should be intelligent, mysterious and deep to lead the movement lines into the store, with a glance of people who pass the street would be naturally drawn to the store. Therefore, I used these two curves together, one is the wall curve expanding from the outside and the other one is the ceiling curve like a cave. Then I studied deliberately how to tie and organize these shapes.

Company : *Case-Real*
Designer : *Koichi Futatsumata*
Photographer : *Hiroshi Mizusaki*
Client : *Alohanine*
Country : *Japan*

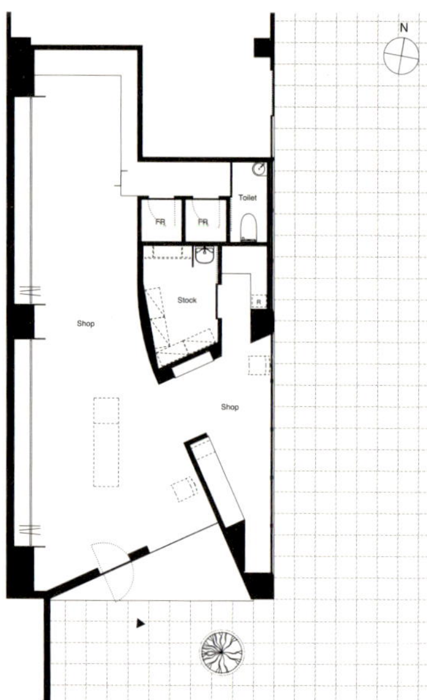

DOUBLE OO'96 "White beams" - There is a small two-storied house which was built a half century ago. And about 40 years ago, a wooden hut with a gable roof was extended on the terrace of the house. The project was to make the hut on the terrace into an office & showroom. The terrace had been extended without any plans for 40 years, and unplanned big and small frames, such as beams, pillars and bunches were running in the air. At first, I took it very negatively. But when I looked at it from a different position, I realized that it could be a unique object. After giving moderate reinforcement, I did a thorough space arrangement by covering all the surfaces, such as floors, walls and garrets with gray painted flooring materials in symmetry. Now only the white painted frameworks run in the air inside of the shape of this gable roof hut. This is a garret office & showroom where only the history of the hut itself and the clothes come to the surface.

Company : *Case-Real*
Designer : *Koichi Futatsumata*
Photographer : *Hiroshi Mizusaki*
Client : *Alohanine*
Country : *Japan*

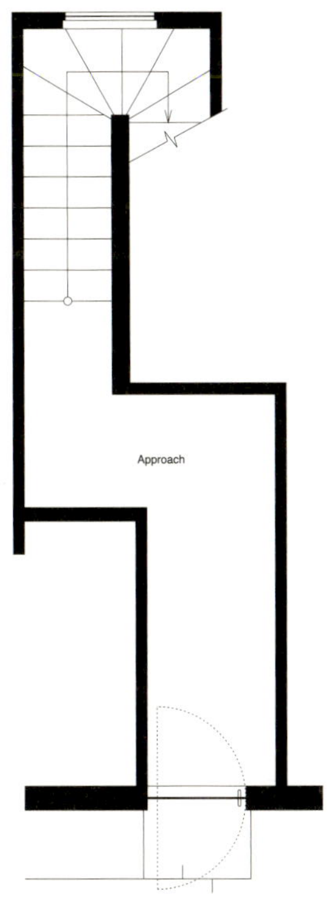
Approach
1st floor plan

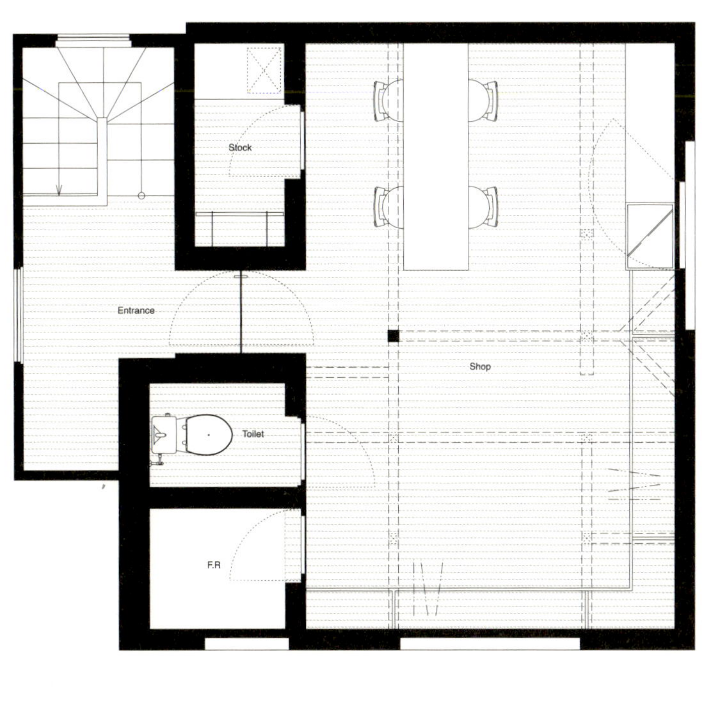
Stock
Entrance
Toilet
F.R
Shop
N
2nd floor plan
0   0.5   1   2M

"A boutique that pursues a memory" - A project to convert a thirty-year-old-zipper factory building into a West Japan maximum level boutique in a residential area about two train stations away from downtown Fukuoka City. The inside, on the first floor I moderately arranged the space by retaining rough and strong factory details and I left as much as possible as there was in the factory of the existing to restore the floor. To take over the memory of a building that has existed in the region for years and to take a part as a new icon in itself, the outline of the building is covered by vines, not renewing its externals. Now a newborn, high fashion boutique covered by green is standing, coming to fit in the region like the green in the park and the trees on the street. Time may give the next value to this building.

Company : *Case-Real*
Designer : *Koichi Futatsumata*
Photographer : *Hiroshi Mizusaki*
Client : *Minorityrev*
Country : *Japan*

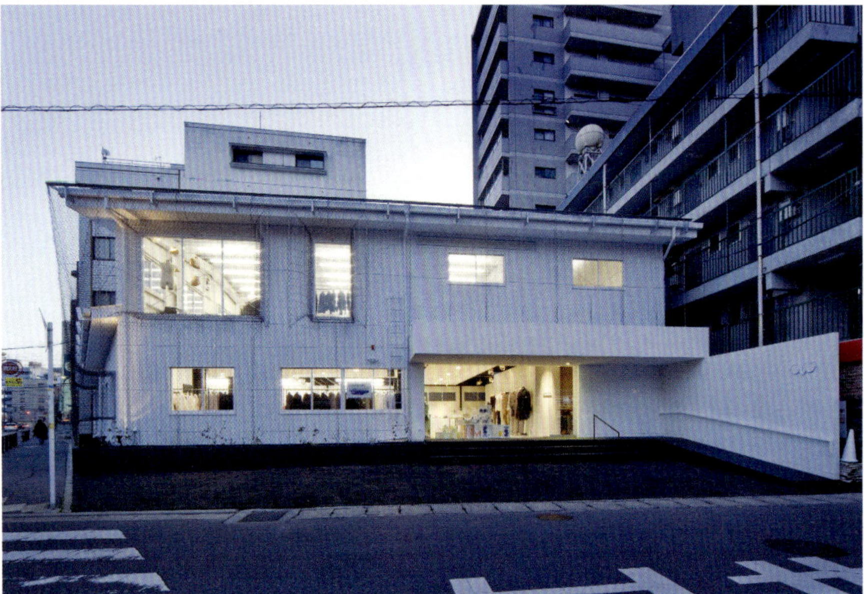

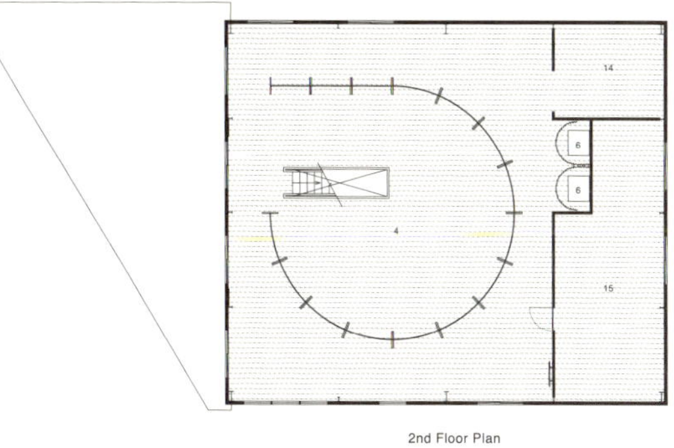

2nd Floor Plan

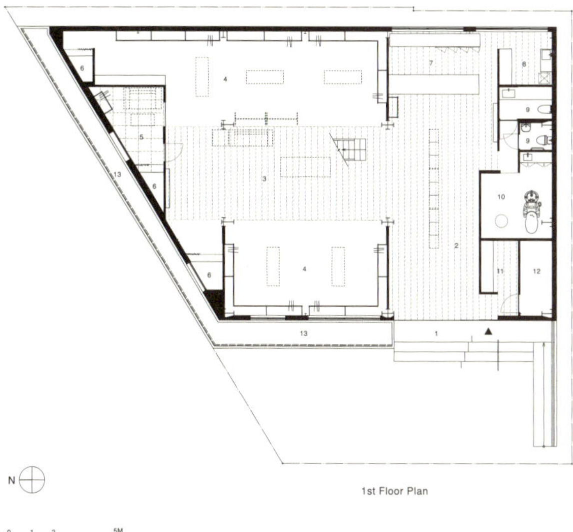

N

1st Floor Plan

0 1 2   5M

LURDES BERGADA & SYNGMAN CUCALA

A Contrasted Space, this is the new creation of Deardesign studio from Barcelona. The new flagship store from Lurdes Bergada, Syngman Cucala, is now installed in one of the best shopping malls in the city centre, L'Illa Diagonal. Deardesign's challenge, is to follow its exploration of a new vocabulary, a research on new architectural codes in retail's universe. The store is divided into two clearly defined areas which, on the one hand, link every technical aspect of a clothes store behind a "wooden skin" and on the other hand, keep clothes as the main focus. The project seeks to preserve the common characteristics of Lurdes Bergada, Syngman Cucala's existing spaces: industrial, different and minimalistic, adding a touch of the contemporary in its architecture. The principal idea was to open the space and allow a view onto the shopping mall's park. This would give clients the sensation of shopping in a space full of natural light, as though they were in a street store. Here Deardesign apply the main philosophy defined by l'Illa Diagonal Mall, interpreting the act of buying in a mall as a "shopping avenue". The park is another decorative piece of the interior. From the park the back façade attract clients in the same commercial way as the interior facade of the shopping centre. Therefore the design team decided to bring together all the technical functions of the store (storage, fitting rooms, electrical quarter, and a 2nd small window) in a huge unique wood structure made from 1000 pieces of wood and put together with 2400 screws. The wooden skin allows all large structures to be hidden, therefore leaving the roof clear. From it's interior, the "skin" reveals to visitors all of its extremely technical constructive secrets, bringing to mind fabric, turn-ups, stitching, etc... This reflects the real importance of technicist in clothes making and enhancing the concepts transmitted by the brand: simplicity, purity, and industry. The installation made of irregular triangles appears rocklike, a contemporary cave. The natural beechwood stands in contrast with the opposite wall, made of concrete. Each triangle is unique and numbered to make the construction easier. Most existing stores of the brand preserve traces of the history of the buildings in which they are installed. The aim of the project is to respect the original context and to re-enforce the industrial characteristics of the building. Basic materials such as concrete for the walls and fine cement on the floor are used. These simple materials simplify the architectural reading of the store and strengthen the concept. Lurdes Bergada and his son Syngman Cucala are well known for the functionality and high quality clothes they design for women and men. The brand is present in spanish market until 1978, when they open their first store. Syngman Cucala is represented internationally in multi-brands stores all over the world, France, Italy, Belgium, Great Britain, Russia, Japan, and United States. With this ultimate launch store in l'illa Diagonal, Barcelona, the brand considers reinforce its capacity to renew constantly itself, and follow avant-guarde in retail and design.

Company : *Deardesign*
Client : *Lurdes Bergada & Syngman Cucala*
Country : *Spain*

SYNGMAN CUCALA
LURDES BERGADA
SYNGMAN CUCALA

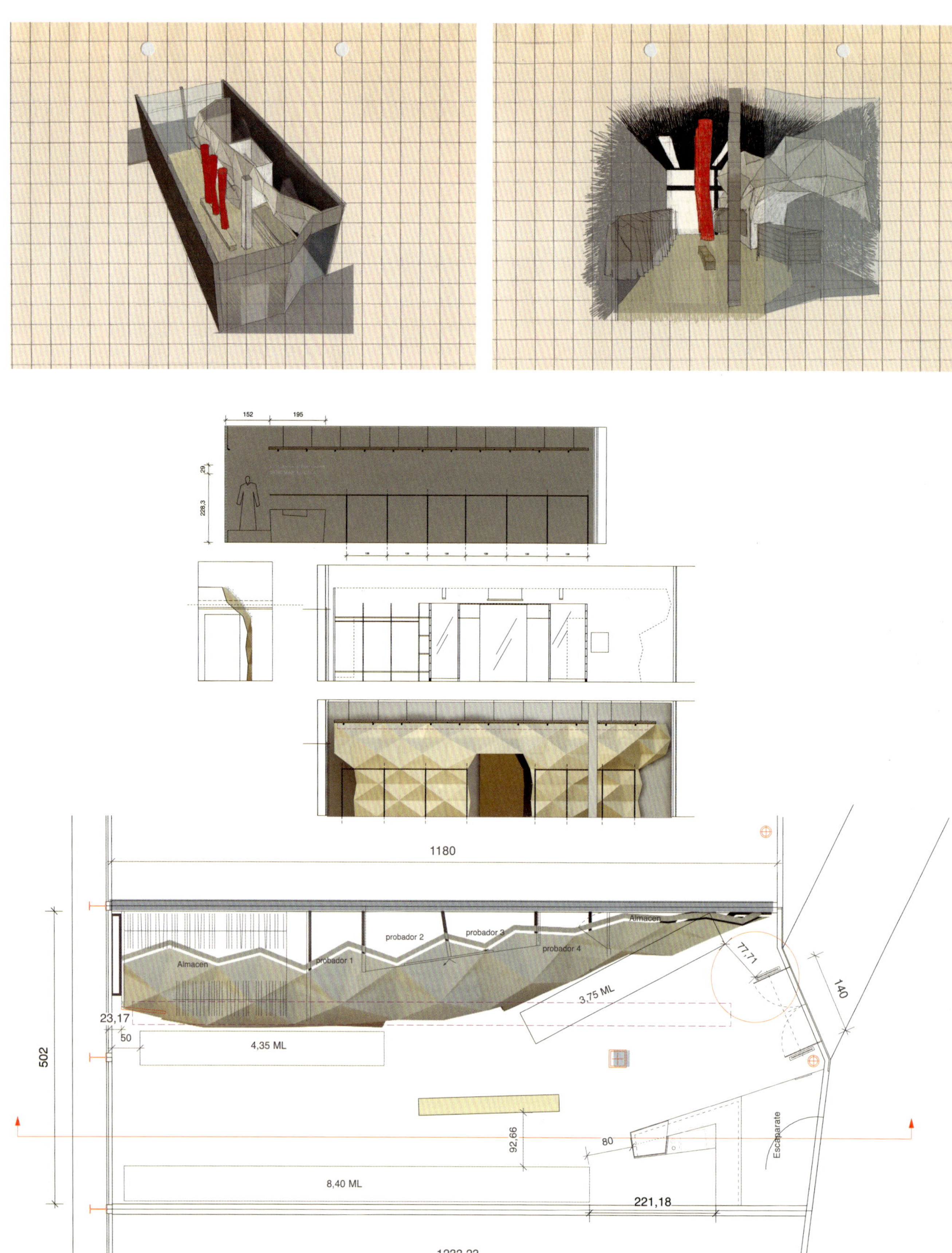

152
195
29
228,3
1180
probador 2
probador 3
probador 1
probador 4
Almacen
Almacen
77,71
3,75 ML
140
23,17
50
4,35 ML
502
92,66
80
Escaparate
8,40 ML
221,18
1233,23

LURDES BERGADA
SYNGMAN CUCALA

LURDES BERGADA
SYNGMAN CUCALA

DIEGUEZ FRIDMAN ARQUITECTOS & ASOCIADOS

The project explores the ambiguity established between object and container, through a faceted form that deploys itself inside the store. The abstract form expresses only its sensuality and a mutating infatuation, escaping in each perspective switch, to the meanings, which from every angle pretend to confine it and explain it.

Contrasts of forms, textures and colors are established between the architectural elements that define the space of the store: on one side, floor, walls and ceiling, on the other side the alien form that invades it. While the empty box is rigorously orthogonal, the alien object avoids straight angles and parallel lines. At the same time as the box is characterized for its rough textures and imperfections as well as for its dark coloring, the object highlights are its sharp form and polished white surface. Corian is the material chosen to materialize this form and to achieve the contrast with the textured wall, the imperfect concrete floor, and the exposed technical ceiling.

Company : *Dieguez Fridman*
Client : *Ayres*
Country : *Argentina*

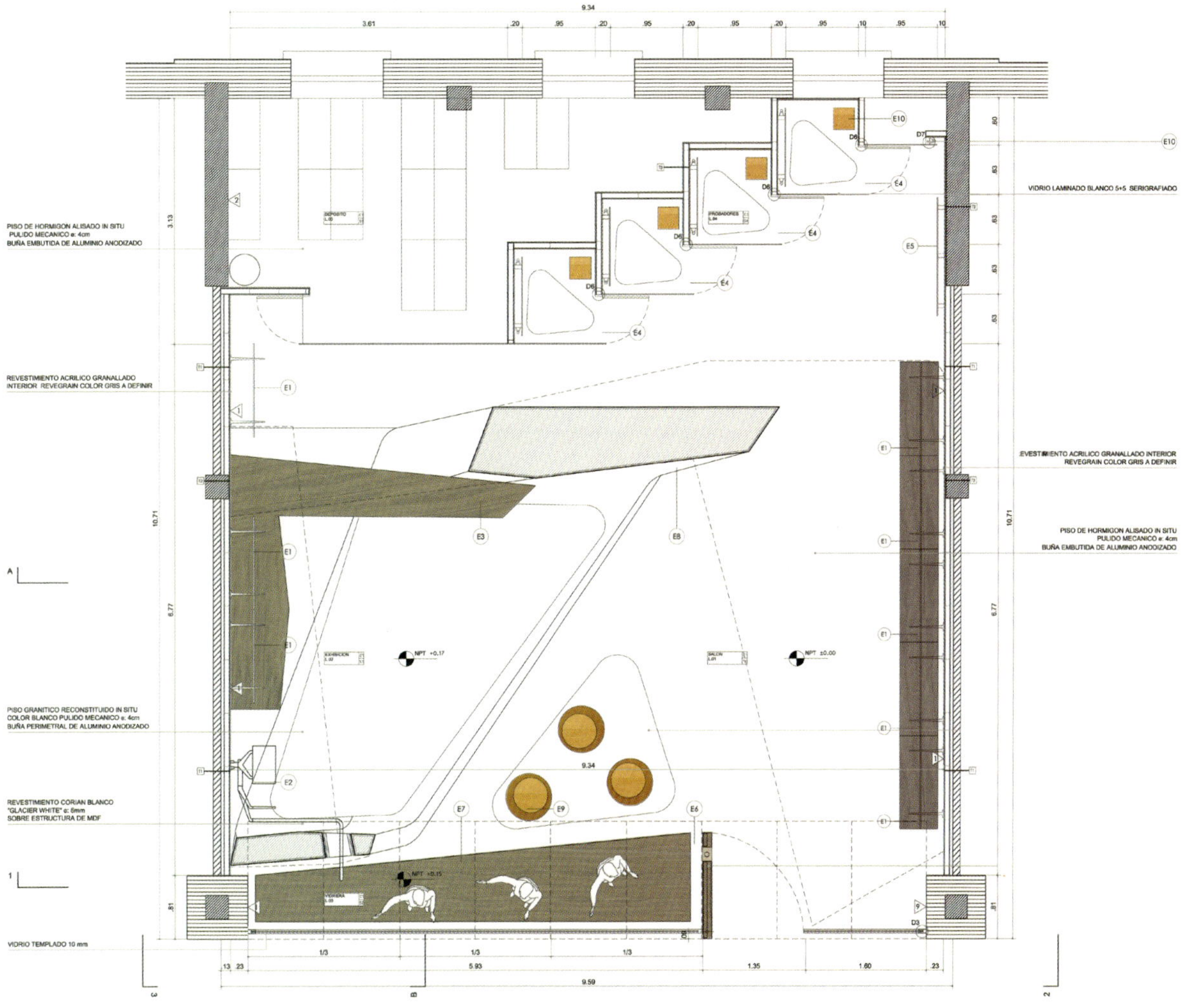
PISO DE HORMIGON ALISADO IN SITU
PULIDO MECANICO e: 4cm
BUÑA EMBUTIDA DE ALUMINIO ANODIZADO
REVESTIMIENTO ACRILICO GRANALLADO
INTERIOR REVEGRAIN COLOR GRIS A DEFINIR
PISO GRANITICO RECONSTITUIDO IN SITU
COLOR BLANCO PULIDO MECANICO e: 4cm
BUÑA PERIMETRAL DE ALUMINIO ANODIZADO
REVESTIMIENTO CORIAN BLANCO
"GLACIER WHITE" e: 6mm
SOBRE ESTRUCTURA DE MDF
VIDRIO TEMPLADO 10 mm
VIDRIO LAMINADO BLANCO 5+5 SERIGRAFIADO
EVESTIMIENTO ACRILICO GRANALLADO INTERIOR
REVEGRAIN COLOR GRIS A DEFINIR
PISO DE HORMIGON ALISADO IN SITU
PULIDO MECANICO e: 4cm
BUÑA EMBUTIDA DE ALUMINIO ANODIZADO
9.34
10.71
6.77
3.13
9.59
5.93
1.35
1.60

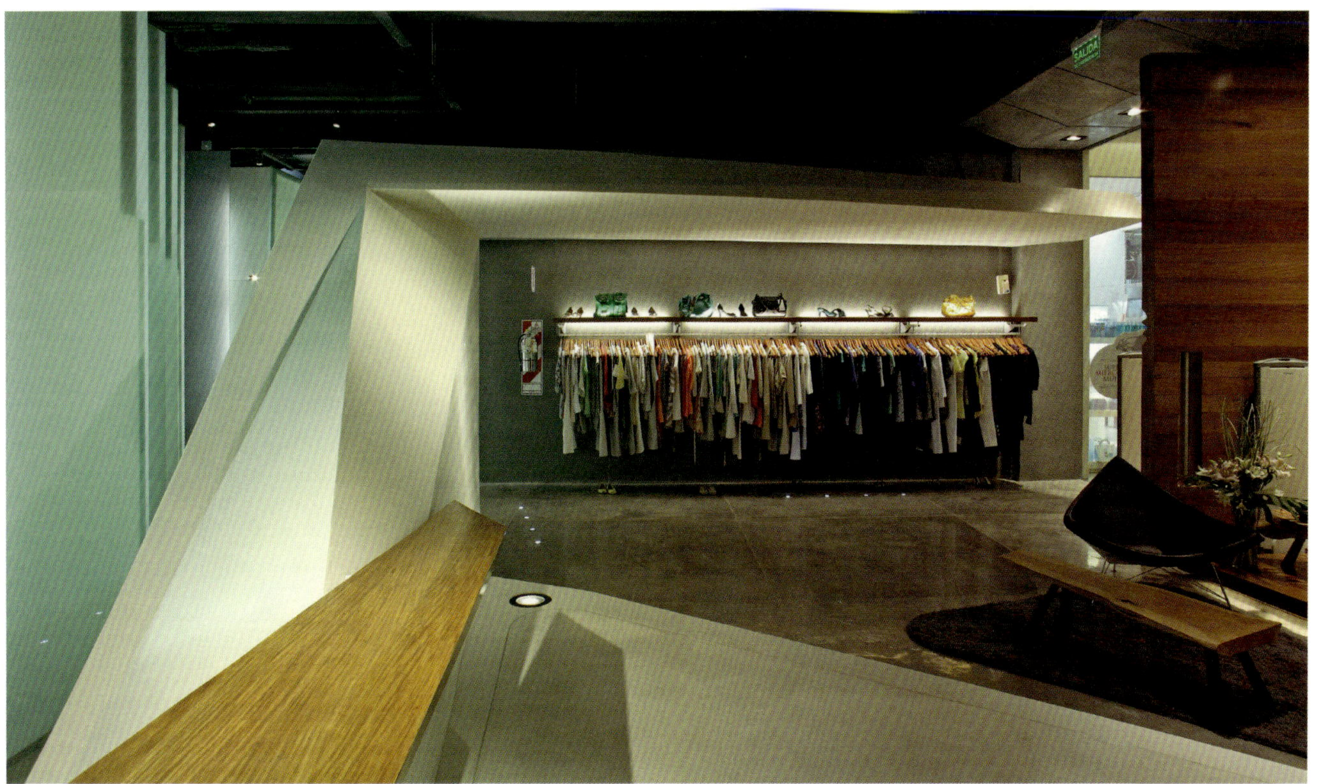

Company : *Eightsixthree Architecture Interiors*
Designer : *Mr. Ed Yuen*
Photographer : *Mr. Elion Yau Ying Ching*
(eightsixthree)
Client : Visual Merchandizing
Country : *China*

The Brief

To create a new concept BMW Lifestyle store that made customers go WOW!

Our Aim

To create a store that emphasized and reinforced the BMW Lifestyle, a store that reflected the luxury and quality of the brand and as such a store that made customers aspire to be part of that lifestyle. To design a store that enhanced the value and recognition of the BMW brand, whilst adding excitement and emotion to the act of shopping.

The Concept

Our concept started by taking the sculptural qualities of our favorite recent BMW sports cars, the M1, Z8 & Z4 and to translate the forms of these cars subtly into an innovative retail environment.

We aimed to create a store that had a strong visually dynamic, elegant and timeless shop front and were inspired by the kidney shaped front grill of BMW cars. We wanted to create a shop front that had the elegance and timelessness of this grill design yet create a design that would make one cross the street to see it closer.

It was important to also create a large see through area into the store that would allow the clients VM (Visual Merchandizing) team a large staging area at the front of the store to create dynamic window displays, as such we have crated slots in the ceiling areas and movable platforms in the base of these window areas to aid with their displays.

As with choosing the colour of a new car, we went through many options, we wanted a classic neutral colour that would allow the colour of products to be shown off to their best. We also felt the colours had to be in tune with current colours used on BMW models and also had to reflect the corporate identity of the client. As such we opted to follow the colours of the BMW motor sport division albeit keeping the colour palette to just two of the three colours reinweiss (white) and signalblau (blue). The diagonal blue stripe running up the wall is an instantly recognizable and direct interpretation of the inclined logo used on BMW M-series cars. All paint used within the store is the same as that used in the motor industry.

Upon entering the store our aim was to allow customers to view from the front to the back of the store easily and to clearly display merchandize at multiple levels. Therefore we created furniture that allowed us to display products in a low, medium and high level format. Our idea was to have products displayed on the floor, at low level in show cases, at mid level hanging from rails or at high level displayed on the feature wall.

All display fixtures and fittings, i.e. podiums, show cases, carbon fibre hanging rails and the feature wall (originally with 156 pull out display shelves) were custom designed by eightsixthree and are all specific to their individual requirement, low level podiums designed to look like fashion show catwalks are used to display luggage and bicycles, inclined (M-series) display cases are based on the BMW roundel logo and allow display of small items within a glass display case.

The hanging rails are black lacquered carbon fibre which provides the strength and rigidity of steel without the weight. We chose to use this material as we wanted to go away from the norm and to show that seemingly expensive and futuristic materials which are being readily used by our client in Formula 1 and America's Cup yatch racing could be brought inexpensively into the store. The carbon fibre tubes are readily available on the market however their hairline finish stainless steel 3 way connection lugs are custom designed by eightsixthree. The whole system can be assembled and checked in the factory for alignment prior to being shipped to site, assuring quick and accurate installation.

BMW Lifestyle

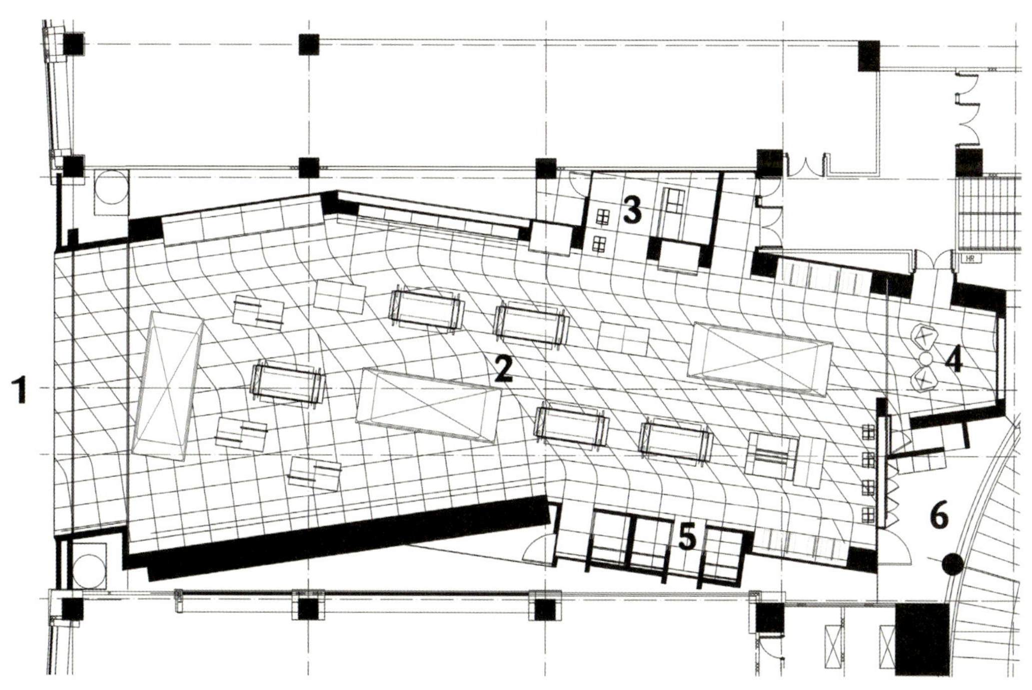

1 shopfront

2 display areas

3 cash wrap

4 VIP lounge

5 fitting rooms

6 BOH

Design shop Lik+Neon has commissioned the designer Gitta Gschwendtner to redesign their eclectic and vibrant shop in London. Lik+Neon sells a unique selection of products including T-shirts, art magazine, interior objects, jewellery and art pieces. The display concept for the varied stock explores a juxtaposition of order and randomness, cleverly integrating bungee cord to create tidy grids showcasing the beautiful covers of the magazines, CDs and records, each of them practically a piece of art in their own right. In dynamic contrast, square display pegs jut from the walls in apparently random fashion, creating sculptural protrusion that function as hocks for prints, T-shirts and jewellery. The pegs create a pixilated effect continued by Gschwendtner's striking one-off ceiling installation a lighting system devised from hundreds of plastic milk bottles, creating three glowing abstract clouds illuminating the white interior.

Company : *Gitta Gschwendtner UK*
Designer : *Gitta Gschwendtner*
Photographer : *Uli Schade*
Client : *Lik+Neon*
Country : *UK*

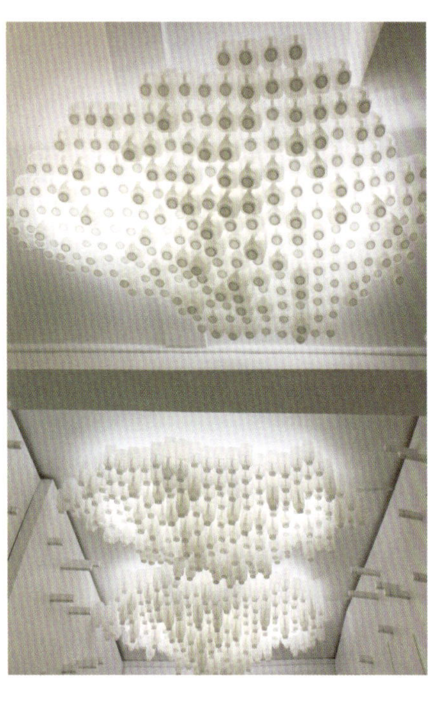

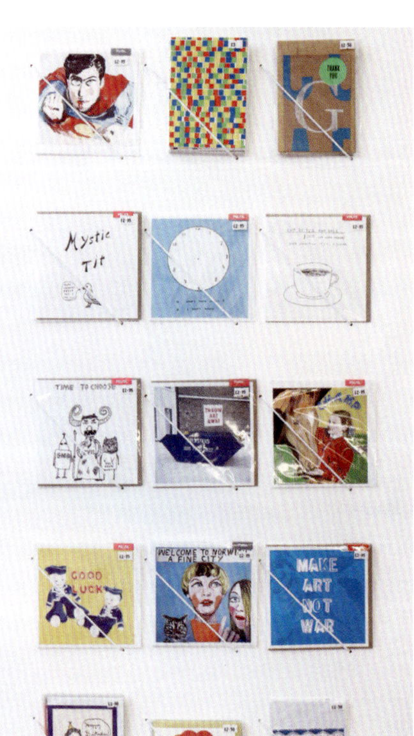

FLUX
love
me

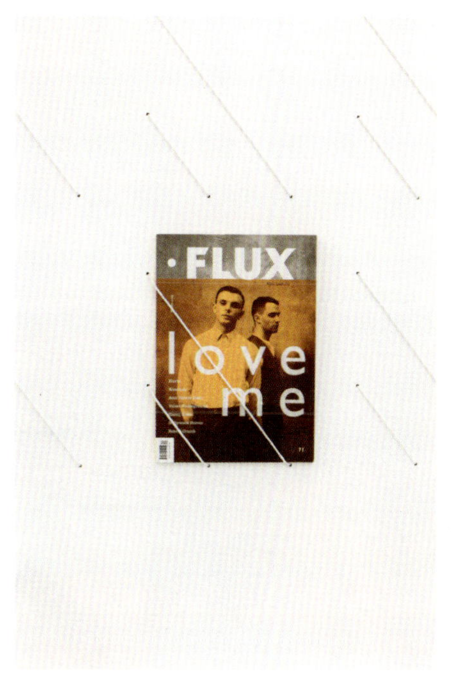

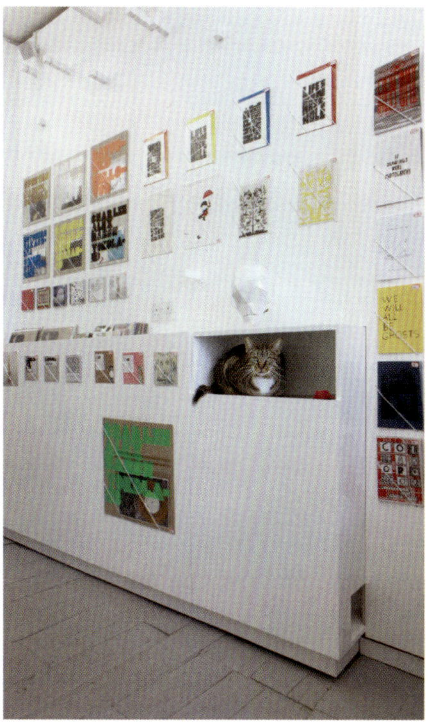

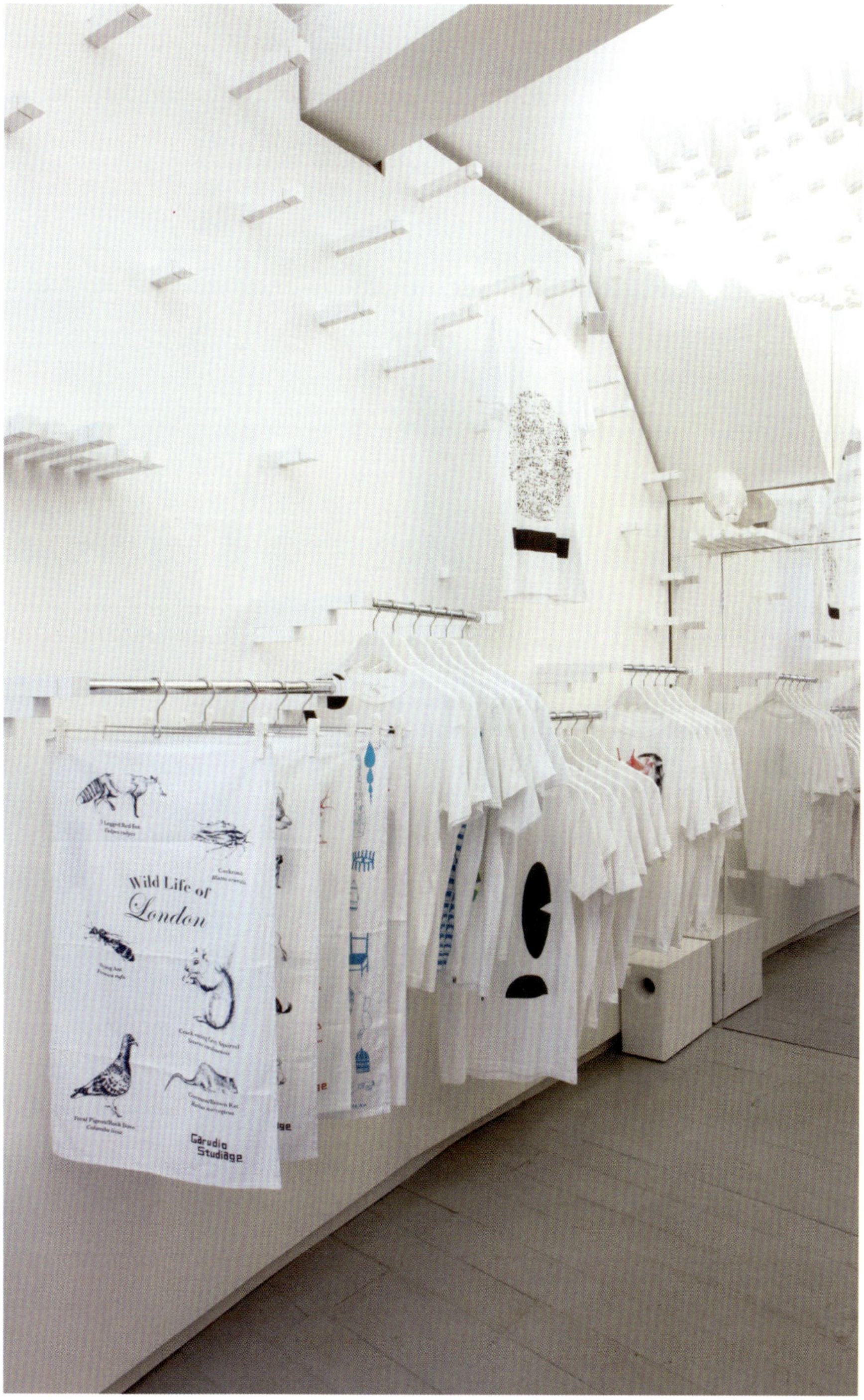
Wild Life of
London

K1p3 architects designed a new flagship store for the fashion label Rhus Ovata in Tel Aviv.

The premises are located on a busy fashion shopping street, the Rhus Ovata brand identifies itself as a subversive brand and therefore chose a shop set back from the sidewalk. The architect's concept for the shop was born from this position, trying to accentuate the depth of the shop. Creating a horizontal layering parallel to the street. The shop façade was redesigned, using steel to close the lower and upper parts of the vitrine and leaving a clear horizontal strip through which the shop shines and draws passersby's in. Openings were introduced in the back wall exposing a back garden. The materiality was kept minimal and basic in its nature narrowed down to a rectangular steel profile and MDF, and the style draws references from contemporary art.

The shop displays both the Rhus Ovata collection and its 'Borrowed' vintage accessories collection. The collections were organized in the space according to the layers concept. The majority of the fashion collection is hanging on a continues single axis across the entire width of the space with three passages crossing it where the steel profile is set into the floor. In the entrance the same steel profile suspends from the ceiling creating a topography within the space.

Along the backdrop of the shop, the 'Borrowed' collection is displayed in a library next to selected art books and alongside it is a wall installation of vintage scarves. Special diamond shaped hangers were designed and hand made to present the bags on a single column.

A great emphasize was given to the design of custom made light bodies. The light bodies generate a dialogue with the floor plan highlighting its orientation and creating a hierarchy in the space. Long horizontal lamps were designed emphasizing the long suspended rack create a 'highway' of light in alternating positions above it. Vertical, mushroom like, lamps were designed to highlight particular points in the space. And pink neon was used for the logo, casually leaning against a wall, repeating around the single column.

Company : *K1p3 Architects*

Designers : *Karina Tollman + Philipp thomanek*

Photographer : *Daniel Sheriff*

Client : *Einav and Hadas Zucker*

Country : *Israel*

SOURCE FLAGSHIP STORE BEIJING

'Source' is a fashion retailer and was established in Shanghai in 2006. This one-stop fashion centre of street culture sells brands from the USA, Italy, the Netherlands, UK, Australia and Japan.

For their new Flagship Store in Beijing, they required that the entire store has maximum flexibility of displaying products with a warehouse-like and industrial atmosphere. In addition a feature was required that could be seen from the street or a sculptural element that would connect the two floors.

A 9-metre high 'Shoe Tower' was proposed at the entrance of the store, which could display the extensive shoe collection. The shoe tower was based on a concept of stacked shoeboxes, which functions as the main display feature as well as a staircase connecting the two floors of the store. The tetris like form of the tower is comprised of shifting boxes that are literally stacked with some left open and others made of glowing light boxes.

The design of the overall racking system is based on a fashion warehouse distribution centre where clothes racking can be easily manually moved around on skids. Some skids are also used for displaying artwork during exhibitions held in the store.

The wall display pieces are also modular which clamp onto the metal mesh wall grid structure that allows for total flexibility and manipulation by their own visual merchandiser. The display boxes are shaped in 'L' and 'T' shapes in the theme of the building blocks of the shoe tower. A floating bar is placed in the centre back of the ground floor to complete the space.

The second floor also features two 'Shoe Walls' in the men's and women's section, each with over 70 standardized L-shaped shoe display elements, which are shifting in different directions to create curved and wave forms.

Company : *Huge Company*
Designers : *Gerald Russelman,*
Betty Zhong, Maia Schulze,
Candy Ma, Frank Xu
Country : *China*

The shop is organized on two floors, on the street level the main display and reception space is a dark gallery like space with a central white stair element leading down to the sewing workshop. The geometry of its walls angled to create movement and to envelope the central white spiral. Nine selected dresses are suspended, hovering from the ceiling around the monolithic staircase, each dress is lit with a single spot and hang on, vintage like, custom made seamstress mannequins.

The complete dress collection of approximately 150 dresses is archived in an illuminated translucent built-in glass cupboard spanning the length of one wall.

A second volume, a bridal dressing room, is kept completely white and accessed via a large cut-out in the wall of the main gallery. The room accommodates the bride and her bridal entourage.

A third room, Hila Gaon's private office, is hidden behind an over scaled pivot door.

The white staircase leads to the lower level workshop where the dresses are fitted on the brides during the process of production. The lower floor accommodates the seamstresses, the cutter, storage, a kitchen and a laundry room.

The walls and ceiling in the first space are textured in dark gray shadows, resembling 30 black & white glamour photo-shoots of divas, an inspiration from one of Gaon's catalogues. The floating dresses are analog to the bride's dream-like state of mind on the day of her marriage, and the spot light reminds one of her being the star for a day.

The vintage furniture is selected from flea markets and antique shops.

The shop is 80sqm on street level and 70sqm on the lower level.

K1p3 architects are responsible for the complete concept design and planning as well as the branding of the shop done in collaboration with graphic designer Nurit Koniak.

Company : *K1p3 Architects*
Designers : *Karina Tollman + Philipp thomanek*
Photographer : *Ardon Bar Hama*
Client : *Hila Gaon*
Country : *Israel*

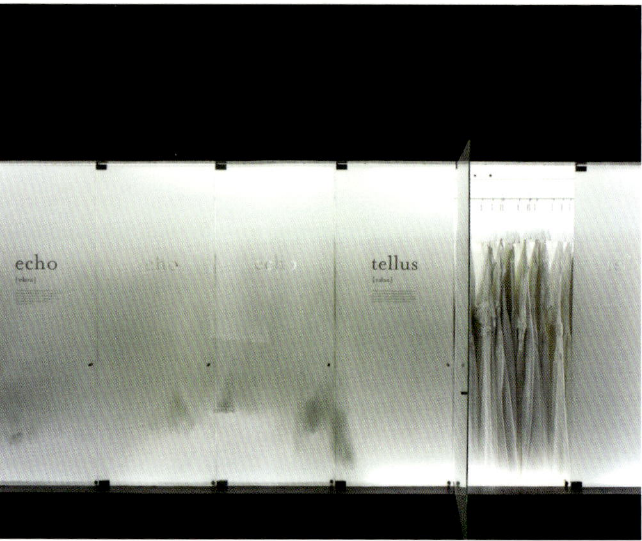

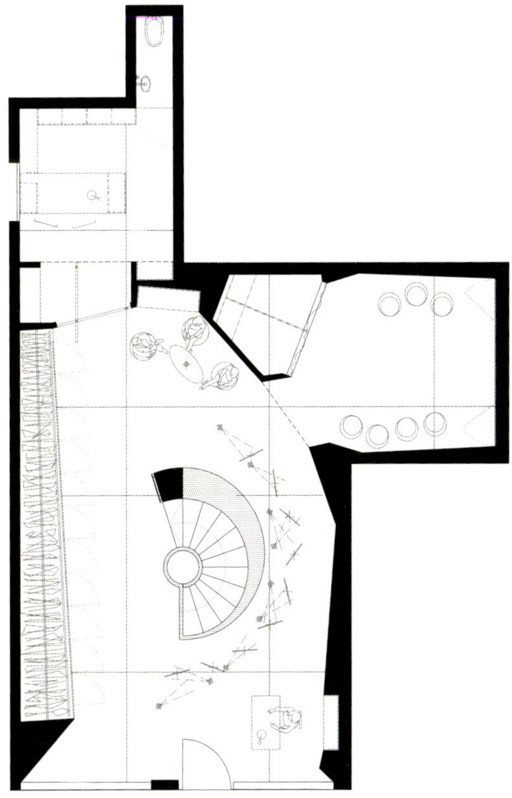

This was a great project as my only limitations were time! I had two weeks to complete as much wall space as possible over 3 floors, adjoining staircases, corridors, doors and changing rooms!! The works were produced from sketches created before and during the project. As the boutique was a unique feminine mix of new and vintage clothing and accessories I really wanted to portray that in my illustration work using influences from various times and places through a contemporary delivery. Using the architechtural detailing over the three floors, the images are seen along pathways, where flowers or cloud elements entice you further towards the beguiling feminine characters. Creating a wonderland of beauty and sensuality female shoppers were invited into an environment of fantasy and play, a very good marketing tool!

Company : *Miss Led Illustration*
Photographer : *Toby Summerskill*
Country : *UK*

Wonderous
Delights
Still
In Sight

Monki's all-new interior concept is a dangerous, dark and gloomy world with tantalizing beauty. It rests underneath the Secrecy, a deep dark damp cave with hidden treasures, dangerous currents, and deceptive breakers. All around you are sunken merry-go-rounds no longer spinning, tangled ropes from long-gone schooners, sparkling jellyfish floating, glowing bubbles, and waterplants taking root on the mirror water surface. Multi-coloured water lilies grow in clusters on the mossy seabed, surrounded by living skin from an ever-present underwater being. Monki is a chain of fashion stores for girls; combining graphics, goods, and store design to form an overall story. The collection is a flirt between expressive Tokyo street style and crisp Scandinavian fashion sense. The label is super priced clothing made for people wanting to express who they are through what they wear, representing individuality, independence, and imagination. Monki started in 2006, and today there are 40 shops in Norway, Sweden, Denmark and Germany. In 2008 60% of Monki was acquired by H&M. Monki opens in its first location outside of Europe this fall, Hong Kong in September 2010.

Company : *Monki*

Creative Directors : *Catharina Frankander,*
Joel Degermark

Designers : *Catharina Frankander,*
Joel Degermark

Photographer : *Fredrik Sweger*

Client : *Fabric Retail Glbl*

Country : *Sweden*

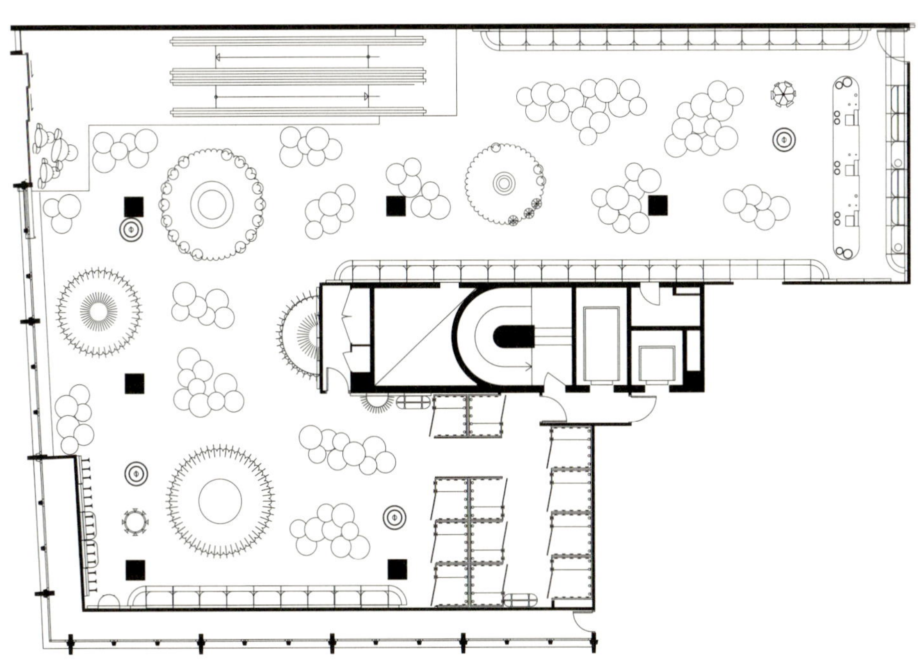

The name geometry makes reference to the client's study of mathematics and was the only guideline for Plajer & Franz studio when asked to develop a design concept. It is a small concept store with collections of fashion designers such as gaspard yurkievich, irie wash, Y3 and won hundred. Accessories from john galliano are combined with home accessories from contemporary designers such as gijs bakker and arik levy .

Since the mass of stores with shabby chic look has become quite tiresome especially in Berlin, Plajer & Franz studio created a whole new ambience. Geometry wants to surprise and implicates to be the apartment of a weird math professor that still has a good taste.

The professor is not only obscure but also has a cultivated sense for proportions and moods. He is collecting all kinds of strange items like skeleton photos, lamps that look like jackstraws having to do with analyzing, exploring and counting. Everything refers to the symmetry and asymmetry. Still everything is very stylish – the mud-coloured wall, the dark wooden floor and the brushed white oak furniture and works well for a men's concept store. Despite of the unique atmosphere combined with homey elements like waiting areas with rugs and dna lamps the design is not playing with the impossible. All aspects of the retail architecture and the associated presentation of the merchandise are planned and implemented right down to the last detail.

With geometry Plajer & Franz studio wants to surprise the client. He is to remember something fresh, positive and unseen. It is a new taste that he can place his trust in.

Company : *Plajer & Franz Studio*
Photographer : *Ken Schluchtmann*
Client : *Raphael Meyer & Carmen Santos*
Country : *Germany*

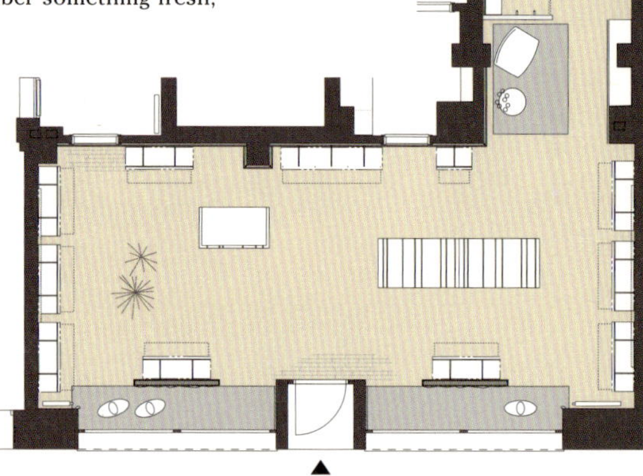

As one of the most successful fashion and lifestyle brands in Europe, s.Oliver caters to all age groups and covers all fashion styles with its broad range of segments including "Casual", "QS" and "Selection". Plajer & Franz studio has been working for s.Oliver for over 4 years and is responsible for the complete design and retail planning of all s.Oliver lifestyle environments worldwide. With the launch of the new store concept, Plajer & Franz studio has once again created an exceptional design with authentic and innovative elements. In the s.Oliver store in Wuerzburg the new concept was now presented to the public. The newly constructed building with which s.Oliver's demonstrates its affinity for the city of würzburg elegantly fits into the surrounding cityscape with its shell limestone facade. The vertical shop window extending over 2 floors and the equally tall prism image that lies behind it accentuating the corner of the plot in this prominent inner city location. The spacious windows as well as the large vertical bay facilitate the dialogue between s.Oliver's lifestyle world and the passer-by on the marketplace. Modular fixtures allow for a varied presentation of products and decorative elements within the visual merchandising and create a fluid transition between inside and outside. Half open spheres with mannequins in the shop windows underscore the lightness of the design and bring into play the 3-dimensionality of the space.

Through the room-in-room approach, each one of the collections retains its unique ambience under the roof of the s.Oliver parent brand. The individual design and use of distinctive materials, some specifically created for the project, underline the singularity of each segment. Tin tiles for example that were used in the early 19th century for ceilings in loft spaces in the U.S., are implemented here as wall cladding at the escalators and highlighted elements in the casual section. Mixed up with the tiles are pixilated photos of the current s.Oliver image campaign. The segment s.Oliver Casual is characterised by natural and stimulating tactile surfaces, which are combined with a warm colour palette to create a cosy atmosphere. The composition of darker wall colours with lighter ones, smooth and coarse saw cut finishes not only creates contrasts but also a strong statement. The pure and unobtrusive character of the wall system with its light oak panels and vertical slotted posts made of black steel further underlines the impact of the product itself. Steel, dark colours and an open ceiling define "QS" for the young urban target group. Wallpapers with graphic elements and altered wood finish designs show a clear segment that also appeals to the older crowd.

"s.Oliver Selection" constitutes the high-end and elegant business outfit. Metallic finishes are combined with black and white surfaces. The specially designed metallic wallpaper underscores that contrast between precious matte finishes and the luxury of high gloss elements such as the highlight wall made of mirror and black glass. The segment "s.Oliver Selection" presents the business outfit in a premium and elegant setting. The classy atmosphere of the space is attained through the combination of metallic surfaces and black and white elements with matte and high finishes, as for instance on the focal wall made of mirror and black glass. Visual merchandising perfectly complements the retail environment. Through its extreme modularity and flexibility as well as through the integration of wall, floor and ceiling, individual islands are formed within the store creating an opportunity for visual barriers as well as highlight presentations.

"s.Oliver Junior" caters to age groups 0-14. Design elements from the casual area are used and redefined with new surface finishes. Brick wall cladding, fresh playful elements such as flowers for babies and bright coloured furniture are characteristic of the youngest segment.

Throughout the store, the consumer continually discovers new and positively charged worlds and emotions, this creates a strong identification with the brand and even more fun shopping.

Company : *Plajer & Franz Studio*
Photographer : *Ken Schluchtmann*
Client : *S.Oliver Bernd Freier Gmbh & Co. Kg*
Country : *Germany*

KABINEN
KO003
MIX COTT
CLENT

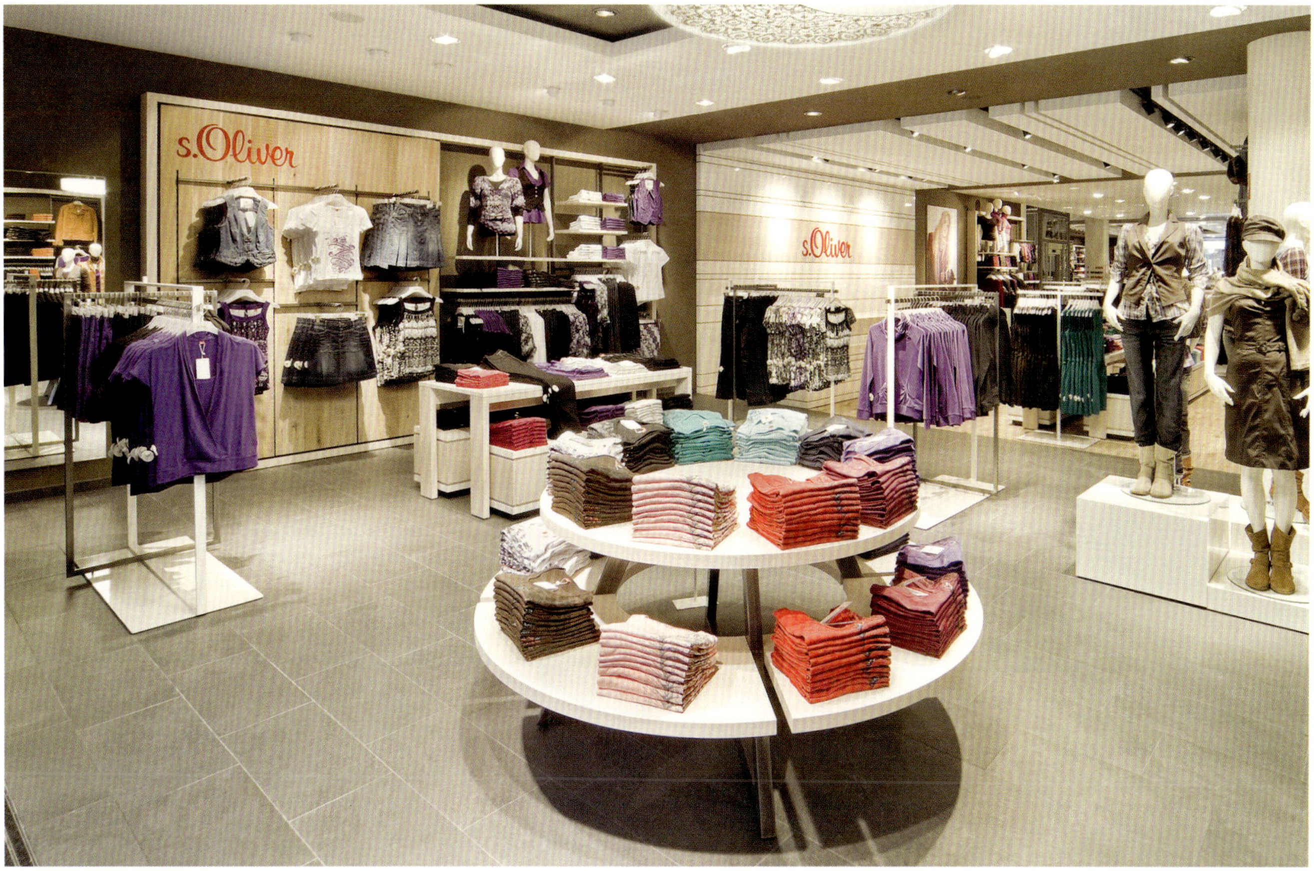
s.Oliver
s.Oliver

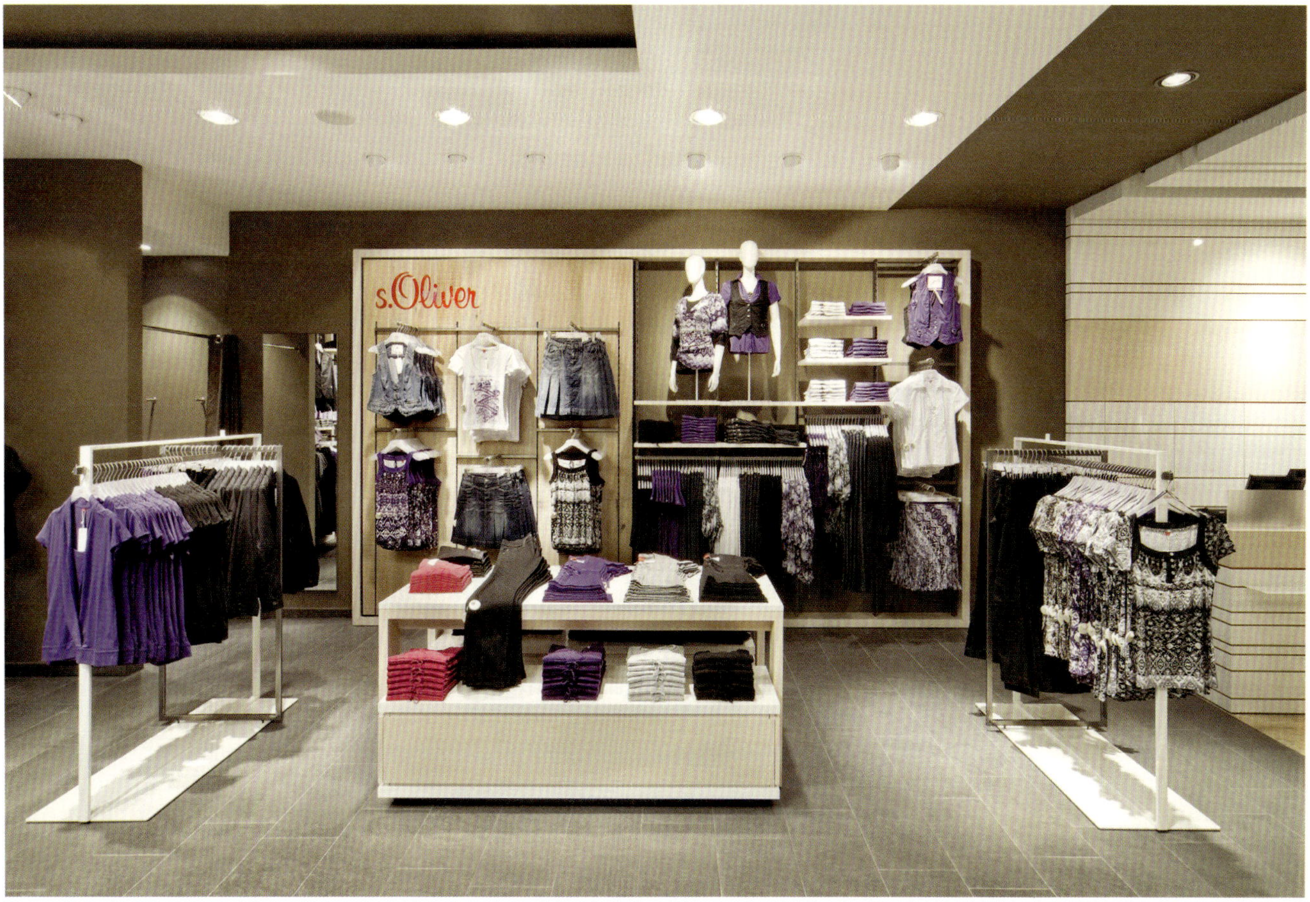
s.Oliver

MASKA – ROCKLAND CENTRE, MONTREAL, QUEBEC

Maska is a prêt-a-porter European women's fashion shop whose feature line is IMPERIAL "pronto moda", Italia.

When the option to relocate to a larger, higher traffic location in the same mall presented itself to the retailer, Maska took advantage of the opportunity and decided to revitalize the store concept at the same time.

From the initial client meeting it was established that the Maska Brand symbolized: Femininity; Freshness; Youthfulness; and Fashion Forwardness. Their target market was the mature yet youthful woman seeking career and evening wear from a collection of European prêt-a-porter brands. The objectives were to highlight the main attributes of the brand and to design a personalized boutique where exclusivity and service reigned.

With the design theme being "elegance meets youthfulness", a modern Baroque style fusing classic architectural elements with modern off-the-wall elements was created. The result: the complete brand experience is felt immediately upon entering the store.

With initial sales far surpassing expected results, the Maska design concept is a definite winner. It tapped into an unaddressed market niche and prime locations in top fashion malls are now being offered by landlords across the nation.

Company : *Ruscio Studio Inc.*
Creative Director : *Robert Ruscio*
Designer : *Ruscio Studio*
Photographer : *Leeza Studio Photography*
Client : *Maska*
Country : *Canada*

Underground was leasing 2 adjacent spaces in Chinook Centre (the first store exclusively for women; the second exclusively for men) when in February 2009 they made the decision to unify the spaces and, at the same time, revitalize their image.

The main problem with the existing spaces was that neither store offered an experience reflective of the brand offerings. The stores also felt like two completely different entities (one was dark, the other metallic). Locating the brands under one roof became the only logical choice.

Underground's main objectives with the new unified design were to (1) better represent the hot brand names carried and (2) to increase the women's sales, which were very weak relative to the men's. The theme took an anti-mainstream approach reflecting more of a hip "underground" world and its urban inspirations.

Following the renovation, the general consensus was that the store finally appropriately represented the brand names it carried. The concept was also so well received by shoppers and mall owners alike that the design has been applied to other Underground stores across Western Canada.

Company : *Ruscio Studio Inc.*
Creative Director : *Robert Ruscio*
Designer : *Robert Ruscio*
Photographer : *Leeza Studio Photography*
Client : *Underground Clothing*
Country : *Canada*

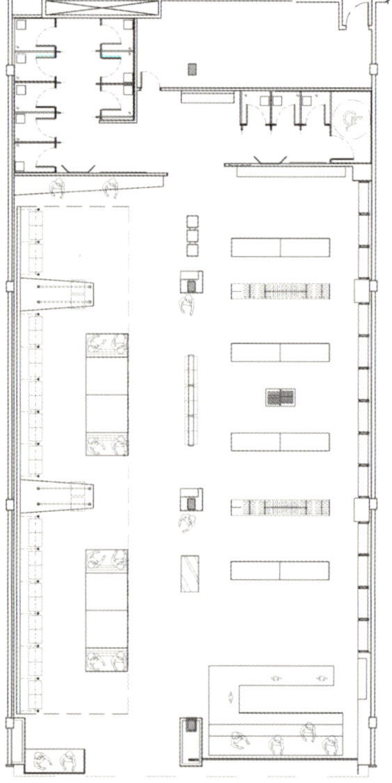

Calgary Transit
2008 System Map
LEGEND

ROMANTICISM2 IN HANGZHOU

The clothes are cut and tailored with quadratic element clothing, then pack and decorate three-dimensional human body. The clothes could adjust temperature, so they could be regarded as the second skin which extended from the body. The space also could pack human body and adjust temperature. But the space couldn't move, thus it has a difference in nature with clothes.

The design idea of ROMANTICISM2, is not lay particular stress on the floor, the wall and the ceiling. It is spread between the space and the clothes, makes it gives play of the third skin. "the skin-like space" or "the space-like skin", will these exist be accepted?

ROMANTICISM2 is very near the West Lake, the central of Hangzhou. ROMANTICISM2 has more than 500 shops in China. This shop is the flagship store of this brand.

The net-stated organic form runs smoothly through the whole space, it looks like a net involved in the inside shop, changing naturally with the extending process, and pack the first floor store totally. And the net gets together at the stairs was unfolded when it enters the underground space, it touches every corner just like in the first floor.

The net keeps changing shapes into counter, stairs, implements and railing and other patterns. And the net which acts as the third skin is consist of bone, fresh and skin. The bone is rebar, the fresh are foamed plastic and glass fibre, the skin are epoxy resin and oil paint.

On the three-dimensional waving white wall, the designer punches many holes to exhibit the samples, expand the theme of body and clothes. Moreover, the ceiling of the first floor uses minor stainless steel, this design is based on the effect to reach visual impact, guarantees the store lighting and the shortcoming that the ceiling is too low. The image is not like inverted reflection made by flat minor stainless steel. It looks like reflection in the water. The water usually appears on land arising in the sky, produce unordinary shadow and light.

Company : *Sako Architects*

Designers : *Keiichiro Sako, Nobutoshi Hara, Kazuya Uzawa*

Photographer : *Koji Fujii*

(Nacasa & Partners Inc.)

Country : *Japan*

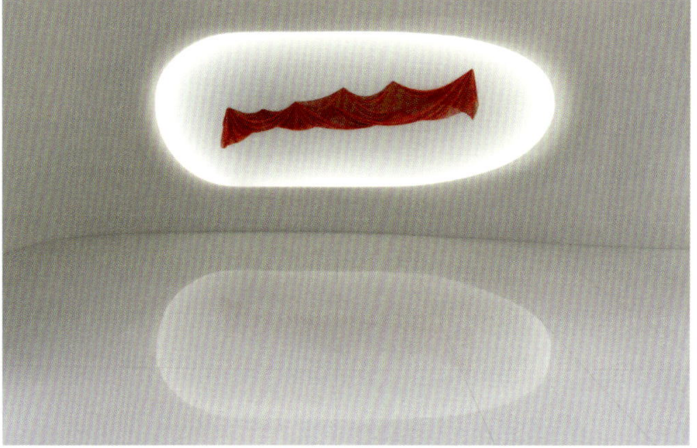

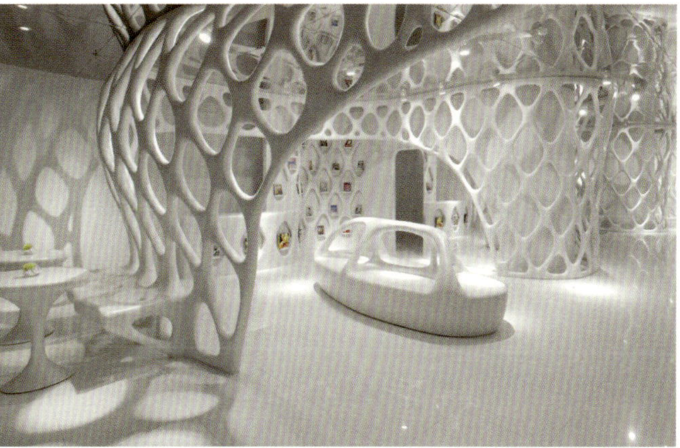

"eifini" is the name of boutique which sells women clothes and they runs about 180 shops in all China. This time we designed its branch shop in Beijing.

First, in order to spotlight the clothes, we painted all the floor, wall, and ceiling in white, and let any other elements to lose their existence. Equipments, like the counter, are made of the same tiles with floor. It designed very simple, so as if a part of the floor rose up and directly became the counter. Then, lastly, we put a whole 180 meter-long hunger pipe into this space.

The pipe goes around the shop freely, and makes out a gently separated, but also successive space. The clothes hung in the pipe color the different spots in the shop, and softly flutter in the air. We punched some holes and inserted the LED tube into the pipe, and then the pipe colored in magenta warmly light up itself. And also, the pipe is held by clear acrylic pole from all directions, and this makes the pipe free from gravity and float in this space.

In addition to displaying the clothes, our pipe has a lot of useful functions. For example, in the entrance, the pipe runs from side to side roundly and it makes out the entrance gate, and if you hang curtains instead of clothes, it will make out the fitting room.

The pipe changes itself one after another, and it seems to be the trace of the conductor's baton in an orchestra. The pipe emphasizes the presence of clothes, but at the same time, it insists the existence of itself, drawing a smooth trace. The concert goes on, while the clothes and the pipe take turns at playing the lead. Visit this place, just feel the melody of our orchestra.

We would like any woman to enjoy the melody changes in every all seasons.

Company : *Sako Architects*
Photographer : *Misae Hiromatsu*
(Beijing Ndc Studio, Inc.)
Country : *Japan*

This is a flagship of a women's wear brand EIFINI which owns about 180 sub branch in China.

In order to highlight the clothes, the designers unified the floor, the wall and ceiling with the color white, so thus to get rid of the sense of existence of the other elements of the shop. The checkout counter and the other prop of the shop are made minimal just like they are raised up from the floor. A 250-meter-long circular tube hanger is placed inside this space.

The tube is supported by YDC-J from all sides, just like liberated from the gravity. It then swims in the space. Widen the space, at the same time keep the scene viewable: overlay several levels to make a tunnel-like entrance; transforming spiral down clothing exhibition area; a curtain cross and turn in to fitting room; and three-dimensional multicurve surrounds and make up a plaza-like rest space. All of these make the shop plentiful and diversity.

It's free to show the clothing, many methods bring more possibility. This open and free space has a total different touch, and it is used farthest. Chengdu EIFINI is a neatly promote clothing diversification exhibition clothes shop.

Company : *Sako Architects*
Designers : *Keiichiro Sako, Nobutoshi Hara, Kazuya Uzawa*
Country : *Japan*

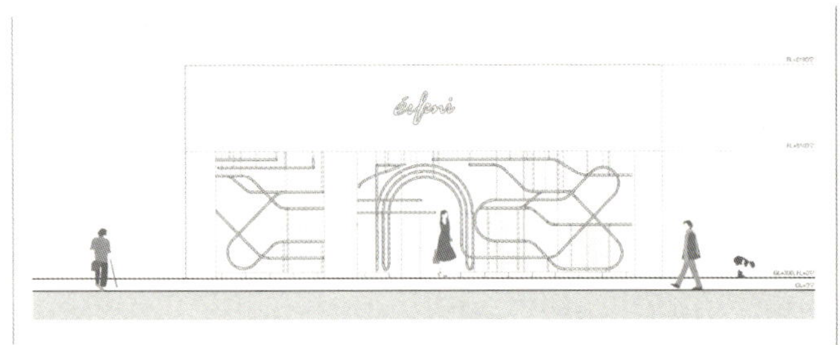

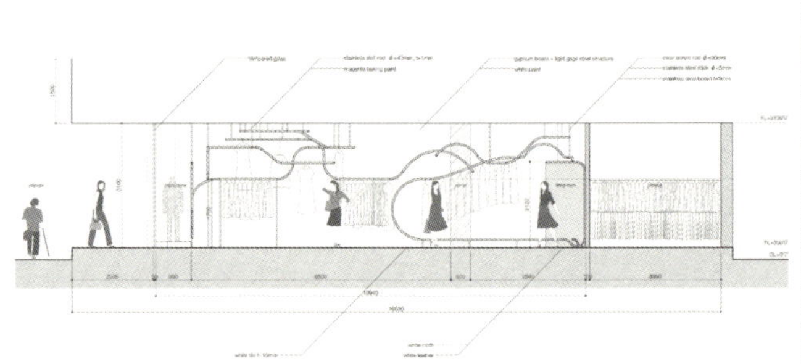

ROMANTICISM3 IN HANGZHOU

The third completed ROMANTICISM shop in Hangzhou.

Company : *Sako Architects*
Designers : *Keiichiro Sako, Nobutoshi Hara, Kazuya Uzawa*
Photographer : *Koji Fujii (Nacasa & Partners Inc.)*
Country : *Japan*

We live in the beginning of the 21st century, and it is the revolution period on the planetary scale. Surround the problem of global warming, only in a year time, people's consciousness about environmental protection has changed a lot. Environmental protection has already become a global and unavoidable problem.

"Huanjue" is a brand based on the idea of environmental protection. For years, the clothes of this brand and the shop design have united and run through this idea. To the founder of the brand, the development of the fashion career and the popularized of the environmental protection are indivisible.

Environmental protection is the most important thing in the movement to create the future. Which change will bring to our future, if we support the developing science and technology? The future space in the science fiction is clipper-built, compact; the floor and the ceiling are divided illegibly. Just imagine, this space is just like cavern. The cavern is the life space which man first acquired. One end of the timer shaft is past, the other is future; time passes by, if we keep look back to the past, may be it will lead us to the future.

The theme of the design is "future space led by the idea of environmental protection".

The fitment of the shop only uses two materials. The floor used linoleum; the wall, the ceiling and others used excelsior-board. Two kinds of these are natural materials, minimize the burden bring to the environment.

It Is the first case that uses a lot of excelsior-board as the main material to decorate the shop. The thickness of the wall of the shop is 600 mm. The designer dig a space to hang clothes on the wall, also the pillar in the shop, and handily uses the lighting, dims the connection of the pillar and the ceiling, makes the wall, the pillar and the ceiling unified.

Company : *Sako Architects*
Designer : *Sako Keiichiro*
Country : *Japan*

AWAKENING

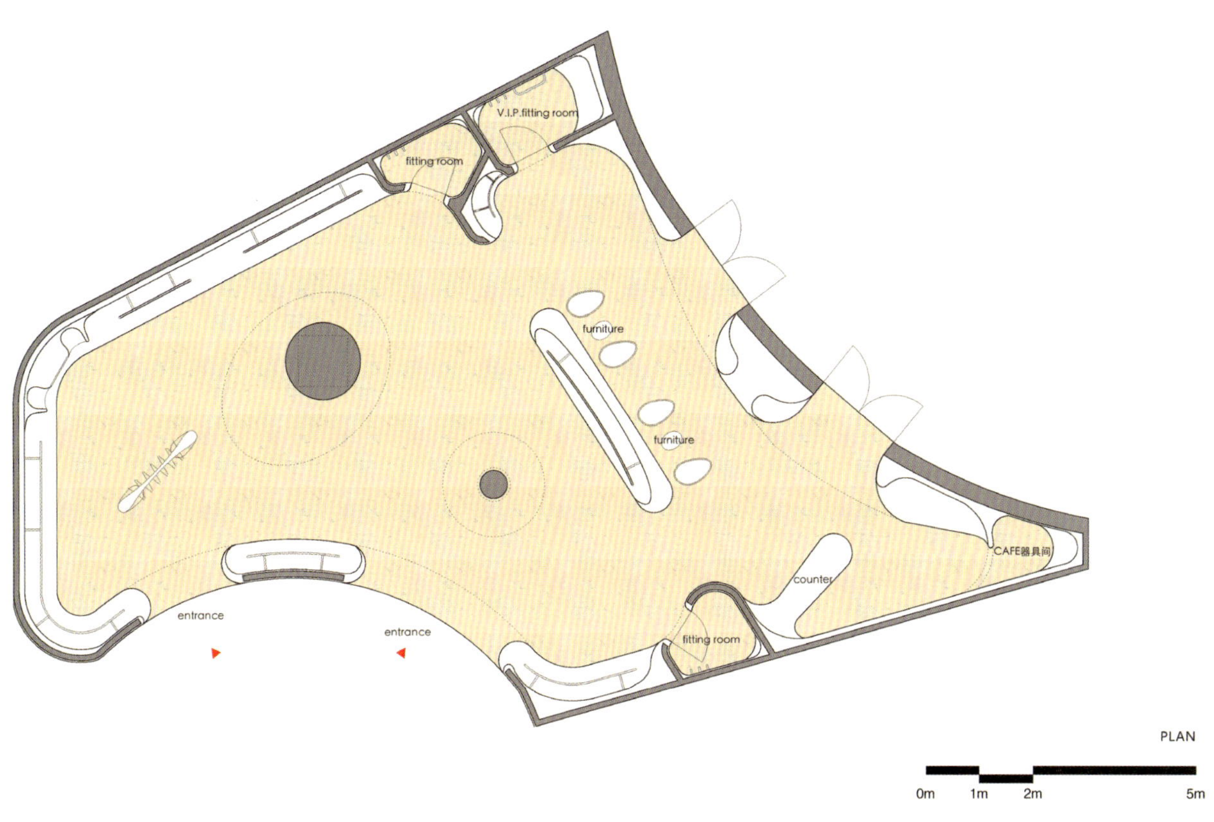
V.I.P.fitting room
fitting room
furniture
furniture
CAFE器具间
counter
fitting room
entrance
entrance
PLAN
0m   1m   2m   5m

Baveg
Go green
Save the
planet

The interior of a boutique in a huge mall.

At first, we have to think how to make use of the 3.65m high-ceiling for this interior. Generally the space above head height is just void for only looking in a boutique, because most of the action for buying and selling is centered close to human body. To avoid this condition, we installed imaginary ceiling made by expand-metal at 2.25m high and set up stepped platform that allows shoppers to reach the attic.

Two stepped platforms as like hills are useful stage for displaying bags, heels and mannequins and give us the choices of flow, the long way by going at floor level or the shortcut by going up some steps.

Mirrors round the edge of the attic visually expand the shop. We expect this illusionary view as a gimmick not to get bored with the shopping in a huge mall.

Company : *Sinato*
Designer : *Chikara Ohno ,Sinato*
Photographer : *Takumi Ota*
Client : *Duras Inc.*
Country : *Japan*

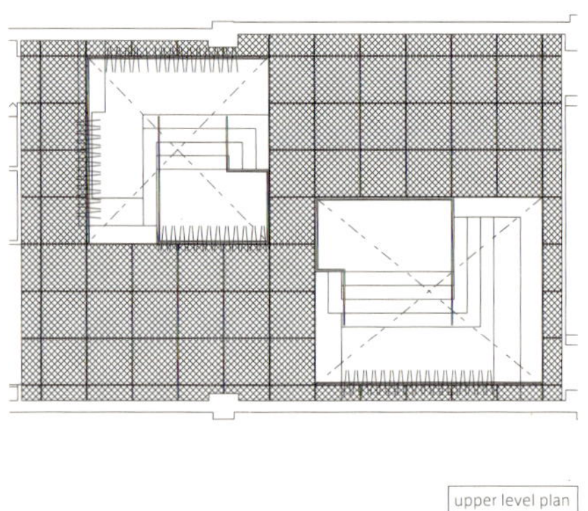

upper level plan

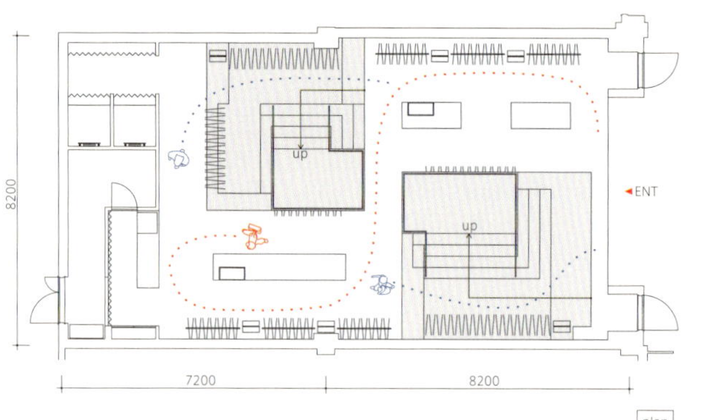

ROLLS

The characteristic of the material used for this installation, which is aluminum, is that it is very thin and easily bent by hands, yet harder than cloth or paper. Therefore it possesses both soft and hard qualities.

By winding and sometimes extending this single, long strip of aluminum from the entrance to the back-end of the store, it creates a beautiful waving form, changing its function and features as the material strength changes.

This flexible quality of the material represents a gentle connection between the softness of clothes and hardness of architecture.

Company : *Sinato*
Designer : *Chikara Ohno ,Sinato*
Photographer : *Toshiyuki Yano*
Client : *Diesel Japan Co.,Ltd.*
Counry : *Japan*

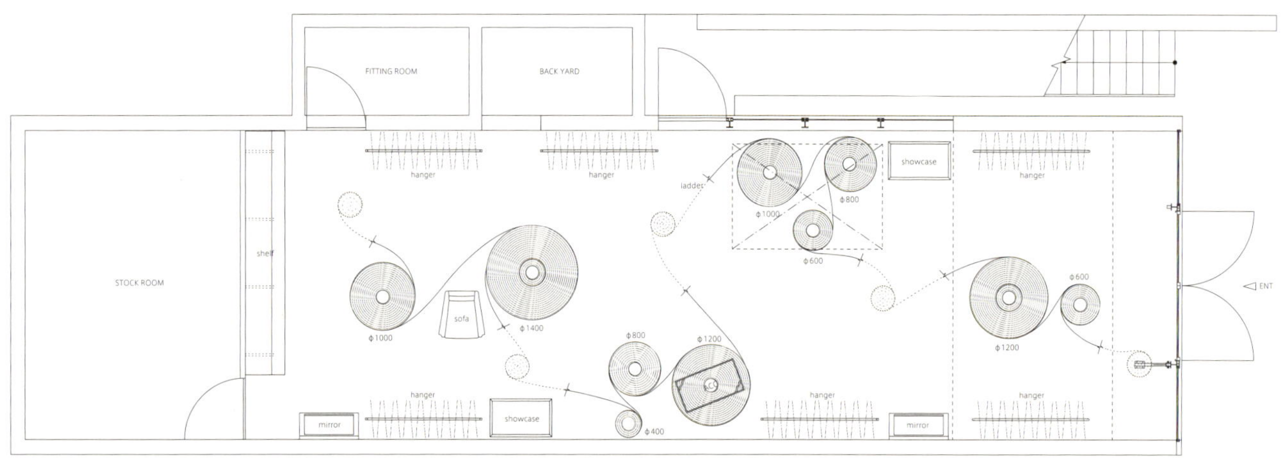

ISSEY MIYAKE AND PLEATS PLEASE ISSEY MIYAKE

ISSEY MIYAKE and PLEATS PLEASE ISSEY MIYAKE. 411 sticks connecting the two spaces. Their colors and shadows float and overlap, creating a new space with a new appearance.

Like flown away into space and floating there, the sticks spread all around the space. As if time stands still, "a balance out of balance" is created.

The concept of sticks was inspired by a European children's game "MIKADO*", which was often played before. The sticks randomly positioned was inspired by MIKADO to create tensions and chance balances, which were designed to become tangible forms. It was designed to be structurally balanced in spite of its unbalanced appearance.

Company : *Emmanuelle Moureaux Architecture + Design*
Country : *Japan*

sticks
by emmanuelle moureaux

PLEATS
PLEASE
ISSEY MIYAKE

PLEATS
PLEASE
ISSEY MIYAKE

sticks
by emmanuelle moureaux
ISSEY MIYAKE

sticks
by emmanuelle moureaux

PLEATS
PLEASE
ISSEY MIYAKE

Sybarite's design for the Marni flagship at the Crystals in Las Vegas was inspired by the image of a cracking whip, seemingly suspended in mid-air as it unfurls. Defining the perimeter, this sinuous "lasso" of stainless steel encircles the boutique, providing hanging space for the RTW collection. At one end it is anchored by the cash and wrap desk, and at the other it morphs into a sculptural wall inset with fibreglass shoe displays.

Painted smooth grey, the curving walls are broken up by an array bubbles in relief - randomly concave and convex, backlit and shadowed - which build up in textural composition. A selection of accessories are displayed in some of the recessed bubbles, enhancing the perception of value and uniqueness. Other sections of the perimeter contain backlit fibreglass display boxes and scattered throughout are suspended mannequin pieces in a mix of natural fibreglass and pearlescent purple lacquer, a new finish inspired by Marni's latest accessories collection. Beyond the walls is a space for fitting rooms, stock room and office. Freestanding elliptical display tables, also in pearlescent purple, offer additional display surfaces and clusters of white PVC stools and soft grey wool rugs provide comfy seating. In the ceiling, giant Barrisol discs echo the bubble motif of the walls and cast soft diffuse light, while the polished concrete floor provides a clean backdrop. Similarly, the exterior treatment is minimalist. Rather than a conventional window display, a simple glass facade with a few hanging mannequins allows a clear view into the shop, putting the collection centre-stage to draw the attention of traffic from the busy escalators nearby.

Company : *Sybarite*

Designers : *Simon Mitchell, Torquil Mcintosh, Giorgia Cannici*

Photographer : *Donato Sardella*

Client : *Marni*

Country : *UK*

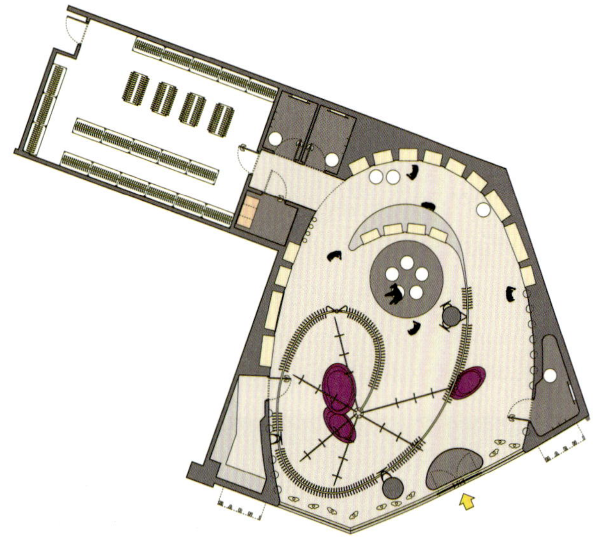

The small Company No Limits is running two Shops in Braunschweig, Germany, selling skateboards, clothing and sneakers.

The illustrations provide the stores with a fresh and very individual urban look with a twist of street art.

The closed doors carry pretty landscape illustration.

The open/folded doors show the same illustrations but by overlaying each other they create a certain 3D feeling.

Company : *Tilogo Germany*
Designer : *Tilo Göbel*
Country : *Germany*

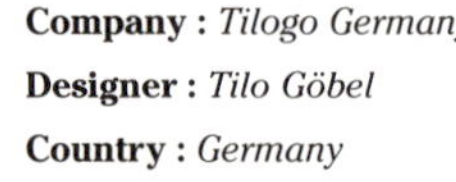

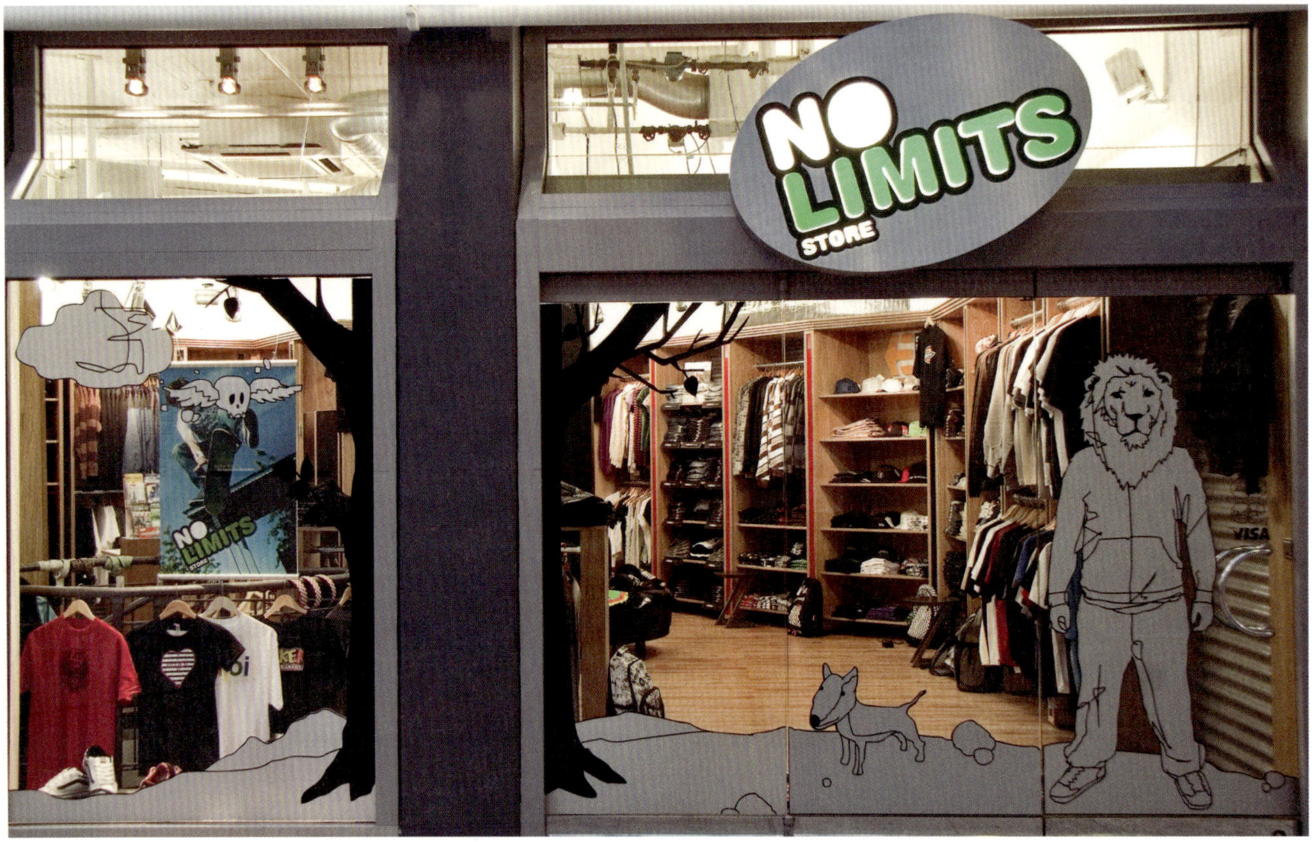

NEW
NO LIMITS STORE
OPENING
FREITAG 18.JULI
BURGPASSAGE · BRAUNSCHWEIG
New Store
Opening
NO LIMITS

NO LIMITS
NO LIMITS
STORE

NO
LIMITS
STORE

The INHABITANT STORE TOKYO opened in Harajuku's Cat Street as the lifestyle/sport brand's flagship store. "Playfulness" and "Japaneseness" are the embodiment of INHABITANT's freestyle expression of modern Japanese taste and which inspired us to envision a space thriving with the spontaneity of a casual stroll through the area known as "the back of Harajuku".

On each of the two floors, long plates cross diagonally the display areas with fitting rooms and counters positioned at a comfortable distance from them. Shoppers are greeted by a long plate on the first floor that can be used as a table to put articles on display, work or serve as a catwalk for special events. The edge of the plate becomes a step to the stairwell leading to the second floor where a suspended plate emerging from the wall welcomes customers like an overhead gate before extending diagonally into the display area holding hanger racks on its bottom side and multi-directional spotlights on its top to showcase the hexagonal tortoise-shell patterns spreading like clouds on the ceiling. Artist Asao Tokolo elaborated two patterns, whose every edge will always match every other, which can be seen encroaching on the floors, ceilings, walls and columns all over the store.

By capitalizing on the mutual relationship of the smaller units composing it, we strived to create a space that would in turn blend in with the small boutiques and residences that make up "the back of Harajuku".

Company : *Torafu Architects*
Designer : *Torafu Architects*
Photographer : *Daici Ano*
Client : *Phenix*
Country : *Japan*

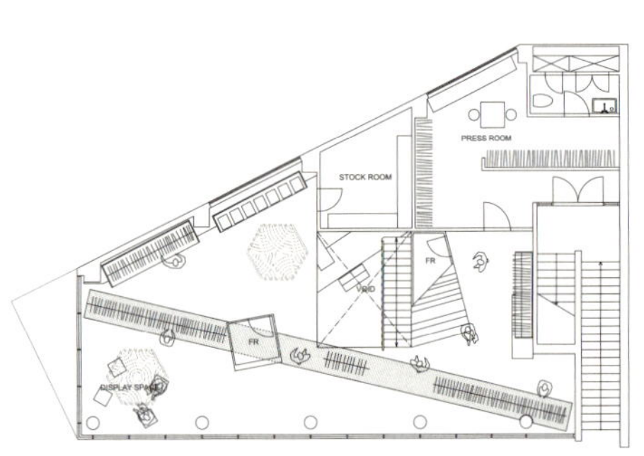

2F PLAN S=1/100

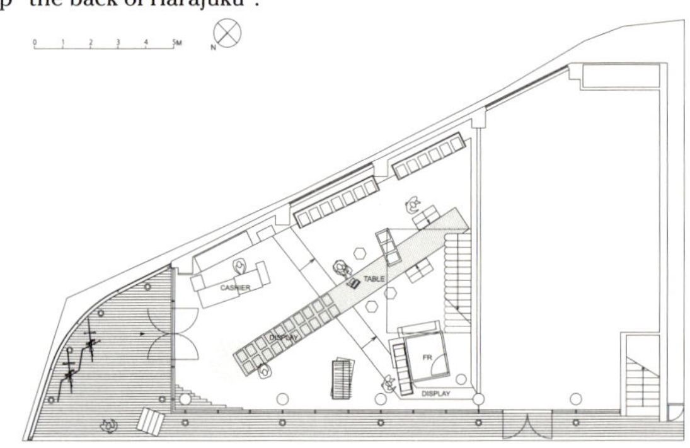

1F PLAN S=1/100

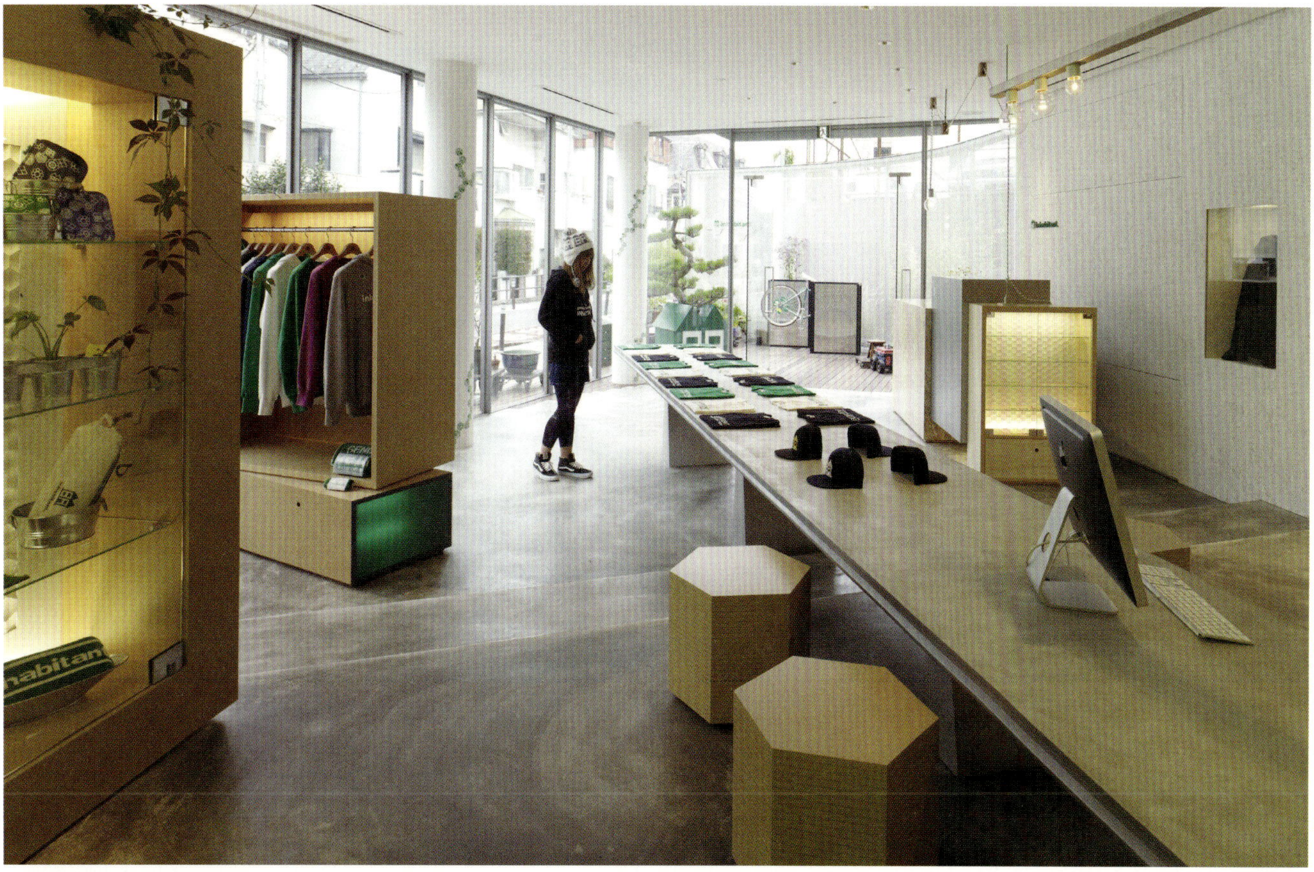

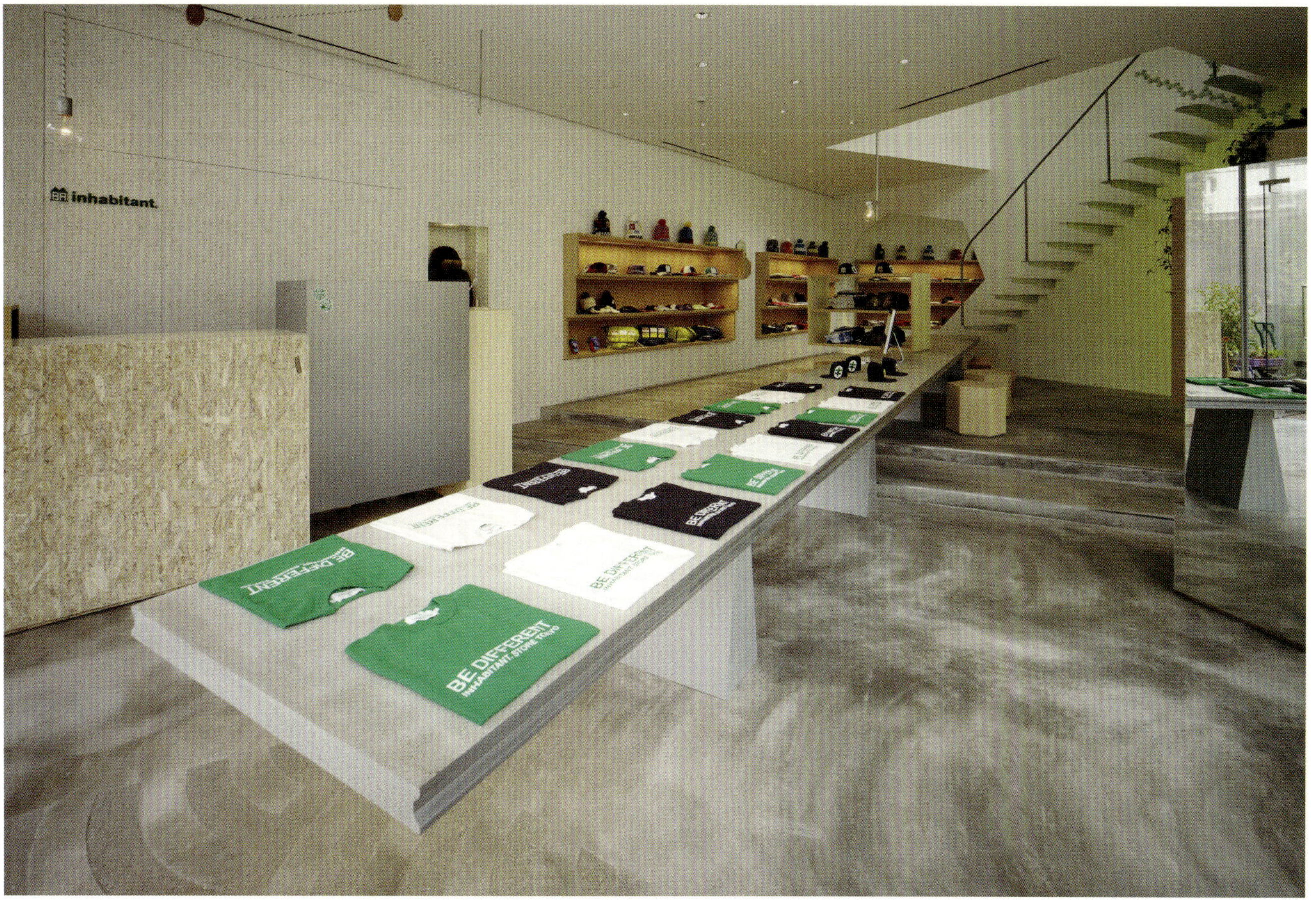
inhabitant.
BE DIFFERENT

GREGORY TOKYO STORE

On The Cat Street of Harajuku opened Gregory's first free-standing store which deals in backpacks and all. The building located at a peculiar corner of Y-intersection, the first floor displays casual merchandize and the second floor displays professional mountain climbing gear. Since the existing building is taper shaped, we had to take a crack at exhibiting a variety of products while giving adequate space for stock items in the limited site area. What we had in mind was a ragged mountain, a dense forest and an Alpine hut to rest in, all of which Gregory backpacks have been utilized in.

We set the hut in the existing blow-by. A part of the hut is sliced by the glass wall of the entrance. The sliced interior of the hut functions as the front display of the store. When going into the saleroom, customers will feel as if they were exiting the hut, and they will see the display shelves all over the wall with a whole lineup of Gregory products. Partition boards shaped as bare rock surface make continuous scenery of a valley with reflections made by the mirrors on both sides of the saleroom. Backpacks between the partition boards remind customers of a scene of rock climbing. Stock products can be placed behind the products that are displayed in front.

Passing through mirrored images of cherry trees and orange trees and walking up the exterior stairs, customers will feel as if they were entering the woods and will be led to the second floor where they sell gear for professional climbers. When they open the entrance door, they see the roof of the hut and the ragged display shelves stretching from the ground floor. These shelves provide a sense of consistency to the separated first and second floor.

The exterior walls that look like carved out rocks function as a symbol of Gregory store. The walls are sprayed with the coating compositions that consist of attention-seeking material usually used for asphalt roads, so that their surface shines like a crystal of a certain mineral when hit by a ray of sunlight.

Company : *Torafu Architects*
Photographer : *Daici Ano*
Country : *Japan*

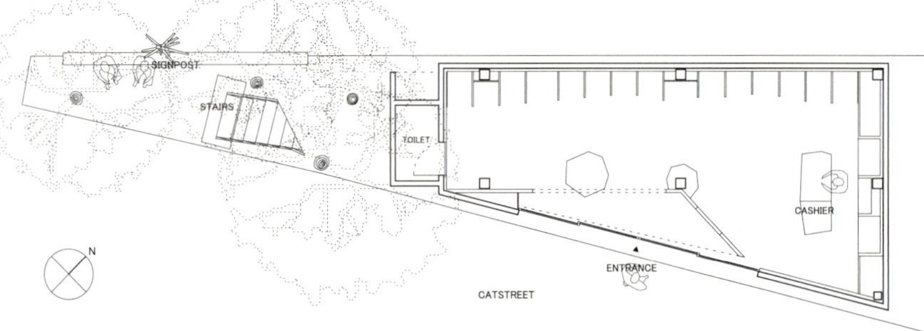

RAINWEAR IN / RAINWEAR OUT

This is mina perhonen's third temporary installation to be held at the stage, located on the 1st floor of the Isetan department store in Shinjuku. This year's theme, "Rainwear In / Rainwear Out", revolves around a booth shaped like a house to highlight the "inside" and "outside" experience of a rainy day. The booth's walls prominently feature mina perhonen's "sunny rain" textile pattern while chairs shaped like rain drops and mirrors shaped like puddles complete the picture for a fun day in the rain.

Company : *Torafu Architects*
Designer : *Torafu Architects*
Photographer : *Daici Ano*
Client : *Mina Perhonen*
Country : *Japan*

Twice a year we design the booth for Blanks new collection presented at the fashion fair gallery in Copenhagen. Everytime we start with a short brief of the theme they have been working on for this particular collection. Most of the time it is quite abstract. A few words and a couple of images all there is for us to interpret. Fashion being maybe the fastest of all art forms gives us an opportunity to design something very fast and intuitive based on a couple of words. So much fun! This particular season we focused on the term art brut. The whole display system was cut out of one original piece of styrofoam by hand.

Company : *Uglycute*
Designer : *Uglycute*
Photographer : *Uglycute*
Client : *ÅF Blank*
Counrty : *Sweden*

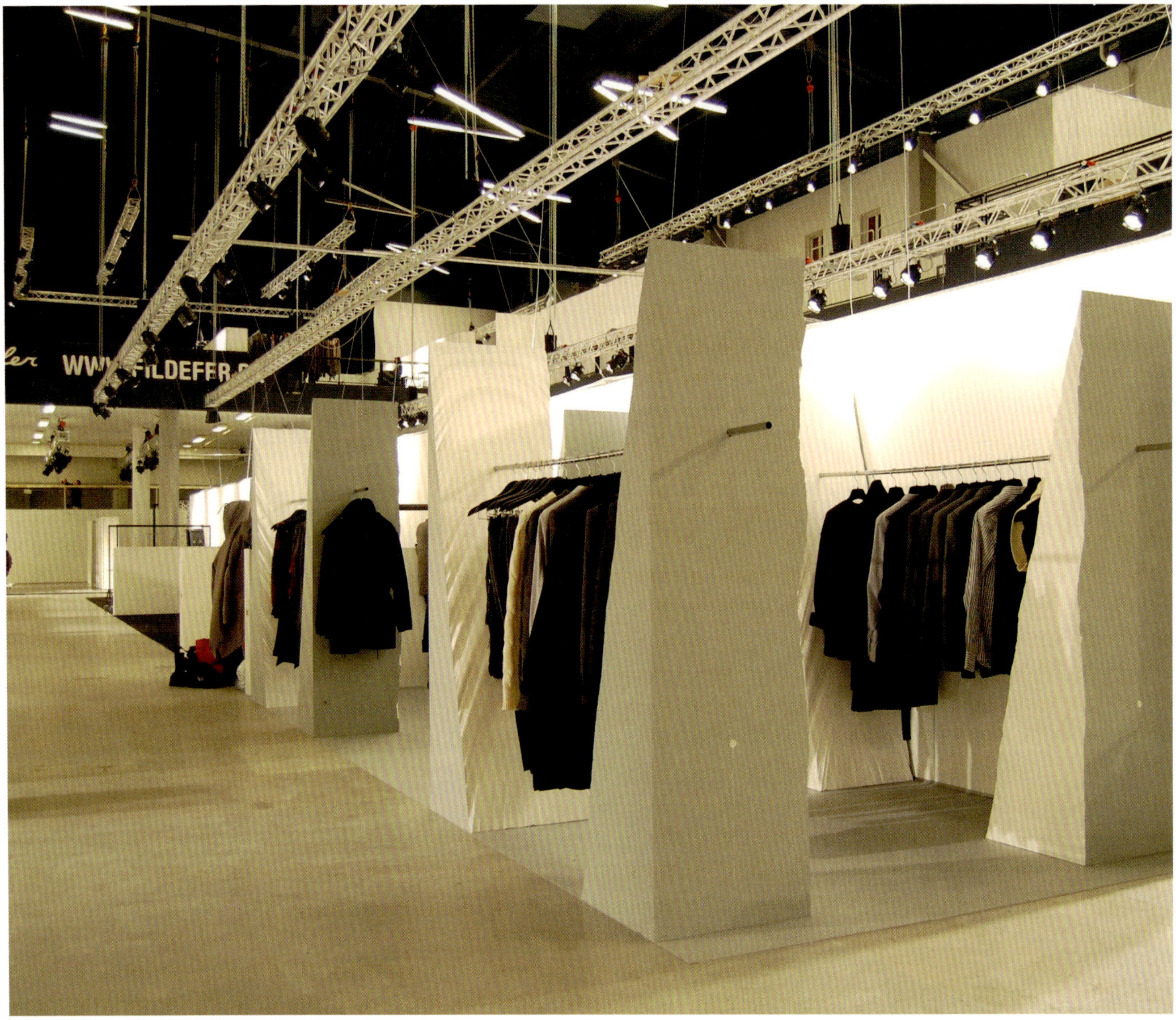

FAIR STAND FOR BLANK S/S 2009

Twice a year we design the booth for Blanks new collection presented at the fashion fair gallery in Copenhagen. Everytime we start with a short brief of the theme they have been working on for this particular collection. Most of the time it is quit abstract. A few words and a couple of images all there is for us to interpret. Fashion being maybe the fastest of all art forms gives us an opportunity to design something very fast and intuitive based on a couple of words. So much fun! This particular season we focused on the term suprematism. The display system was made out of plywood pieces glued together with a black glue. The glue was allowed to leak creating a graphic contrast to the white painted plywood.

Company : *Uglycute*
Designer : *Uglycute*
Photographer : *Uglycute*
Client : *ÅF Blank*
Counrty : *Sweden*

Shop for ANTEPRIMA wire bags. Rich colors in nearly 300 colors, and distinctive bag by sparkling light. I thought can be made to control the density change of spatial arrangement of the bag. The bags are lined so close by the wall, so you can see the beautiful color bars lined the entire figure. In contrast to the middle of the shop, the bags hanging from the ceiling, the space looks like from the stage around 360 degrees, and looks as the sparse space. We thought let's put the accent not only the products but also the lighting. It was black and white gradient color for the walls, I feel like becoming increasingly brighter as you go around the back of the store from the moment you enter. It also overlaps with elation when you enter the shop. Stainless steel mesh suspended ceiling, the impression that almost the whole space into the wire bag.

Company : *Yuko Nagayama & Associates*
Creative Director : *Yuko Nagayama*
Designer : *Kana Oshiki*
Photographer : *Daici Ano*
Client : *Anteprima*
Country : *Japan*

DELTA is a store located in Tokyo, Japan.

Company : *Yuko Nagayama & Associates*
Creative Director : *Yuko Nagayama*
Designer : *Reiko Negishi*
Photographer : *Daici Ano*
Client : *Delta*
Country : *Japan*

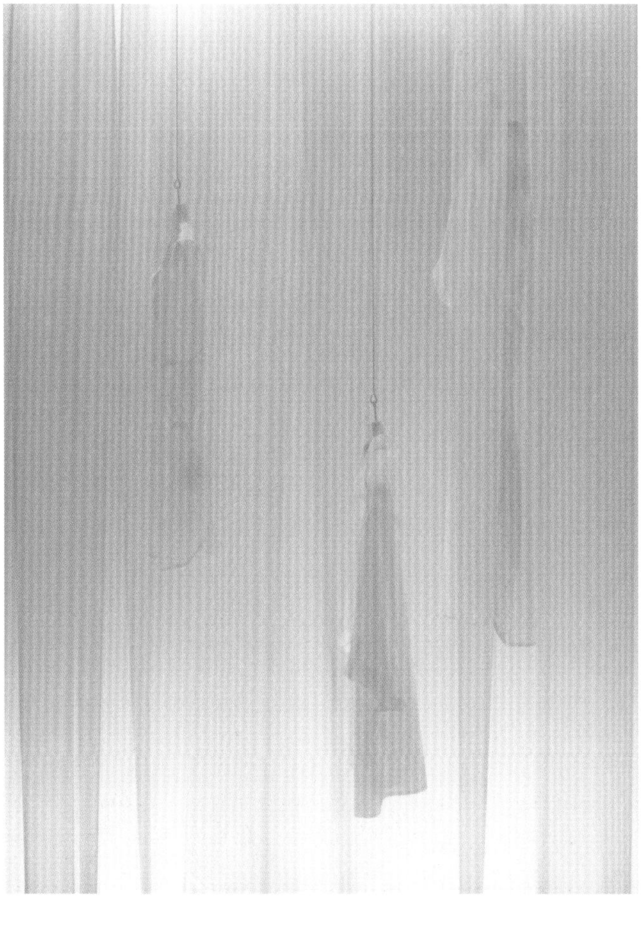

YLANG YLANG is a store located in Tokyo, Japan.

Company : *Yuko Nagayama & Associates*
Creative Director : *Yuko Nagayama*
Designer : *Kana Oshiki*
Photographer : *Daici Ano*
Country : *Japan*

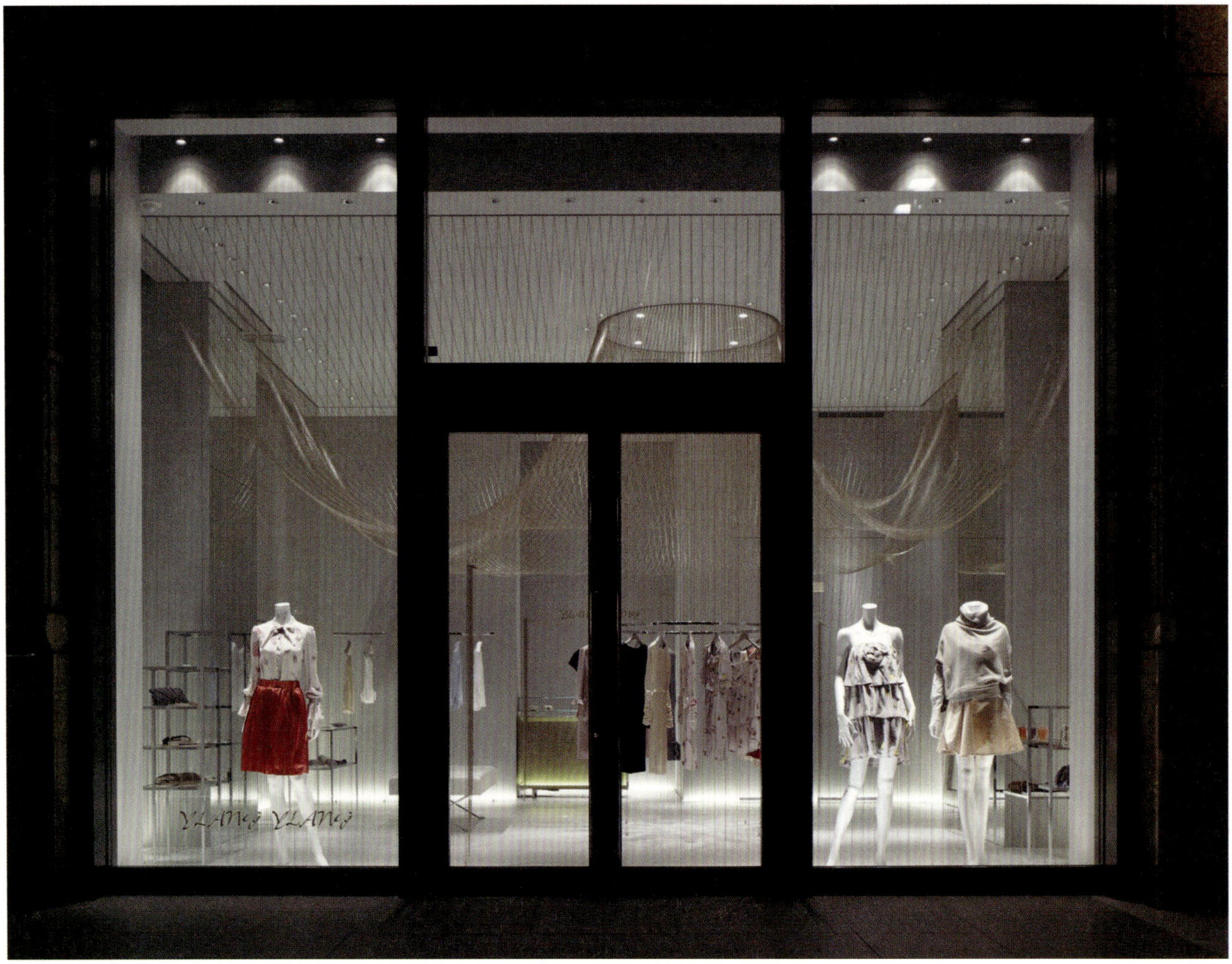

By mounting the pegboard on the entire 5m tall space, and lighting it from behind, this rough hardware store material turned into an ephemeral, lace-like dress that wraps around the space. In addition to the vertical pegboard display, horizontal display fixtures, made of found and recycled furniture pieces were cut of the pegboard dress and pulled of the wall revealing the yellow undergarment. The pegboard material was selected because it is the most basic flexible display infrastructure, which allows the constant change, growth and mutation.

Company : *Z-A studio*
Country : *U.S.A.*

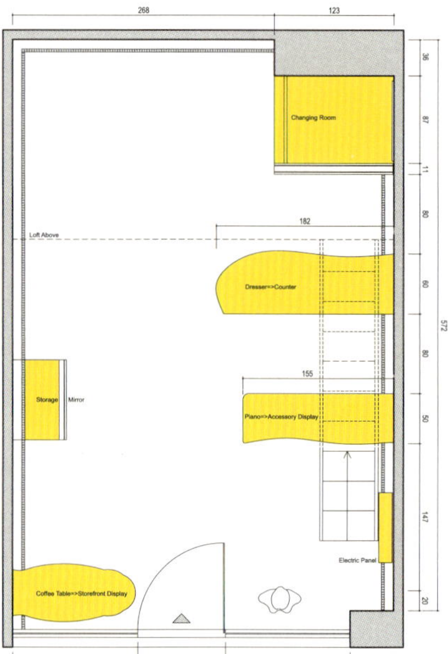

DELICATESSEN CLOTHING STORE

Every consumer of fashion is aware of the fact that he/she is paying for design rather than material. Furthermore, the pace at which an item of clothing becomes obsolete is dictated by the change of fashion trends and seasons and not by the quality of the item. Therefore the capital invested in design exceeds the funds invested in quality. In architecture the balance of investments is reversed, the cost of materials far exceeds the investment in design.

The design for the Delicatessen clothing store follows the economical logic of fashion design in an attempt to invert this typical condition. Two main strategies were brought in from the world of fashion and introduced into the space: the use of transient materials and the idea of a disjointed layer that would cover the space.

As a result all the elements in the store are made of linoleum and cardboard tubes exploring the use of thin, ephemeral and readymade materials, relative to the way they are used in fashion. By cutting, folding, rolling and wrapping, the original purpose of the material is transformed to create the display elements, fitting room, desk and store front. The space is dressed with a thin layer that can be peeled off and replaced on demand. Change of seasons or fashion trends can induce the redesign of the entire space. The reoccurring customer who is used to the change of goods can encounter an immersive transformation and the spatial design can become a commodity consumed on a regular basis.

To keep this scenario feasible the materials, which are taken out of their original context, are contrasted with their new environment. They don't blend in by producing minimal detailing or elaborate features; rather they are draped over the raw space for an easy removal. In order to maintain spatial quality without the use of fine details and materials a strong coherence is generated through the strict use of two materials, which transforms their pedestrian nature.

The organizational scheme enhances the physical connection between the production studio of the fashion designer at the back and the store space in the front. Through the existing openings between these two spaces three linoleum strips climb over, stretch and wrap around the cardboard tubes like conveyor belts. The gray linoleum belts carry all the goods while serving as their background.

Choosing the material at the beginning of the design process reverses the typical design process where materials are applied onto a concept. In this case the materials dictated the forms and functional possibilities of the elements. The display elements were shaped following the structural abilities of the cardboard tubes, the display fins utilize the flexible qualities of the linoleum and the fitting room folds the linoleum to open and disappears back into the wall when not in use. Playing with the yellow and gray double-sided linoleum accentuates these operations.

Fashion design is a creative field that has managed to completely merge with contemporary life. The entire industry is based on global reality and constant transformation. Architecture has to confront the same reality of ever-changing programs, budgets and building uses. If we want to learn from fashion design, we have to change our expectations from architecture. If we don't expect all architectural products to become monuments, if we can invest less in 'high-end' materials, we might be able to give more importance to the manipulation of material and the quality of design rather than the cost of matter, to the designer rather than the contractor.

Designer : *Z-A / Guy Zucker*

Photographers : *Naomi Yogev,*
Shay Ben Efraim

Fashion Design : *80% design / 20% material.*

Architecture : *20% design / 80% material.*

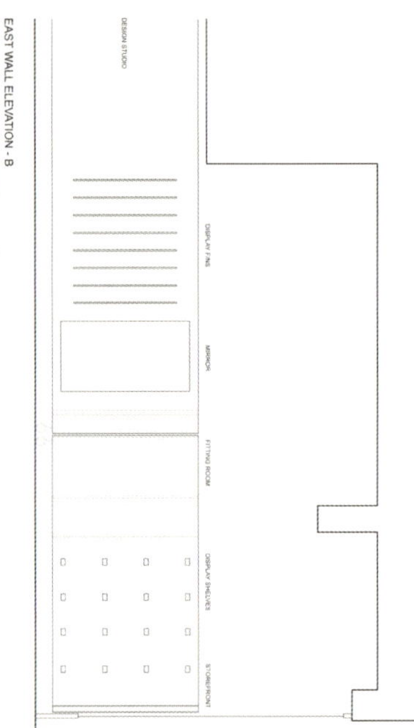

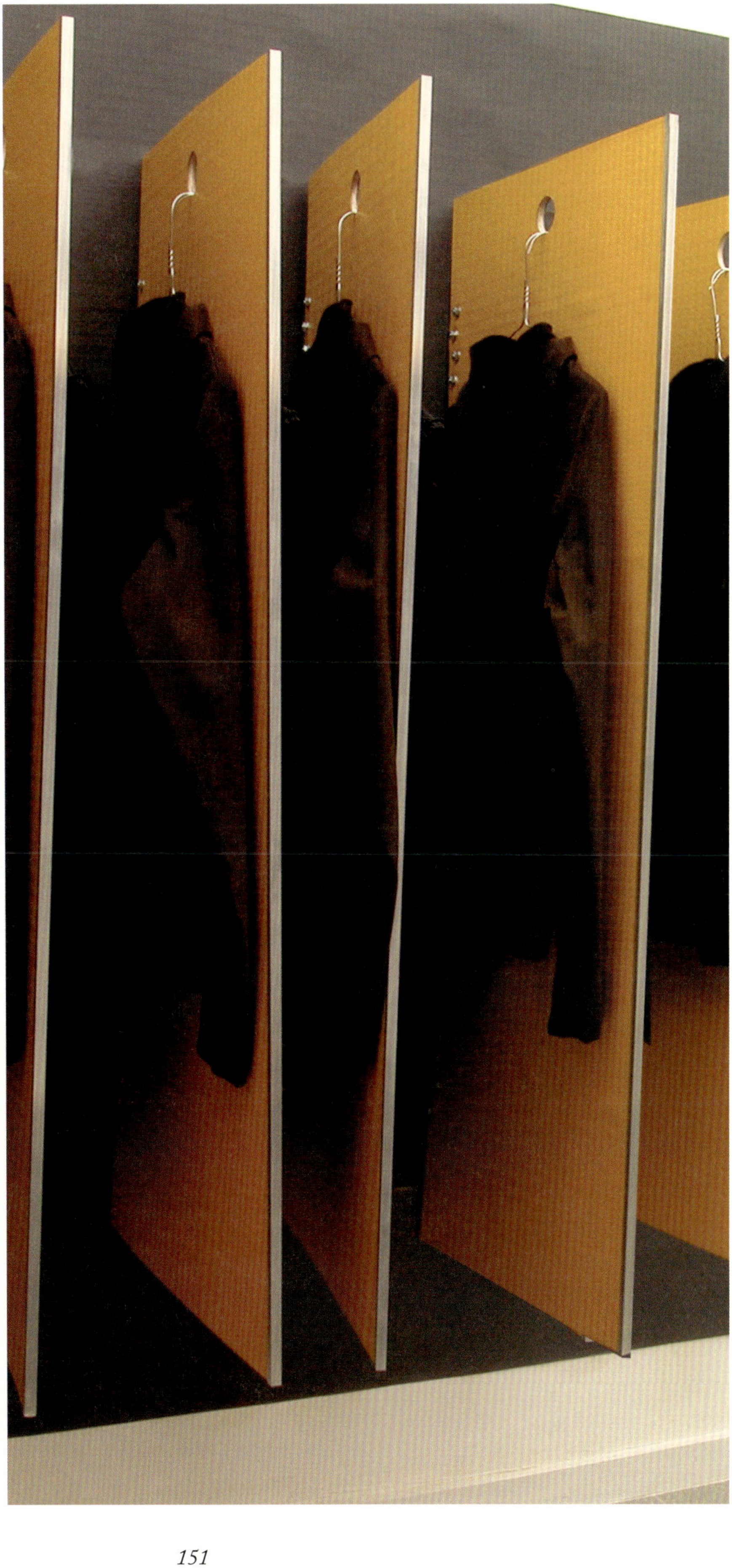

As the top brand of fashion leather products, DISSONA has cooperated with us for a long time in the image system. A series of excellent image designs have completed together for 15 years. With the long development and innovation, DISSONA brand image has grown with the progressive spirit, laying the foundation for the free expression.

Space Design Strategy

At present, needs of commercial terminal image are increased daily in the fashion industry. We provide not only the pure space aesthetics, but nice shopping experience. E.g. when DISSONA establishes a flag store in Seibu, we need to create an atmosphere with the completely luxurious value conception, to show the cut-edging sense of this brand: pure elegance.

The purpose of the image of DISSONA Flagship Store is to create a pure environment which can better foil the products and provide consumers the unique consumption experience. Besides, we will adopt the curve element to create an aesthetic feeling of arc surface. The result of challenging the domestic construction difficulty is the successful integration of future elements. A special DISSONA logo will be wove into the ivory Masland 100% wool carpet. The huge Swarovski classical ceiling pure crystal lamp will be the extremely clever decoration. The white-grey chamois European chaise lounge will emphasize the unique and luxurious quality of DISSONA.

Company : *Hallucinate Interior Design Co., Ltd.*
Creative Director : *Leo Wang*
Designer : *Leo Wang*
Photographer : *Hallucinate*
Client : *Dissona*
Country : *China*

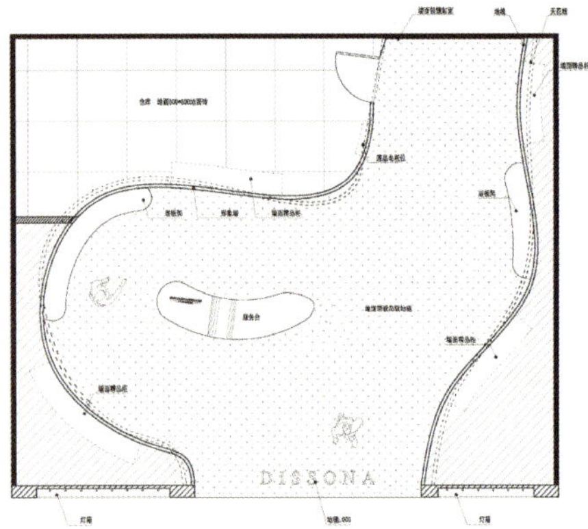
俯视图

DISSONA

Serbian design studio reMiks has completed Supermarket, a concept store inspired by the "golden years of communism". Hosting a bar, restaurant, salon and fashion boutique, the store is located in a former discount supermarket in Belgrade. Found objects including a fridge, hospital screens and a camper van are used as display devices.

The 1400 m² site of the Supermarket concept store is an actual former discount supermarket, the first one ever to be opened in former communist Yugoslavia. reMiks' relaxed attitude toward the "Golden years of Communism", coinciding with the period of brutalism in architecture, was the constant source of inspiration for the reMiks team.

The interior is intentionally raw and seemingly unfinished, so various delicate or luxurious objects or hedonistic activities that take place in an extremely ascetic environment. The installations are visible, concrete floor is cracked, toilet doors were taken off a derelict freight elevator. Retail modules were produced from recycled wood material (OSB). According to the designers, their intention was to create an "imperfect background for the educated consumers' perfect fetishes".

The interior is divided into functional areas:

Bar area is 25 meters long, along the length of the retail area.

Fashion Lounge covers more than 150 m².

Spa and hair salon covers 350m².

Restaurant 200m².

Art & Design Exhibition space intervenes with all these areas.

Intentionally raw approach plays an important part in introducing contemporary art and design into commercial, retail spaces. Supermarket is on a fast tract to become an arts & culture destination of regional importance. Supermarket is one of the locations of the first Mikser Design Expo, another brain child of reMiks / Mikser collective, taking place on 6-12 June, 2010.

Supermarket concept store improves the existing retail concepts in Belgrade in several ways:

Slow shopping enriched with various experiences, flexible space, perfect for various events, cultural content, Promotion of young designers, inventive ways to showcase the products, influencing the consumers' tastes, more interaction with consumers and more high-quality information about brands, eco-friendly high quality/high style merchandise.

Improvements in retail experience are achieved by inventive consumer education. Serbia moved from Communism to market economy during the times of Balkan wars in the 1990s, which followed the prosperous 1970s of Marshall Tito's Yugoslavia and unstable and declining 1980s, of the post-Tito's Yugoslavia. Basically, the market is still relatively undeveloped - the mass consumerism is a recent phenomenon, along with the typical obsession with big brands: Nike, Gucci, big flashy brands with large advertising budgets. On the other hand, this is a small market, where even those big budgets don't sell many pieces.

But, even in a market this small, there is people who have lived abroad, travelled a lot, and are now past the mass consumers' tastes. These are the people that Supermarket is targeting, offering them a place where they can buy certain things that are a little more suited to their more refined tastes. On the other hand, to the mass brands consumer, Supermarket is offering something else, but they do need to be educated about niche brands. For example, a line of perfumes called Escentric Molecules. They're enough of a niche brand to be obscured/sought after by those in the know (depending on your prospective) even in New York, where you can have ANYTHING, but we've managed to convince them to sell their merchandise in Serbia, in Supermarket. And those who knew about the brand were ecstatic to be able to buy it without having to travel abroad. For those who didn't know it took some in-store promotions, PR, product placement etc. to get them to notice it.

Company : *Studio Remiks*
Country : *Yuhoslavia*

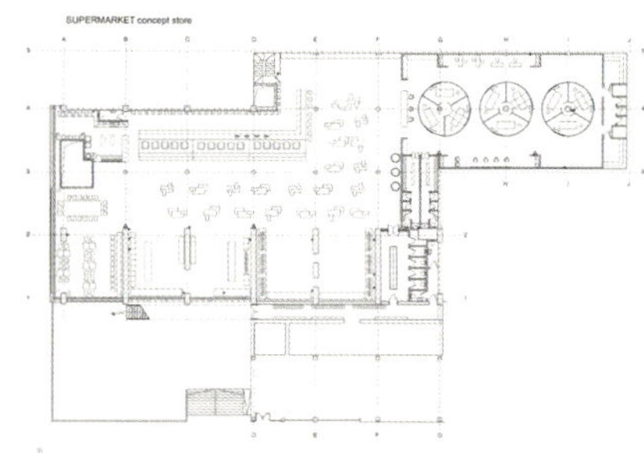

The Richard Chai store is a temporary retail installation created by Snarkitecture in collaboration with designer Richard Chai as part of the Building Fashion series at HL23, presented by Boffo and Spilios Gianakopoulos. Carved from the confines of an existing structure beneath the High Line, the installation envelops visitors within a glacial cavern excavated from a single material.

White architectural foam is cut by hand to produce erosions and extensions of the sculpted walls and ceiling to create a varied landscape for the display of Richard Chai's collection. The range of shelves, niches, hang bars and other moments embedded within the form encourage the designer's curatorial eye for display. At the close of the temporary installation, the material was returned to the manufacturer and recycled into rigid foam insulation.

Company : *Snarkitecture*
Designer : *Richard Chai Paired With Snarkitecture*
Photographer : *David B. Smith*
Country : *U.S.A*

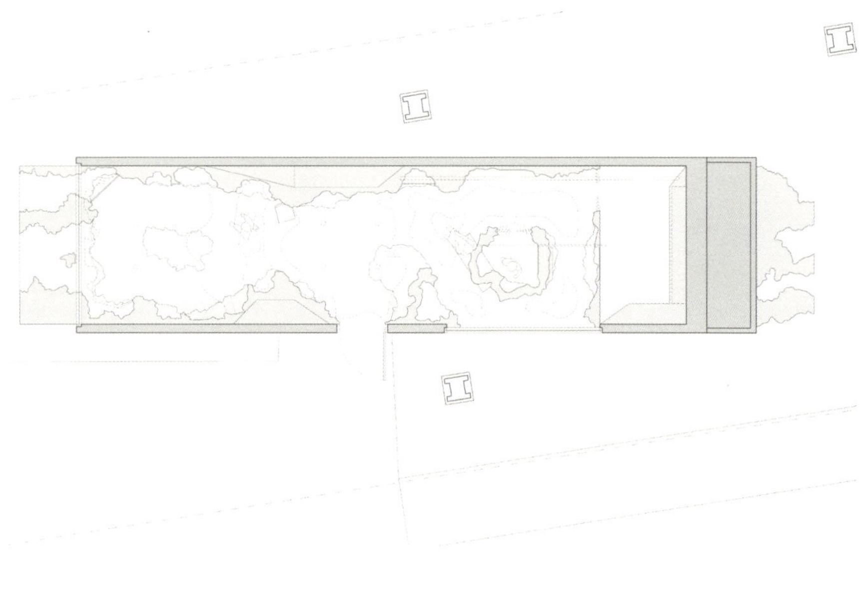

RICHARD CHAI × SNARKITECTURE

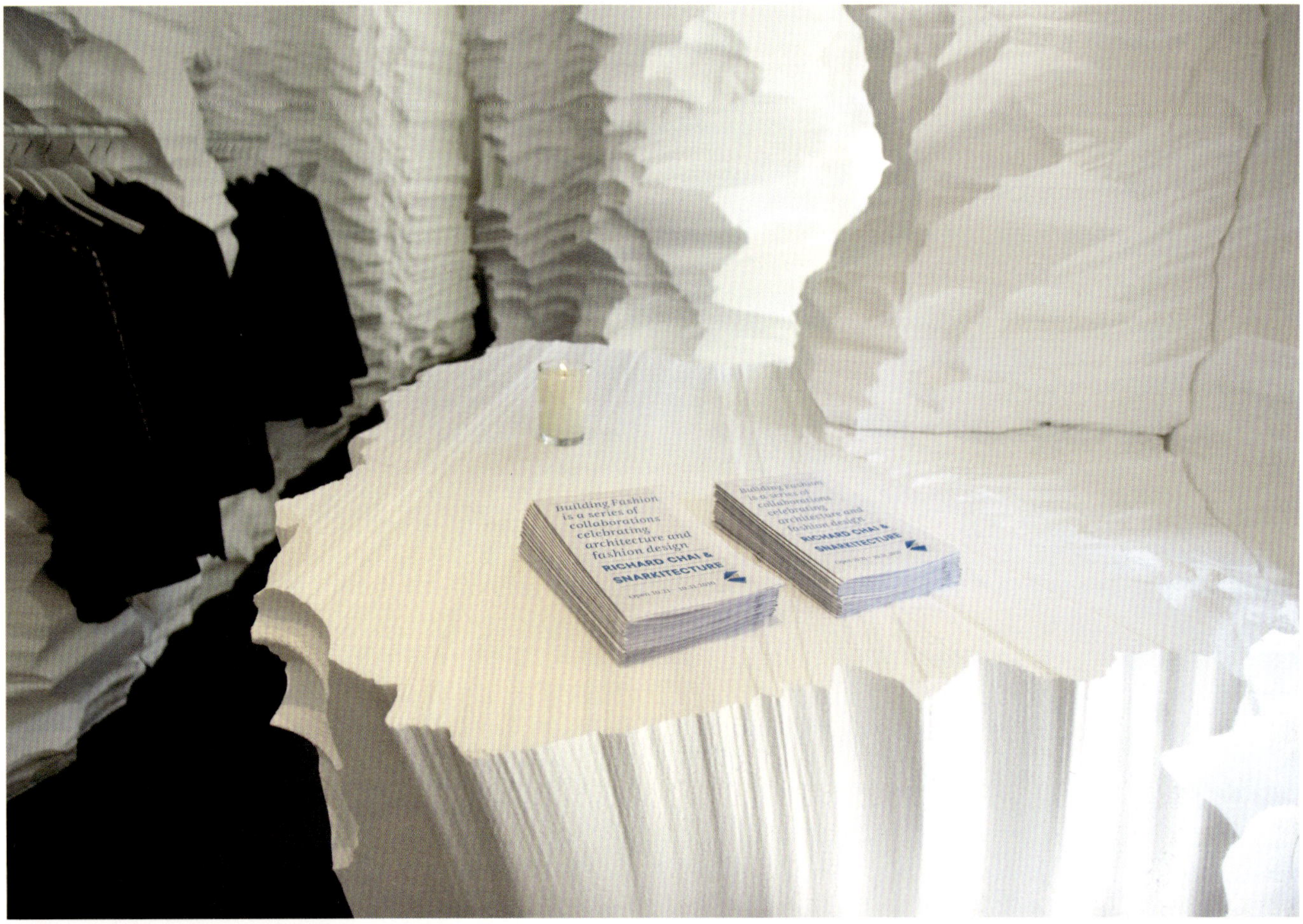

Building Fashion
is a series of
collaborations
celebrating
architecture and
fashion design
RICHARD CHAI &
SNARKITECTURE

UBIQ

UBIQ is a store located in Philadelphia, USA.

Company : *Architecture At Large*
Country : *U.S.A*

Boutique by many scattering boxes:
In now days huge logistics supports our consumption lifestyle.
Nowadays, we cannot live without huge logistics that supports our consumption lifestyle. In this boutique, we use boxes, the symbolic element of shipping, to create interior space that arouse consumer's appetite. We brought 150 boxes into over 350 s/m white space and arranged those boxes three dimensionally by using laying off and interlock system. People will walk around as if they try to find bargains in a warehouse.

Company : *Sako Architects*
Creative Director : *Keiichiro Sako*
Designer : *Tomoaki Murata*
Photographer : *Zhonghai Shen*
Client : *Jeanswest International(Hk)Ltd.*

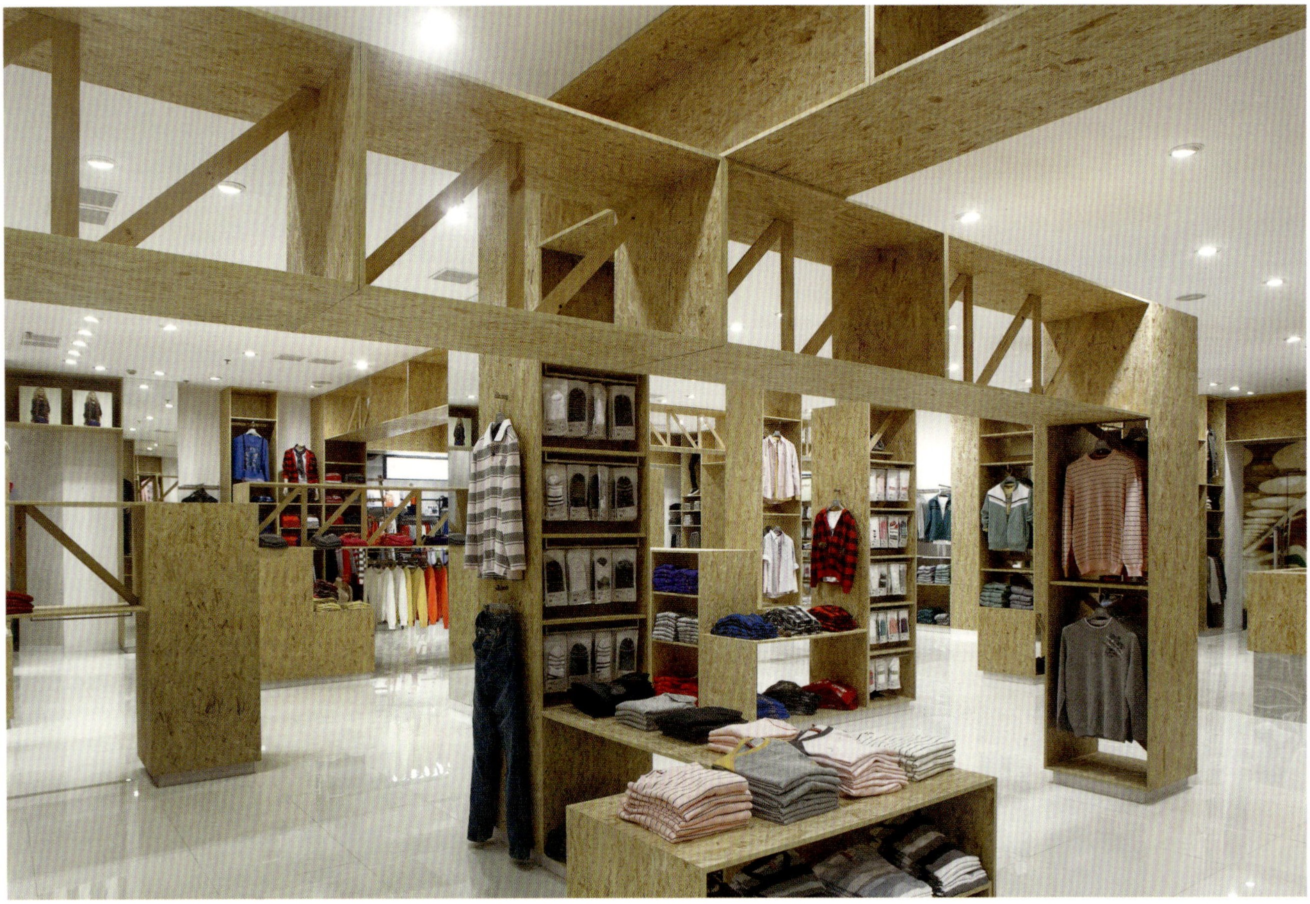

THE ALV SHOWROOM is a boutique.

Designer : *Fabio November*

Jean Charles de Castelbajac, the most British French designer, just opened his new concept store in the fashion heart of chic Mayfair, at the corner of Conduit Street and Saville Row.
JCDC Flagship Store is designed by Christian Ghion, who is already responsible for JCDC store in Paris.
A mix of tradition and underground on two levels, the 300m² London space is organized in such a way by Christian Ghion that it can adapt itself to JCDC's strong graphic sense and the diversity of his collections. Through a kaleidoscope of fabrics and flashy primary colors (which are Castelbajac's trademark), his wallpapers, furniture and tableware, his men's and women's fashion and his art, are all presented in a deliberately "work in progress" atmosphere. This Rock n' Roll attitude qualifies JCDC's work as well as the Rubik's cube cash register, the neon lights and his portrait overlooking the stairway and made out of…Lego The façade is reminiscent of those in the theater districts of London or New York.
One more time, the complicity between Christian Ghion and the iconic french fashion designer has created a very unique "pop punk teddy bear" world !

Company : *Christian Ghion Studio*
Creative Director : *Christian Ghion Studio*
Designer : *Christian Ghion Studio*
Photographer : *Christian Ghion Studio*
Client : *Pierre Gagnaire & Intercontinental*
Country : *France*

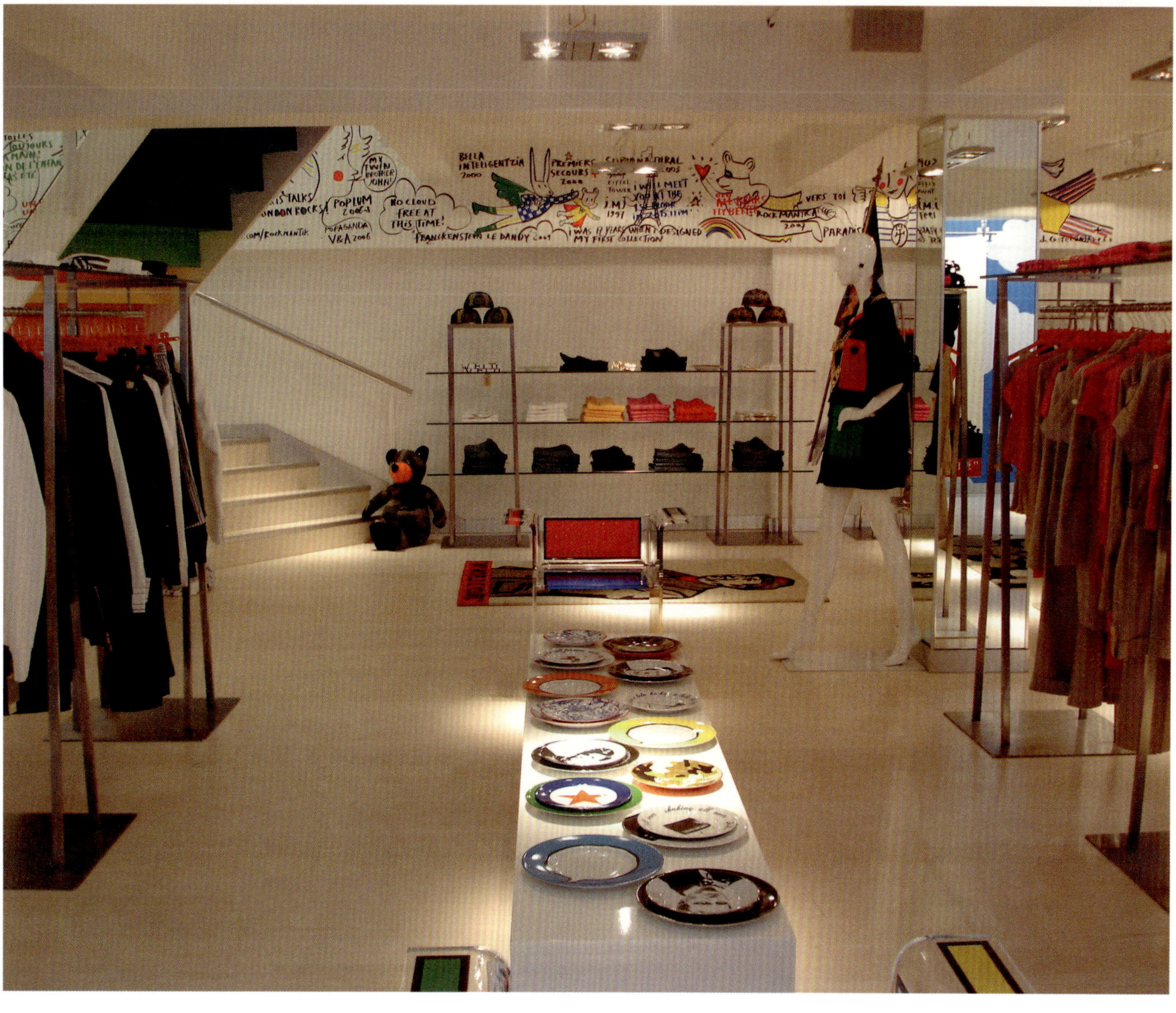

This new branch of Vakko, located in Istanbul's new shopping mall in Istinye Park, features women's, men's and couture apparel, in the long rectangular 1500 m^2 space. This project pairs the avant garde style of Vakko with classical modern elements. The travertine walls reach down to a black and white granite floor and upward to a ceiling composed of laser cut ornaments. Brass display units are an eye catching addition to the couture section, while a billiards table punctuates the men's section.

Company : *Autoban*
Photographer : *Ali Bekman*
Country : *Turkey*

Dooney & Bourke turned to Jeffrey Hutchison & Associates to create a bold new visual language for the brand while simultaneously maintaining respect for the heritage of the company. This retail concept is brought to life in a sophisticated freestanding store that occupies approximately 2,500 square feet on one level in the new Venetian Macau Resort. JHA created a modern yet warm environment that updates the Dooney & Bourke image while expressing the richness and detail found in its product.

The front of the store incorporates a dramatic wall sculpted out of wood slats, creating a front entry for the space and highlighting key products to passerby. JHA utilized nautical inspired details and forms, interpreting them in a modern way for an experience that is both somewhat familiar and fresh. The curved, slatted wood walls provide a rich backdrop for the Dooney & Bourke product.

The interior of the store is separated into two rooms which allows for a variety of product stories. Transitioning from the dramatic curved wood entry into the front space, this first room incorporates beautiful lacquered wood cabinetry with lighting details which focus on and highlight the merchandise. Moving into the next space feels like another room in this sleek "yacht" with its long lit wood shelves and vaulted ceiling. The more intimate proportion of this room allows customers to experience the finely detailed product at close proximity.

The primary materials utilized include travertine marble floors, Venetian plaster, cherry wood curved slatted walls, and antique brass highlights.

Company : *Jeffrey Hutchison & Associates*
Creative Director : *Jeffrey Hutchison*
Designer : *Jeffrey Hutchison*
Photographer : *Charlie Xia*
Client : *Dooney & Bourke*
Country : *U.S.A*

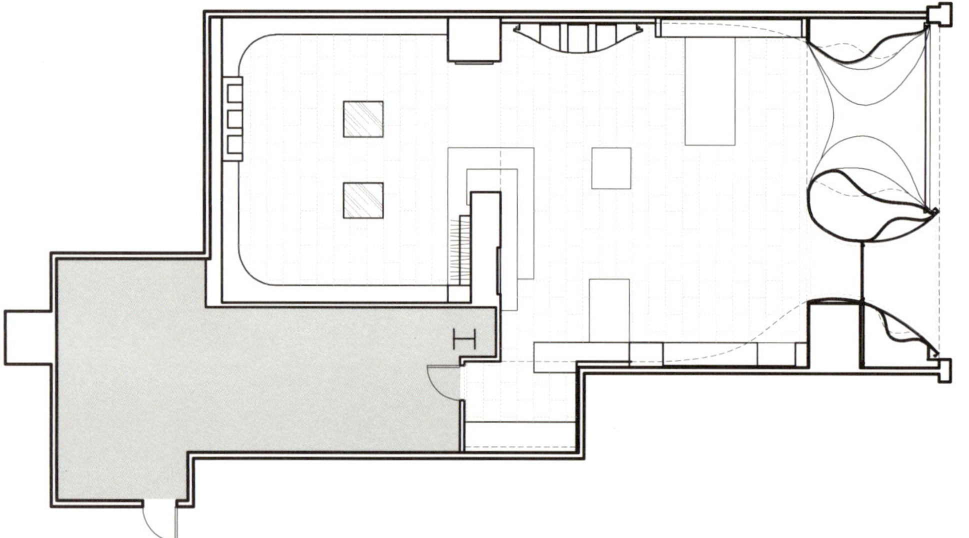

In the heart of Chicago's fashion district, at the corner of Oak and Rush streets, Barneys New York offers this great city a new 91,500 square feet elegant and unique fashion retail emporium designed by Jeffrey Hutchison and Associates.

The six story integrates architecture, art and merchandising into one language, while respecting the city's great architectural heritage. The classic design, evoking such iconic structures as Louis Sullivan's Carson Pirie Scott store, is enhanced through the use of Indiana limestone and bronze-framed windows.

This newest Barneys New York outpost features seven floors of the Barneys trademark mix of pulse-quickening merchandise, each level conveies a distinct feel and experience that coordinates with the wares:

The striking first floor (devoted to women's accessories and jewelry) is inspired by the grand shopping emporiums of the early 20th century. For fragrance and cosmetic fans, The Foundation is located in the lower level, down a geometric, sculptural staircase. The Foundation features a beautiful white marble floor in a geometric pattern accented by back-lit decorative murals, highlighting the product and conveying a clean, fresh sensibility.

Traveling up the angular floating staircase clad in glass and stone, clients reach the "Women's World" on the second floor. To display the tantalizing selection of footwear, JHA created variegated acrylic shelving on which shoes appear to nearly float. Women's designer apparel fills the remaining gallery-like space highlighted by a contrasting gray limestone floor designed in a graphic triangular pattern. The space is further enhanced through the use of bold light coves throughout the ceiling, creating a strong visual pattern. Arriving at the third floor, featuring casual women's wear, customers are greeted with an industrial-inspired design scheme – featuring oak, raw steel and whimsical painted furniture.

The fourth floor showcases men's designer clothing and sportswear, with its roughly hewn "end grain" wood floor and rich materials such as white lacquer, bronze, oak and mahogany. The classic man will find a welcome home on the fifth floor with a modern, clubby vibe exhibited in its white wenge wood walls, bronze metal accents and teak floors. Chelsea Passage sits in the clouds, resting on a portion of the sixth floor next to Barneys' signature eatery, Fred's. This light and airy space is a perfect backdrop to the beautifully edited home and gift product.

Company : *Jeffrey Hutchison & Associates*
Creative Director : *Jeffrey Hutchison*
Designer : *Jeffrey Hutchison*
Photographer : *Adrian Wilson*
Client : *Barneys New York*
Country : *U.S.A*

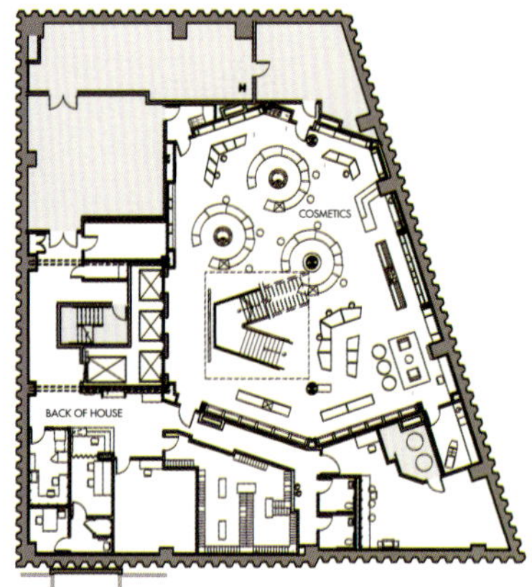

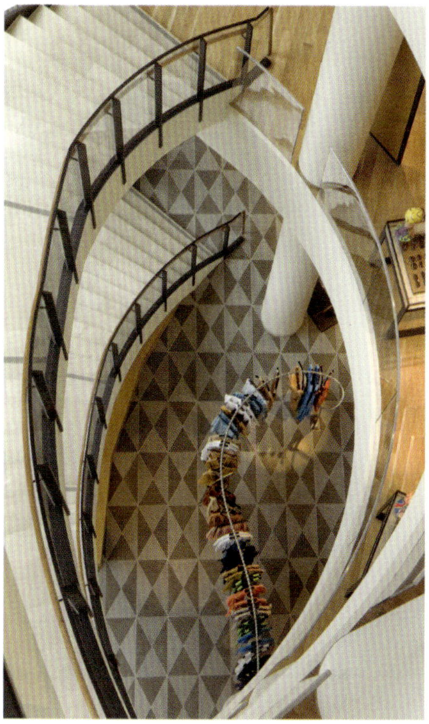

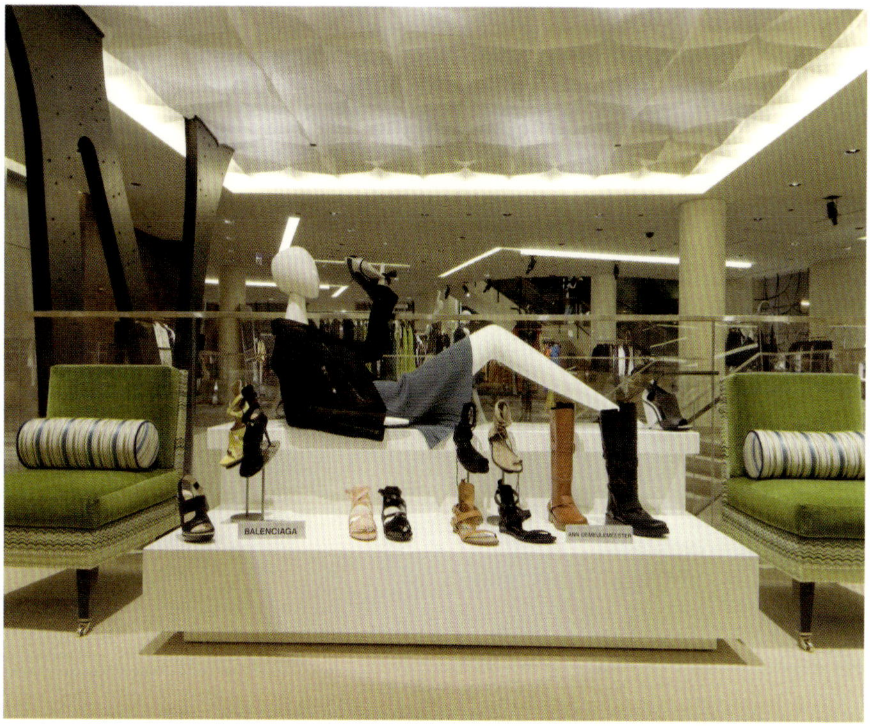
BALENCIAGA

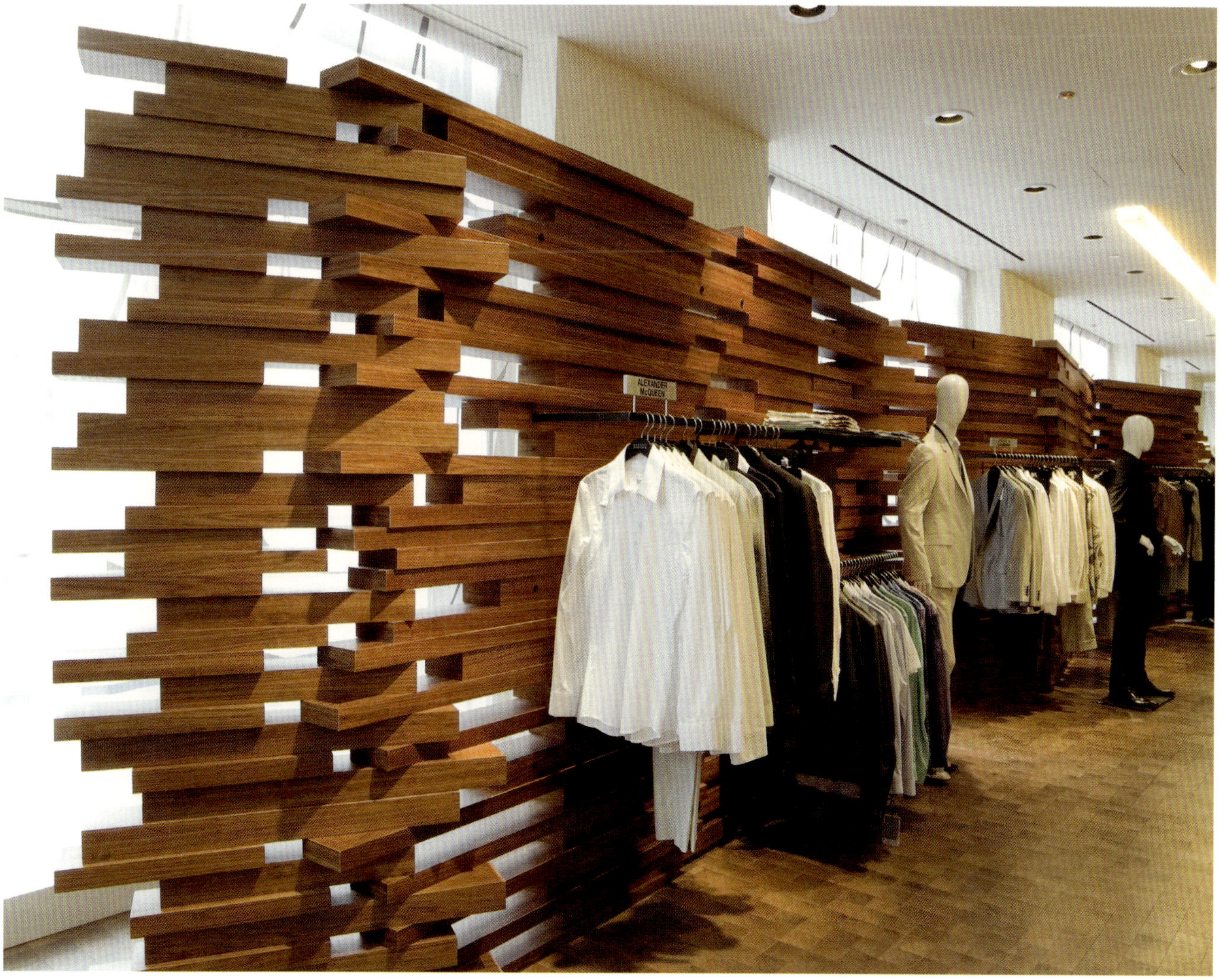
ALEXANDER
McQUEEN

BALENCIAGA
BARNEYS
NEW YORK

CANDIDO1859 DEPARTMENT STORE

The last of three floors, the men's department of Candido (opened 1859) is among the first designer-label store to open in Southern Italy.
The mirrored ceiling heightens the space which grabs the visitor before enticing them down a coloured path of light.
The raised central patio modifies the surrounding space through a combination of perspective and illusion, one blue tumbling into another.

Company : *Local Office for Large Architectures.*
Designer : *Local Office for Large Architectures.*
Photographer : *Francesco Prato*
Country : *Italy*

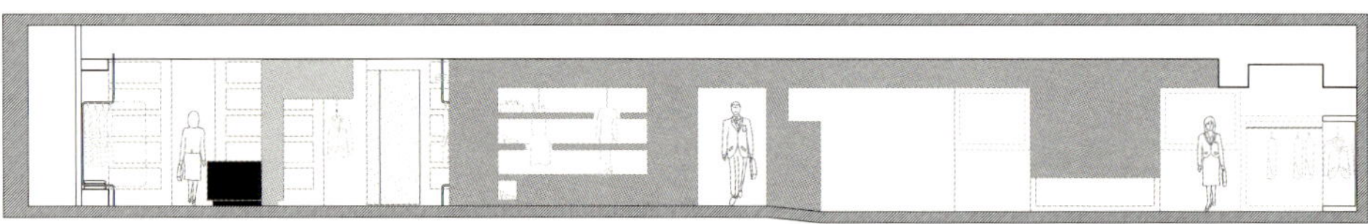

SECTION.**2**

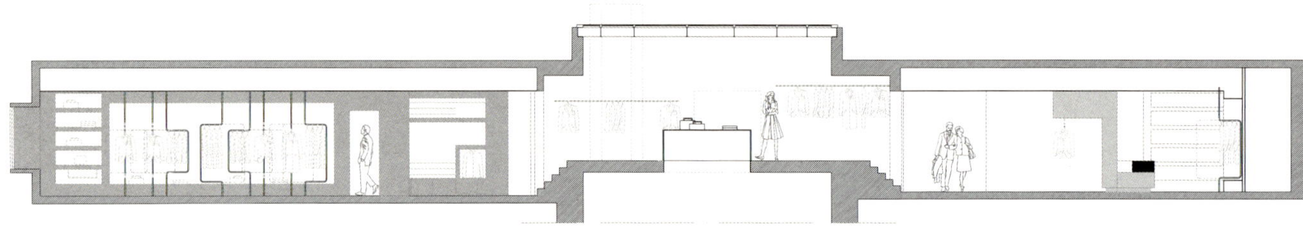

Located in a new luxury mall among top international and Indian designer shops the client wanted his store to make a strong design statement and set itself apart from other stores.

Keeping this in mind we consciously chose a different approach to the interpretation of luxury – rather than using opulent materials and symbolic artifacts to represent luxury we sought to create a sleek, uncluttered space that through its dynamic, understated articulation of space would convey a sense of high-end design.

The concept for the store was based on Origami – an idea of a space enclosed by folded planes of paper and initial forms were explored by making rudimentary studies in paper. The permutations of these forms were then studied and reconfigured using numerous scale study models of the space. Eventually the design was finessed using 3-D modeling software that was instrumental in generating the 28 sectional profiles that served as the basis for the working drawings.

The design consists of two folded white planes suspended inside a dark wooden box. Contained within these planes are various functional requirements, from the main garment display racks [lit from above] to the AC ducts and vents. The cash counter was also tucked behind one of the planes, as the large dressing area which is closed-off with a thick red curtain. Suspended from the metal trellis false-ceiling are hundred of flowers, lazer-cut from sheets of acrylic - a boisterous assemblage that offers a striking contrast to the straight lines of the folding planes below.

Company : *Romi Khosla Design Studios*
Designer : *Martand Khosla*
Photographer : *Saurabh Pandey*
Client : *Suneet Varma Designs Pvt. Ltd.*
Country : *India*

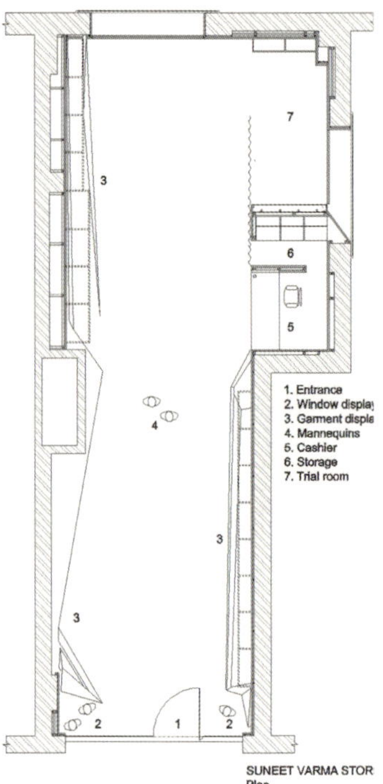

SUNEET VARMA STOR
Plan

ORNAMENTS SHOP

ISE Jewellery was an existing family business that approached HEAD for a re-branding exercise and moved of location within the Peninsula Hotel in Hong Kong. The traditional serve over counter style was retained but the rest of the store was modernised. By developing the existing logo into a repeat element, this simple effect was then used on double sided glass throughout the store. The exterior of the store was treated with strong matching grooved glass and one-off male and female mannequins were designed for the show window to specifically showcase individual pieces of Jewellery.

Company : *Head Architecture And Design Ltd*
Designer : *Head Architecture And Design Ltd*
Client : *Ise Jewellery*
District : *HongKong (P.R.C)*

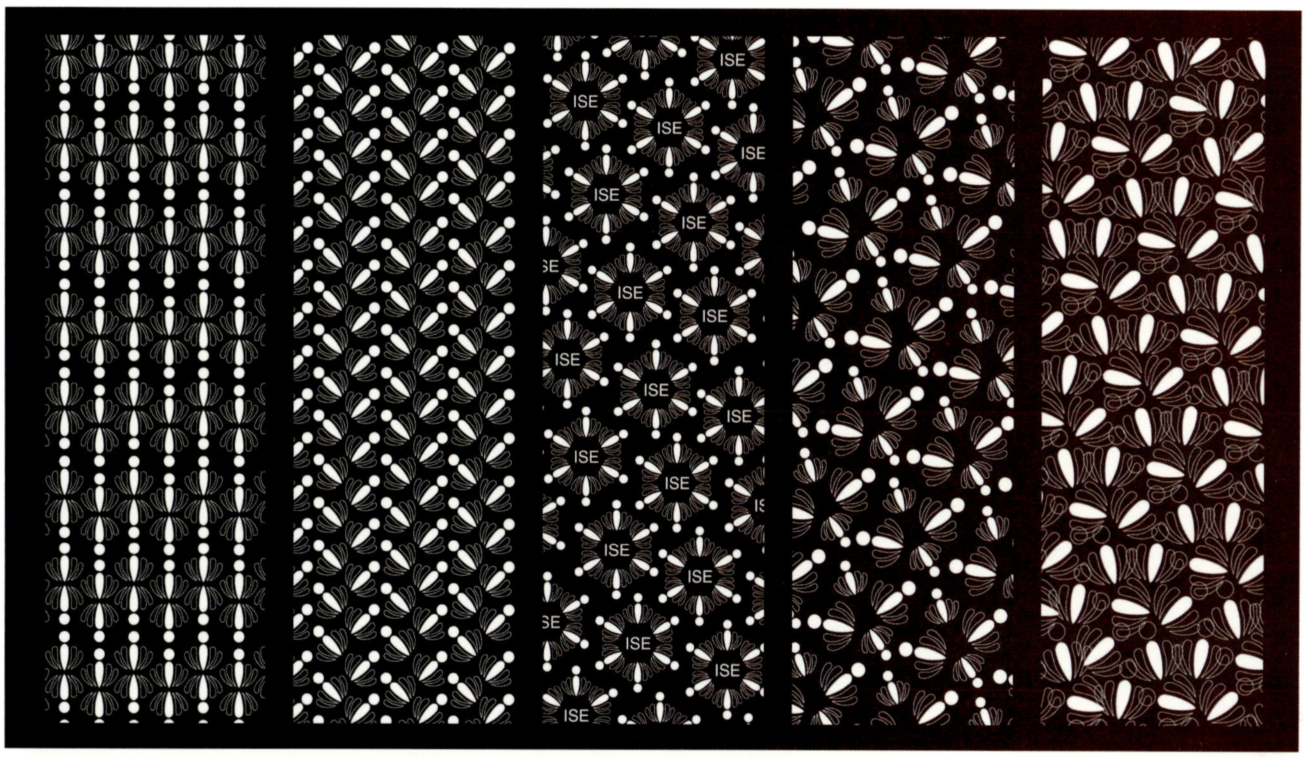

MAUBOUSSIN U.S. FLAGSHIP STORE

For the renovation of the five story townhouse, Rockwell Group is creating an experiential environment in which guests can discover the imaginative fashion jewelry. With the objective of evoking an emotional connection between the customer and the jewelry, Rockwell Group is focusing on playfully displaying the merchandise and capturing the magic of the brand with many layers of surreal and unexpected design details.

Façade/Entrance

The spirit of discovery is introduced. Even before entering the store, visitors will find a glass vitrine with perspective "trompe l'oeil" framing beautifully lit jewelry cases. Inside is a dramatic corridor with a sparkling glass wall on one side and another glass vitrine on the other side. After hours an interior kaleidoscopic projection, designed especially to illustrate the magic of the color and geometry of Mauboussin jewelry, is visible by passersby outside.

First Floor: Lifestyle Jewelry

The journey through the store commences on the first floor, a dark dreamscape space provides a dramatic backdrop to the spot-lit colored lifestyle jewelry glittering in glass treasure boxes. At the entry, a bouquet of stars features Mauboussin's signature rings. Rockwell Group plays on the traditional notion of a townhouse with walls clad in dark sandpaper with copper stitched moldings. For a twist on this classical reference, the stitched moldings are not complete, adding to the surreal nature of the environment. In the center of the space is a lit sparkling, faceted glass wall rising through all three retail floors. The sales pods are intimate areas identified by comfortable wingback chairs and custom designed ceiling features such as sparkling beads or rich tulle to provide privacy for the store's patrons. To proceed to the upper floors, one can either take the grand stair, or the elevator, which surprises the shopper when the doors open as it is designed as a little personal boudoir or powder room complete with a dressing table, pouf and mirror.

Second Floor: Diamonds

The second floor showcases Mauboussin's diamond jewelry. Each case has a magnifying glass on top to encourage customers to lean in, and engage with the jewelry. The silver stained wood floor and the etched graphite plaster walls serve to complement the sparkling diamonds.

Third Floor: Bridal

The third level is the bridal floor. It is a glamorous, feminine environment, featuring light satin, lace, tulle, feathers and antiqued mirror.

Fourth Floor: "Salon de Gourmandises"

On the fourth floor, guests will be able to combine the pleasures of trying on jewelry with tasting chocolate delicacies and "gourmandise" and enjoying delicious hot beverages. On the dining tables are cases that fan out to reveal various layers of jewelry. The space boasts exposed brick walls, contrasted with amber onyx counter tops, pickled white oak millwork, and white cerused chocolate-brown oak floors.

Fifth Floor: Loft

The top floor is an open loft space featuring reclaimed wood floors, exposed brick walls, and an eclectic mix of vintage and custom modern furniture and lighting. This space will be used for private dinners, and will be the site of a monthly dinner hosted by a top Parisian chef.

Company : *Rockwell Group*
Designer : *Rockwell Group*
Photographer : *Barbel Miebach*
Country : *U.S.A*

GLOCKENTURM TASCHKENT / BELFRY TASHKENT

Ippolito Fleitz Group has designed the interior architecture of the Uzbekistan International Forums Palace, located on Amir Timur Square in the heart of the Uzbek capital Tashkent. The palace was ceremonially opened in September 2009 to celebrate the occasion of Tashkent's 2200th anniversary. A jewellery shop, housed in one of two historic bell towers providing the design prelude to this representative ensemble on Amir Timur Square, was also designed as part of the project. Entering the space is like stepping inside an ornate jewellery box. The rooms translate the exclusive nature of the goods on display both thematically and functionally. Dark walls are completely overlaid with laser-cut decorative ornamentation, made from highly-polished stainless steel panels that depart from the wall surface and enter the space itself. The effect created is that of a second skin that develops unexpected depths of light. The length of the rooms is optically elongated by means of ornamental, tinted mirrors on the end walls and a dynamic lighting element crossing the ceiling. Only a few selected openings such as windows and display cases break the boundaries of this shimmering casket. Precisely illuminated jewellery display cases, in part equipped with monitors, offer the ideal stage on which to present precious collections of jewels.

In the historic setting of the bell tower, Uzbekistan's design traditions melt and merge with a contemporary design language. The historical ornamentation at the tip of the pointed arch windows casts its reflection upon the stainless steel patterns in the interior. Interior and exterior, old and new are thus con-joined and intermingle in a fascinating synthesis.

Company : *Ippolito fleitz group*
Designers : *Peter Ippolito, Gunter Fleitz, Tilla Goldberg, Steffen Ringler, Alexander Fehre, Christian Kirschenmann*
Photographer : *Zooey Braun*
Client : *Republic of Uzbekistan*
Country : *Uzbekistan*

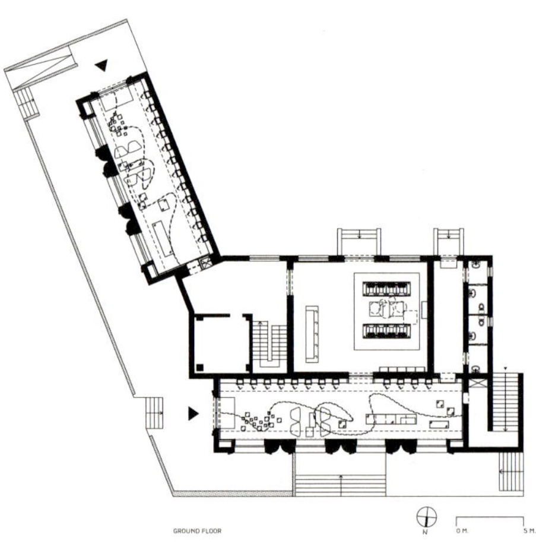

A CLOCKWORK SNOW

Mechanical gears seem to drop from heaven like icy snowflakes, crystallizing into a magical machine frozen in time. The gears represent our rational world, but here they transcend the purely utilitarian to become a romantic, haunting dream.

Tjep. was invited amongst six other international artists and designers to create a Christmas window for Italy's most famous department store: La Rinascente on Piazza Duomo in Milano.

Company : *Tjep.*
Designers : *Frank Tjepkema, Leonie Janssen*
Country : *the Netherlands*

CONTEMPORARY
CHRISTMAS
ART

The LADG designed a luxury retail space with custom lighting and flexible display fixtures in Frank Gehry's Edgemar Retail Complex in Santa Monica, California.

RK Apothecary is a spatially effcient and visually engaging retail space. The product is taken off of the shelves and displayed on a series "outré fruit" tables so the customer can engage with it.

The RK Apothecary space before the redesign was small and dense with structural and mechanical elements that could not be altered. The LADG's design had to respond to the existing interior because the client did not have the luxury of gutting it and beginning fresh. The double-height ceilings required them to develop hanging lighting fixtures to activate the space.

Square or rectilinear tables were either too big to allow customers to pass through the store or too small to accommodate the large number groupings of product desired by the client. Given the constraints, the LADG experimented with water filled ice bags - reminiscent of those used by British nurses to sooth the fever of an ailing patient in a 1950's film. They observed how the bags slumped, folded and wallowed around obstacles. The displays were designed to imitate the posture of ice bags in order to navigate through difficult fits between columns and oddly planned corners.

Company:

The pragmatic problems served as a point of entry to design. They drew parallels between the large display "pods" and the anatomy of fruit. Take the strawberry as an example. The exterior gives little clue to the structural nature of its interior. By peeking inside the relatively plain skin of the displays, the "outré fruit" could reveal a very different, exotic interior.

As this line of thinking matured, the architects looked at still-life paintings by Caravaggio and Rubens. Designers Andrew Holder and Benajmin Freyinger describe the inspiration, "These artists used fruit as sumptuous, scene-setting devices in exactly the way we hoped to deploy our outré fruit to present product in the store. In that sense, the outré fruit is set afloat inside the environment and piled with tempting objects to browse."

Company : *The Los Angeles Design Group*
Photographer : *Todd Weaver*
Country : *U.S.A*

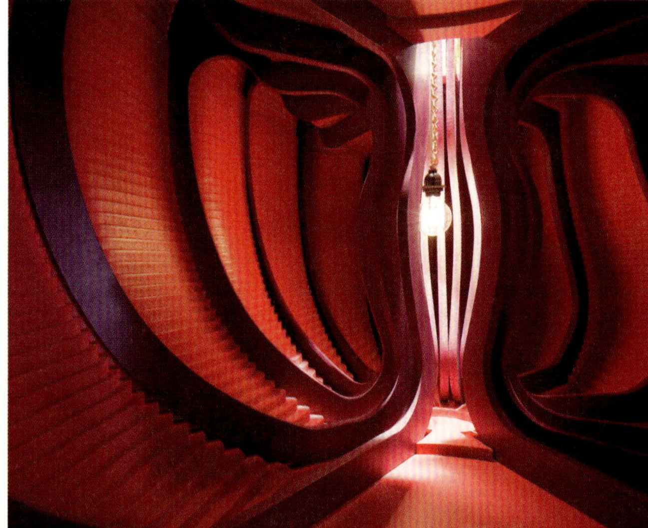

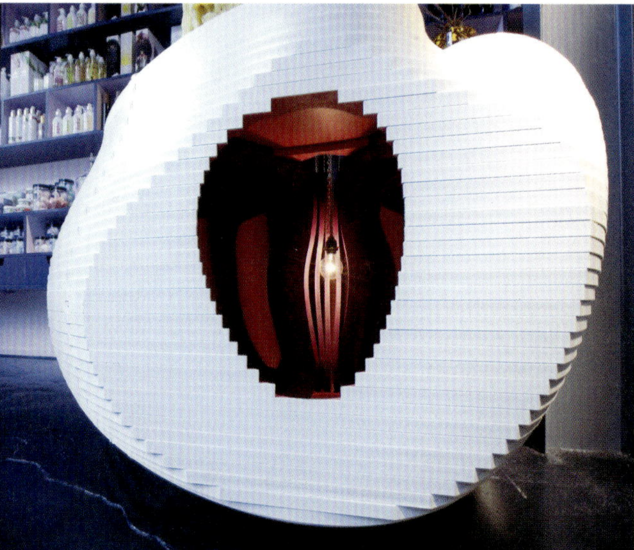

Estée lauder founded this company in 1946 armed with four products and an unshakeable belief that every woman can be beautiful. Today, more than 60 years later, which simple notion has literally changed the face of the beauty business. The main objectives of Plajer & Franz studio were to create a contemporary image for the traditional brand name. Designed for an a-list hosting event in the foyer of Berlin's most glamorous department store: the KaDeWe. Despite the extroverted appearance, the choice of clear colours and clear forms also suggest to bauhaus and art deco style, the whole high quality optic provides allusions to the story of the maison. The creative design of Plajer & Franz studio managed to seduce both, the visitors at the ism, and the exhibitor whose expectations have been by far outranged.

Company : *Plajer & Franz Studio*
Designer : *Plajer & Franz Studio*
Photographer : *Ken Schluchtmann*
Client : *Estée Lauder Companies Gmbh*
Country : *Germany*

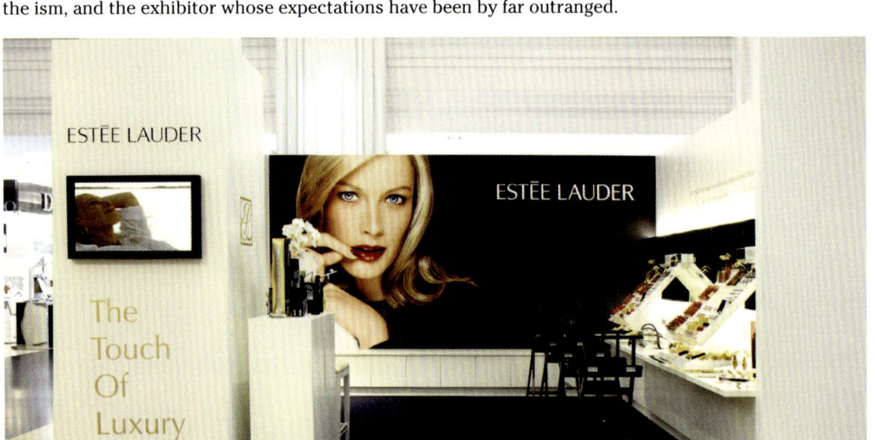

ESTÉE LAUDER
ESTÉE LAUDER
The
Touch
Of
Luxury
ESTÉE LAUDER
The
Touch
Of
Luxury
KaDeWe

The town of Mosbach lies around 30 km north of Heilbronn and is an important medium-sized centre for the region. Conradt Optik is an established specialist opticians located in the centre of the town's pedestrian precinct. After many successful years of operation, the business is now being handed over to the next generation of owners. The new owners are looking to differentiate themselves from the competition through focusing on a select segment of brands and individual customer care. This new direction has been further underscored through a comprehensive refurbishment programme. The entire building façade was renewed as part of the renovations, thereby making the shop's new profile immediately evident from the outside. Long windows stretch down to the ground, giving maximum insight into the representative interior, which in itself becomes the window display. An adjacent shop space was incorporated into the existing space, producing an elegantly elongated floor plan. The space opens straight onto the pedestrian precinct on two sides. Both entrances lead towards the main service counter, which serves as the centrepiece of the room.

The rear wall merges seamlessly with the ceiling, which contains a recessed area giving onto the longitudinal side. This design differentiates the area for browsing from the customer service area, as well as connecting the two entrances with each other. The recessed ceiling is decorated with a fine structure of lines in subtle tones of brown, mauve and blue, evoking associations with the stroma and play of lines in the iris. The room is encapsulated by an organically curved rear wall, which brings a generous dynamic to the space. It conceals existing fittings such as the stairs and workshop, and is connected with the ceiling via a wide-radius cavetto. Its soft contours formulate the wideopen horizon of the space, while at the same time dividing it into individual zones, which group the product line naturally into glasses for women, men and children. The glasses are displayed in three recessed horizontal bays, which span almost the entire length of the rear wall. Precision front and rear lighting creates a stunning presentation space for the glasses. Flush-set storage space for the entire product line runs beneath the display bays. Parallel to the windows on the longitudinal side are three floating displays. These are set at a slight angle and are reserved for the opticians' range of sunglasses. Continuous rear lighting ensures that the eye is drawn to the beauty of the products themselves, while simultaneously giving a rhythm and depth to the space.

Various free-standing display cases provide space for special presentations. Oval displays set in eye-catching places in the rear wall create attractive focal points for customers entering the shop.

Customer service takes place at two conference islands at each end of the longitudinal axis. Arching tabletops continue the soft lines of the design idiom, while at the same time creating an open and transparent atmosphere for discussion and customer proximity. In the rear area of the shop, steps lead up to separate refraction rooms. The entire shop space is fitted with a deep-pile, anthracite-coloured carpet. This ensures good acoustics while enhancing the soft and flowing character of the interior. The complete redesign of Conradt Optik supports the opticians positioning within the high-end segment. The exciting inter-play of light and dark sets the stage for an attractive display of products. Colourful accents are subtly set by the products and the structure of lines on the ceiling. The latter also delivers a unique key visual, which is employed in various settings in the company's communication, for example on the paper bags.

Company : *Ippolito Fleitz Group*
Designers : *Peter Ippolito, Gunter Fleitz,*
Alexander Fehre, Tim Lessmann,
Christian Kirschenmann,
Vincent Gabriel, Anne Lambertz,
Axel Knapp (Graphics),
Yuan Peng (Graphics)
Photographer : *Zooey Braun*
Client : *Conradt Optik GmbH*
Country : *Germany*

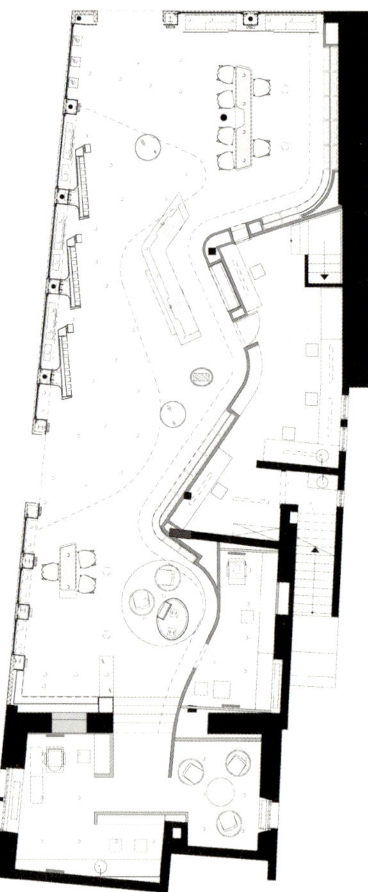

CENTRE VU, MONTREAL, QUEBEC

Centre VU is a full service optometry centre, offering brand name high end frames and sunglasses. In 2008, the call to update and refresh the entire store's image came to fruition and Ruscio Studio was once again called upon to take on this challenge.

The existing store design had 3 major design issues to address: first, after 12 years without renovations, and with the overwhelming success of the Signature Collection Department redesign, the mandate to update the whole store image was inevitable; second, the layout, with its tall floor units, made it difficult to have a clear overall view of the store; third, too many random brand images (POP) created clutter and took over the merchandise.

Successfully taking away the clutter and putting the merchandise back in the spotlight via lighting, graphics and a unique eyewear display system, the new design for Centre VU is simplistic and stylish and once again well represents the high end brand name products being sold.

Company : *Ruscio Studio Inc.*
Creative Director : *Robert Ruscio*
Designer : *Robert Ruscio*
Photographer : *Leeza Studio*
Photography
Client : *Le-Centre VU*
Country : *Canada*

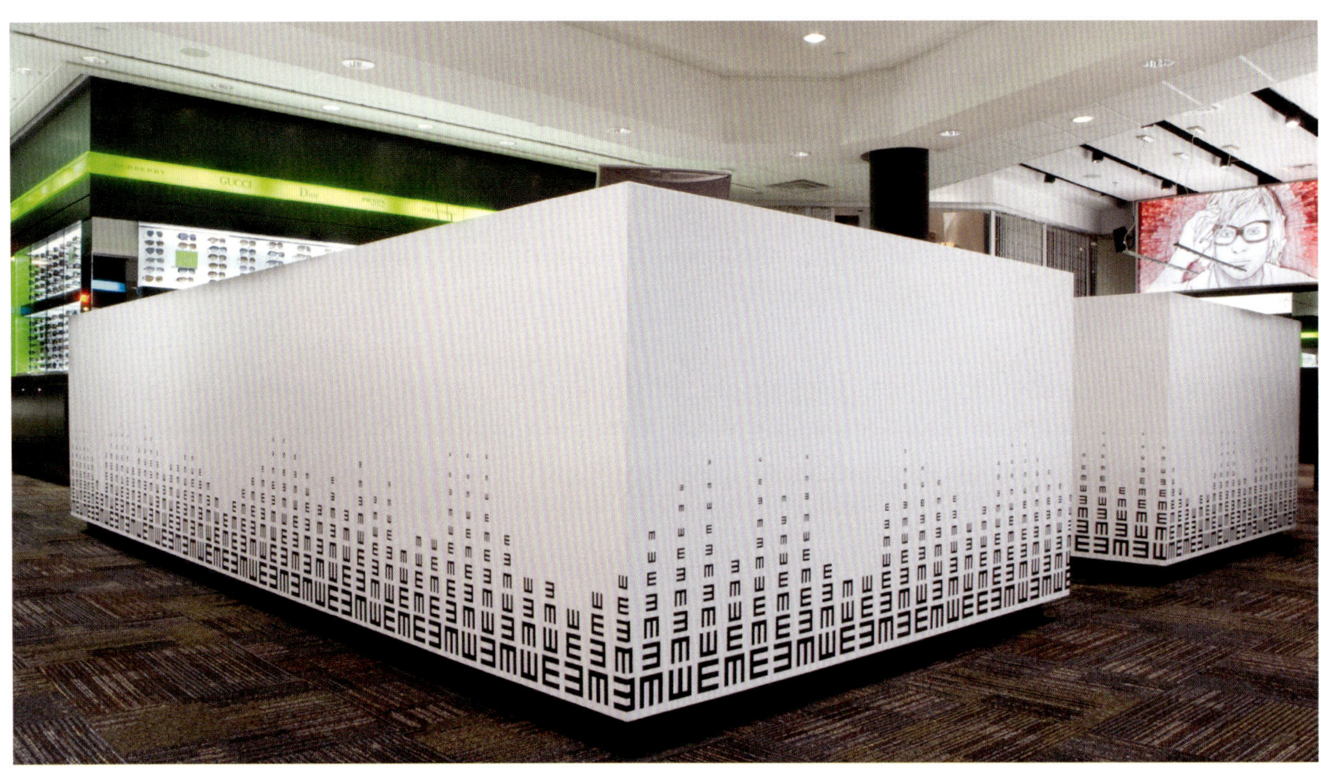

Alberto Apostoli has designed the concept retail for the Flagship of Comete Jewels in Milan. Thanks to the experiences consolidated in various fields of project, the Italian architect was able to rielaborate a place of traditional purchase in a place of multisensory and emotional design. The idea is born from the "claim" of the well known brand Comete - "Romanticamente schierati" (lined up in a romantic way) - that places side by side a rich intimate dimension of feelings and emotions and a rational and pragmatic attitude. The space assumes a double dimension, which allows to communicate truth and dream with creativity. Emotion and colour are the key words of the plan, mainly interpreted through an important use of forms, light, sounds and aromas. The sale point becomes a luminous backdrop "punctuated" by illuminated (led) circular display windows of three different dimensions that seem to fluctuate on a hypothetical horizon. The light of the backdrop keep changing creating itself emotions and games always different during not only the day but also based on the seasons or to the various periodic or thematic occasions. The integrating sound is part of the plan and bound together to the use of essences perfumed used for the packaging, constitutes a special and evocative sensory unicum. The white colour dominates in an important way but they are the colours and the light that create the best scenarios.

The external window is instead pure form that alloy the inside to the outside in natural and nearly geometric way. A game of empty and full circles that want to read Comete world through a magnifying lens intentionally alienated from the real world. The plan could not be born without a deepened acquaintance of technologies RGB and to a background of experiences tied to the Wellness and the multisensoriality that Apostoli has made in the past few years. The concept, in conclusion, wants to impose a new way to conceive the sale point of the jewel; a way that tries to stimulate the customer much through the product and "the romantic" feeling as well as through emotions.

Company : *Alberto Apostolic Architecture&Design*
Creative Director : *Alberto Apostoli*
Designer : *Alberto Apostoli*
Photographer : *Luca Morandini*
Client : *Comete Gioielli*
Country : *Italy*

TRADE FAIR STAND FOR STOCKHOLM FURNITURE

The stand was designed for &tradition for the Stockholm Furniture Fair 2010. It has been built entirely from the metal book case system NORM BLOX designed by norm. The system consists of two different sizes of metal book cases that are connected with ultra strong magnets. The back and the front of each case can be changed in color and material according to the use and the NORM BLOX can be used as tables, podiums, etc.

For this stand space, which was relatively long and narrow, the obvious choice was to go vertical to give a sense of impression. The cases were stacked in rhythmically to obtain a playful but strict character that suited the brand identity. For the fronts and backs the &tradition brand colors were chosen as well as prints of all the designers as marble busts. The products were fitted nicely into the over dimensioned shelves giving a distortion of the proportions. Towards the front of the stand five big BLOX were used as podiums with concrete tops and leg in natural oak, transforming the BLOX into small designer tables. From the ceiling were hung formations of different lamps in groups functioning almost like a transparent curtain.

Company : *Norm.Architects*
Creative Directors : *Jonas Bjerre-Poulsen &Kasper Ronn*
Designers : *Norm.Architects,Jonas Bjerre-Poulsen &Kasper Ronn*
Photographer : *Jonas Bjerre-Poulsen*
Country : *Denmark*

&tradition
&TRADITION. THE NORDIC HERITAGE
IN CONTEMPORARY DESIGN
ANDTRADITION.COM
MILK
SHUFFLE TABLE

FLOWERPOT
BULB

BOOK SHOP

Drawing inspiration from stepping patterns commonly found in Navajo blankets, Rafael de Cárdenas constructs a new retail space for OHWOW, the creative collective spearheaded by Al Moran and Aron Bondaroff. OHWOW Book Club is located below street level in a landmarked historic brownstone on Waverly Place. At 150 sq ft, this pocket-sized store was conceived by de Cardenas to echo a classic black & white, pre-war NYC bathroom. Its shelving units appear stacked one atop the other and the negative space behind the shelves lends a floating sensation. A layered pattern of stream-lined brushstrokes on the walls, coupled with reflective angular mylar shapes and sharp fluorescent lighting give the space a sense of disorientation and chaos, fitting in OHWOW's vision of creating a heterotopic arena for cultural projects.

Designer : *Rafael De Cárdenas*
Photographer : *Floto + Warner*
Client : *Ohwow Book Club*
Country : *U.S.A*

The NEW PEOPLE J-Pop Culture complex opened in the heart of Japantown, San Francisco; an area home to a five-storied pagoda that offers a curious and exotic sight even to the Japanese visitor. It is in this extravagant setting that we designed the interior of the new building, set to become a center showcasing modern Japanese popular culture, at the request of the owner, a manga (Japanese comics) publisher and president of the company managing the complex, VIZ Pictures, a distributor of Japanese cinema in the USA. We were primarily involved with designing the interior of the public spaces such as the lobby on the 1st floor, the NEW PEOPLE THE STORE retail shop on the mezzanine, as well as the gallery and VIZ Picture's offices located on the 3rd floor. The building also houses a movie theater in the basement and various tenants on the 2nd floor.

The side panels of the mezzanine shop's displays feature faces of characters appearing in manga by artist Yuichi Yokoyama to bring out the flat 2D quality of the medium and represent the company's colors, whose growth has paralleled that of Japanese comics.

The "Face Furniture" characters seem to engage in a lively dialogue with each other as speech bubbles, like those found in comics, adorn the horizontal displays on the floor and the vertical displays on the walls.

On the 3rd floor, a display area lined with movie posters and film crates separates the president's office from the rest of the office space where we find three islands of desks, curved as to avoid uncomfortable gazes, and a kitchen counter placed by the window, giving the whole area the welcoming atmosphere of a big dining room.

Due to the limited execution time available and quality assurance concerns, all pieces of furniture were made in Japan so as to be readily assembled on site.

By integrating the 2D motifs of manga to the 3D depth of architecture, we produced an abstract yet intriguing effect. Furthermore, we were inspired by the building's name to create a space where one can experience a unique and rather surrealistic worldview to foster the appreciation of modern Japanese popular culture by all visitors to "NEW PEOPLE".

Company : *Taiji Fujimori Atelier*
Photographer : *Daici Ano*
Country : *Japan*

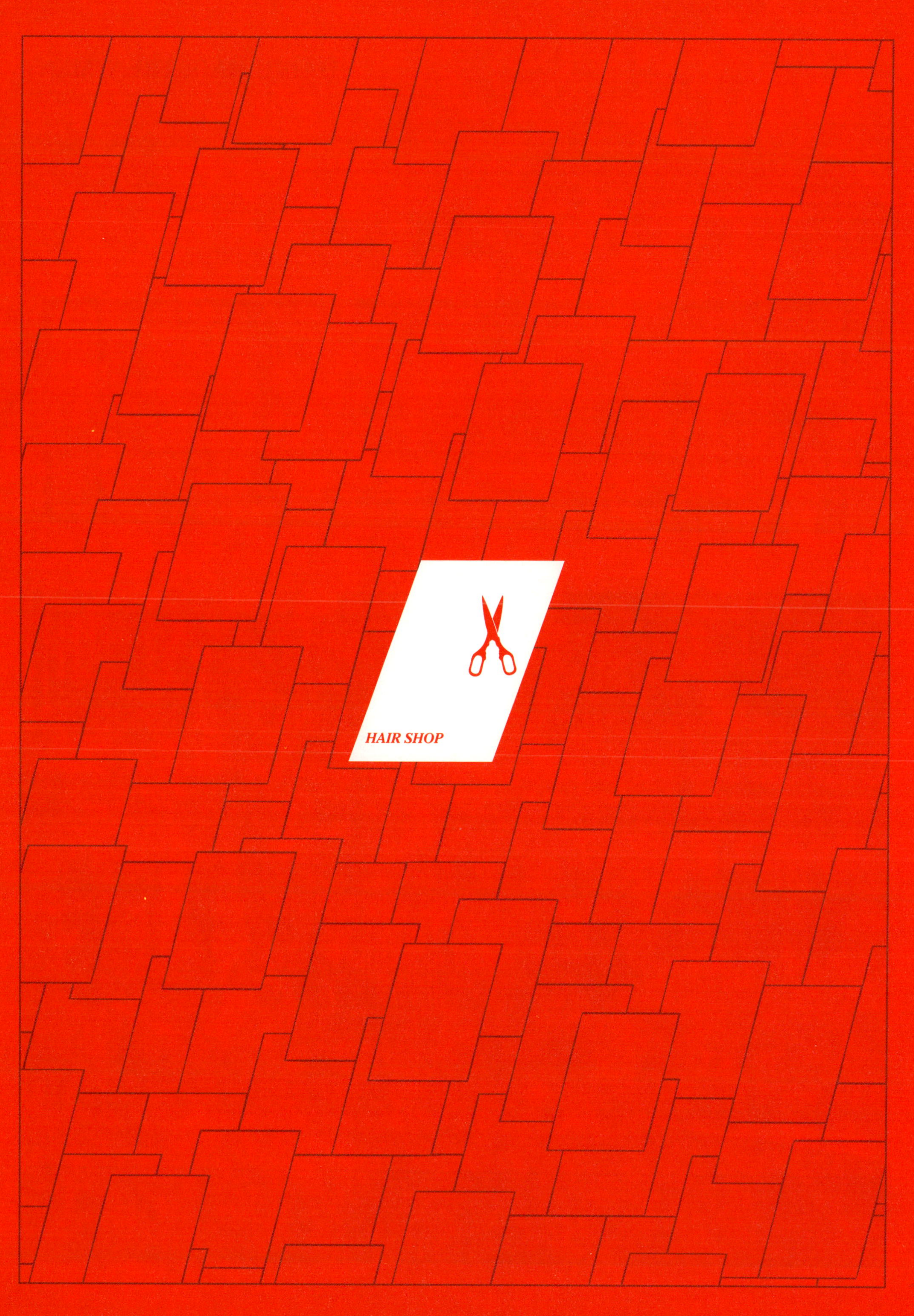

HAIR SHOP

HAIRU HAIR TREATMENT

Started with modular design and built through generous clean and simple detail, perform in natural material scheme and color, brought you to the difference experience of leisure. It may look like a salon, but hairu is a hair health-care, such as treatment for losing hair, hair spa & massage.

The vocal point is the 2 (two) faced rough balian stone which also as a transition door to the wash area. The ribbon mirror on the both side wall is carried through the view of all the space with the private sight just for the client without having eyes contact with the therapist.

The soft material, vitrage, is acting as a divider which could be moved to get along with the other. And the hard material, cotton, is as a permanent divider from the main corridor.

Company : *Chrystalline Artchitect*
Designers : *Febrian A. Wijaya,*
Nelly Candra
Photographer : *William Sebastian*
Country : *Indonesia*

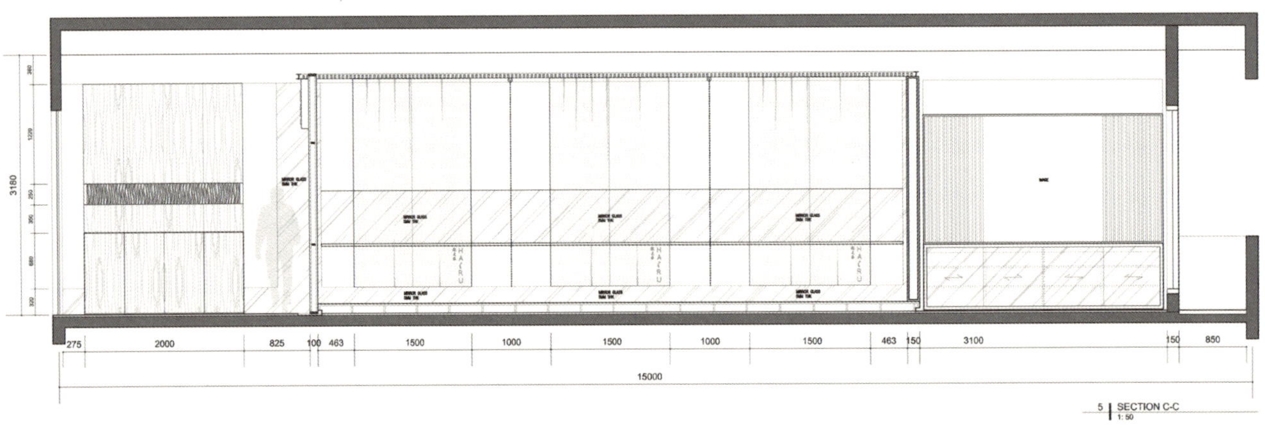

HARU

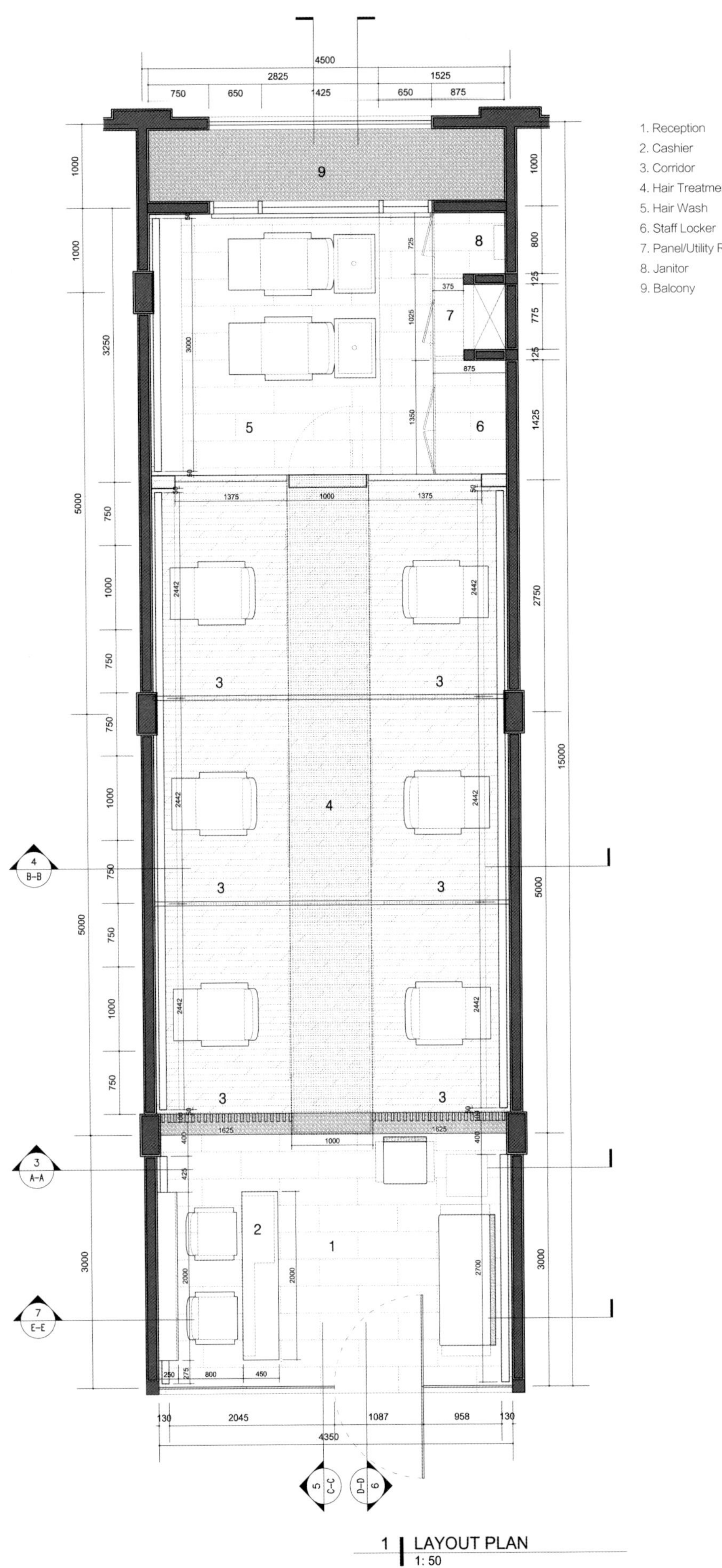

1 | LAYOUT PLAN
1 : 50

The new interior of "Boa Hair" is giving the impression of entering an own world, a new identity of the hairdresser's salon - the space has given a hair cut.
The complete underside of the ceiling is covered with hanging white-transparent fibres. A slight movement circulates in the fibres when hairdryers blowing air through the space.
The development and production of the material and elements took place together with Wasag AG Switzerland.

Company : *Claudia Meier Architektur*
Designer : *Claudia Meier*
Photographer : *Claudia Meier*
Client : *Manuela Daluz*
Country : *Switzerland*

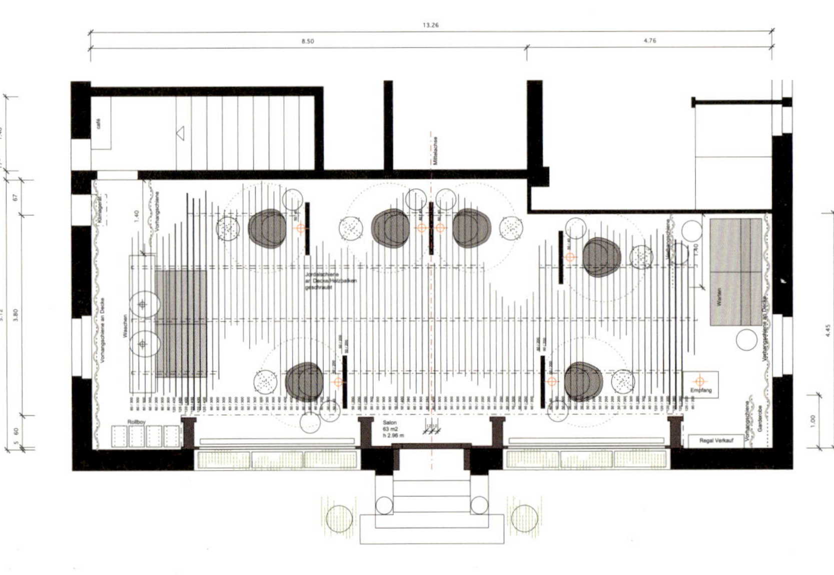

ERIC PARIS SALON KERRY CENTRE

The remodel of Eric Paris Salon started with the need for a connection between the newly acquired second floor space, which will house the hair cutting stations in the future, to the existing saloon entrance, retail space and reception located on the ground floor. GRAFT introduced a continuous fluid staircase, linking these two spaces together and creating a vertical "cat walk". This main vertical circulation becomes the central spine which branches off and connects the different functional areas throughout the salon. The manicure and pedicure stations are set off as galleries for clients to admire the other roaming customers; hidden beauty rooms contain custom designed massage tables and leather wall patterns.

As the stair ascends, it morphs from staircase, to wall panel, until it loops over to become a fully enclosed corridor before it spills out onto the second floor. The sculptural stair is accentuated on the inside by cladding of colorful metal panels, mimicking the salons shiny and sensuous, bold, fingernail colors, while the polished stainless steel on the outside will provide customers with distorted reflections of themselves after their beauty treatment.

Company : *Team Graft*
Client : *Eric Paris Salons Ltd.*
Country : *China*

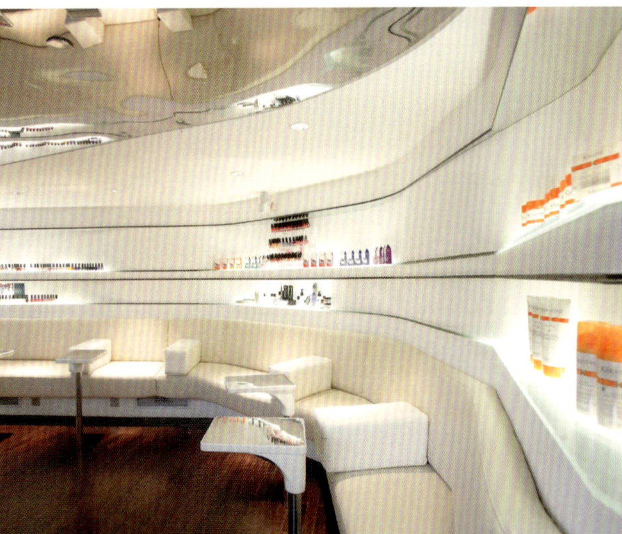

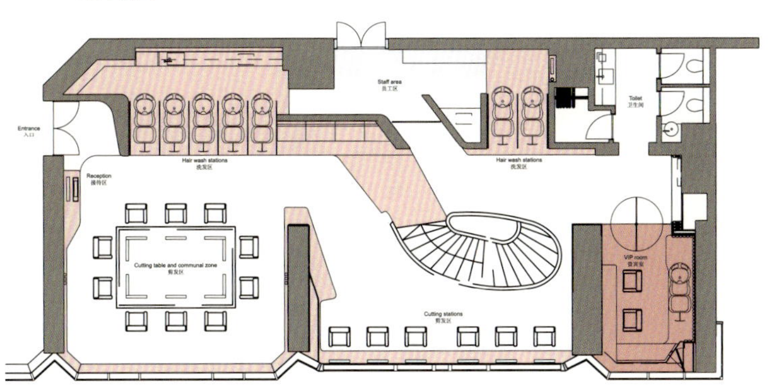

2nd Floor Plan
二层平面图

Mezzanine
夹层
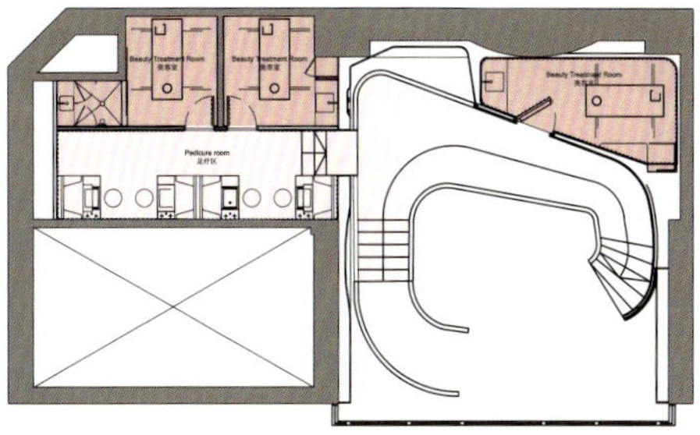

1ST Floor Plan
一层平面图
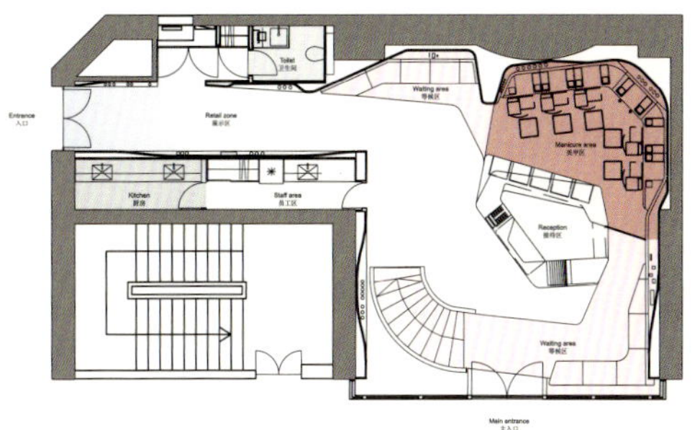

BURANO

BURANO is a hair salon.

Company : *Inly*
Designer : *Takahiro Fujii*
Photographer : *Seiryo Studio*
Country : *Japan*

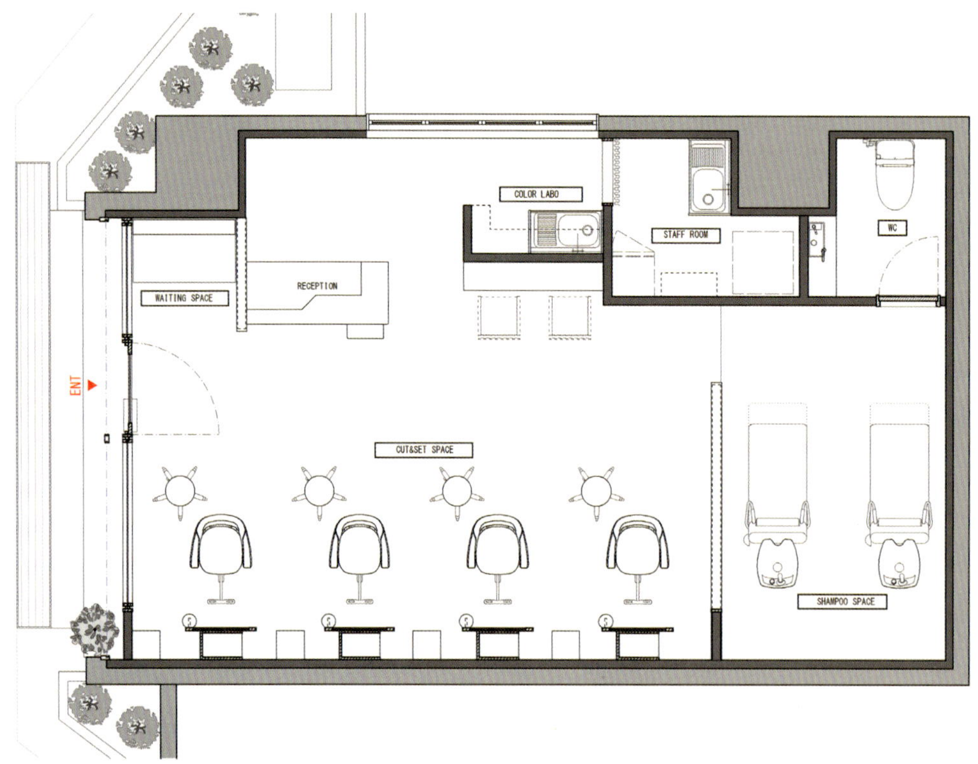

TIARA

Item to be displayed is different at shop by shop. At Fashion boutique, that is Clothe. At watch shop, that is watch. So what is at hair salon? The answer is customer.

I intended to make customers displayed and look beautiful at this shop.

"Only one" - Place just for me. This is the shop concept from the client.

People consciously make barriers to outside and make their own territory at anytime and anyplace.

However, their barriers are changing by following their motions, not solid objects like walls or partitions.

I designed floating ceiling which changes by chairs' shape to make customers feel vague and invisible barriers at this salon.

By doing this, people will recognize their own barriers at this empty space.

Through all lighting which is designed as ambient light towards the ceiling, this featured ceiling work as board reflector to make customers look beautiful.

I hope all customers can recognize "involuntary barrier" and feel "only one"- place just for me.

Company : *Kamitopen Architecture-Design Office*

Designer : *Masahiro Yoshida*

Photographer : *Keisuke Miyamoto*

Client : *Tipa Co.,Ltd. Manabu Konno*

Country : *Japan*

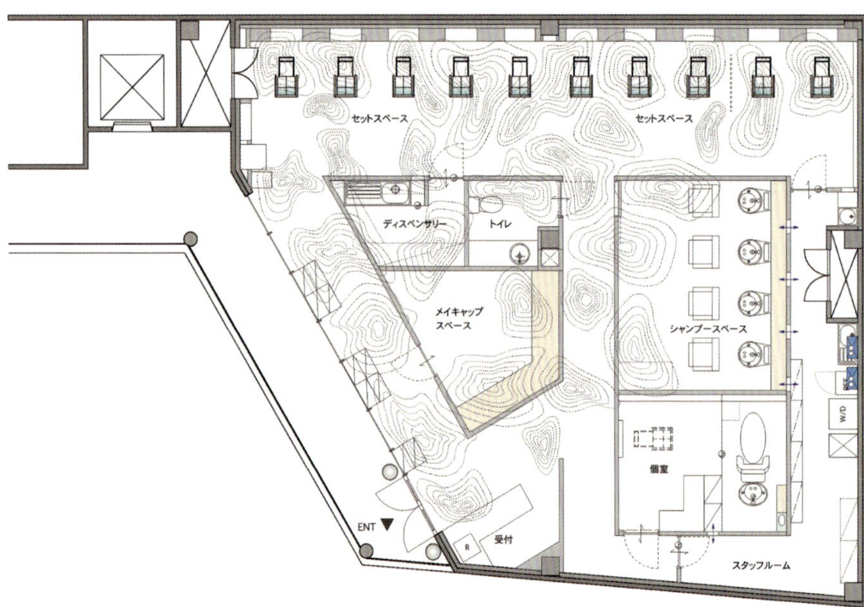

MOOMOO ARCHITECTS

The initial client's request was to add a retail space to salon area. The salon therefore carries a secondary function - it also serves as an exhibition space for young designer's garments hand picked by a famous Polish designer. A fitting room is concealed behind the curtain wall which visually separates the retail function from the hair dresser's zone. Inclined wall planes are bisected by horizontal cuts which open shelf space for the exhibited hair products along with the functional sink surface. Tall slender mirror columns serve to both clients and the stylists, offering abundance of storage and function inside. Spacial dynamism and multiple reflections offer multiple perspectives into the space resulting in a playful creative environment for hair masters. Plenty of waiting space is provided for along the window openings as well as at the entrance.

Company : *Moomoo*
Country : *Poland*

BARTOSZJANUSZ

CURE SALON MONSIEUR

A complex of a beauty salon and a cafe, whose site has a narrow frontage.

The site is a little way off the main shopping street and on a lane. In addition, it is narrow and deep, which we Japanese call "unagino-nedoko" (means "a bed for an eel").

The client desired it to be like a retreat. So we focused on utilising the depth of the site sandwiched between two buildings and creating an interior space in which people can feel light.

Thus we divided the building into three parts and slightly shifted them each other. Additionally, we used different materials for each part and alternate their roof pitches so that people can feel it extending far back.

Furthermore, we put its entrance on the side and people just feel what is happening inside in its front. This should make people want to peep into the room.

The space for hair dressing is located in the middle and has the other two parts' exterior walls as its interior wall. Moreover, it is facing the small garden and the customers will see it over the mirrors. Consequently, they can enjoy being hair dressed inside the building just like outdoors.

Company : *Upsetters Architects*
Photographer : *Yusuke Wakabayashi*
Country : *Japan*

LA GUARDIA SALON

The sensation of viewing yourself and the people taking care of you provided the conceptual basis for the design. All the components of the salon are defined by outlining their perimeter and focusing your view on the person in the frame. The different functions of the salon, such as waiting area, reception desk, cutting stations, espresso bar and lounge, dissolve into the red frame that defines them. This leaves a framed void space, which draws your attention to the specific activity that takes place within its boundaries.

Company : *Z-A studio*
Country : *U.S.A.*

BARTEK JANUSZ HAIRDRESSER

Design of the place is based around a simple concept derived from the jagged, angular forms created by free falling hair which can be found on the floor of any busy salon. This striking arrangement which occurs on the floor will now be transformed throughout the interior to create a dynamic, vibrant space. The salon carries a secondary function - it also serves as an exhibition space for the work of young designer's, the clothes hand picked by a famous Polish designer Gosia Baczynska. A fitting room is concealed behind the curtain wall which visually separates the retail function from the hair dresser's zone. Inclined wall planes are bisected by horizontal cuts which open shelf space for the exhibited hair products along with the functional sink surface. Tall slender mirror columns serve to both clients and the stylists, offering abundance of storage and function inside. Spacial dynamism and multiple reflections offer multiple perspectives into the space resulting in a playful, creative environment for the hair masters. Waiting space is strategically located along the window openings as well as at the entrance to offer a unique viewing experience for customers.

Company : *Moomoo Architects*

Designers : *Moomoo Architects ,*
Jakub Majewski,
Lukasz Pastuszka

Photographer : *Malgorzata Pstragowska*

Client : *Bartek Janusz*

Country : *Poland*

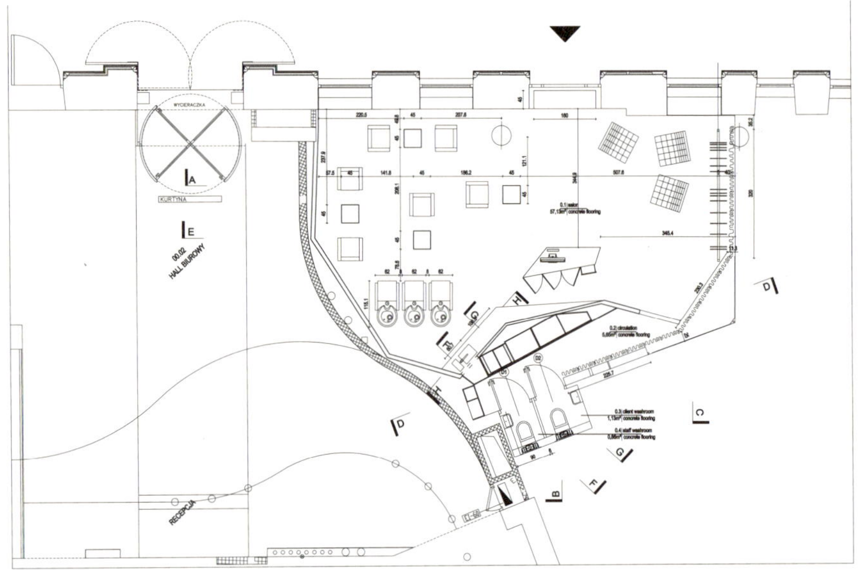

DRUG SHOP

What is a pharmacy? The signifier leads us to ponder not only on the word pharmacy, but also on the object and relationships that connect the conscious and unconscious dimensions of the term. Illusion becomes the trigger. Three questions propel us into action:

Where do we draw the line between reality and the space of illusion? Can one concentrate this boundary along a zero-thickness plane? Can light be captured in this space of no thickness? The experiment begins with the search for an intercalary material capable of capturing the illusion of light. A material made up of a myriad fibres accumulating on a virtual plane. Light rushes over it as if it was a massless fluid. Limits are dissolved in a liquid plane. References to the object disappear. The luminous symbols float in the form of ephemeral traces as abstract elements in the dark.

The project embraces the new demands for relationship and proximity of the customer with the product, breaking away from the classic formula of direct sales and creating an ambiance that places the medication on the same plane as the consumer. The interior and exterior zones are connected through a first filter that is interrupted to form shop windows, spaces for visual exchange where the façade increases in density and specificity. These captured voids become magnets to attract the attention of the customer moving in the vicinity of the pharmacy. A second filter, designed to showcase the products for sale, will delimit public and private areas, multiplying the relationships between them both. Light shines through the programmatic sequence. Space becomes deep once again.

Company : *BUJ+COLÓN Arquitectos*
Photographer : *Luis Díaz Díaz*
Client : *Pharmacy "La Puebla 15"*
Country : *Spain*

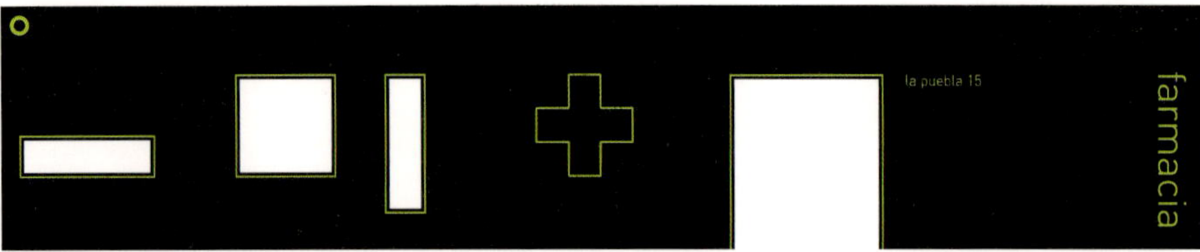

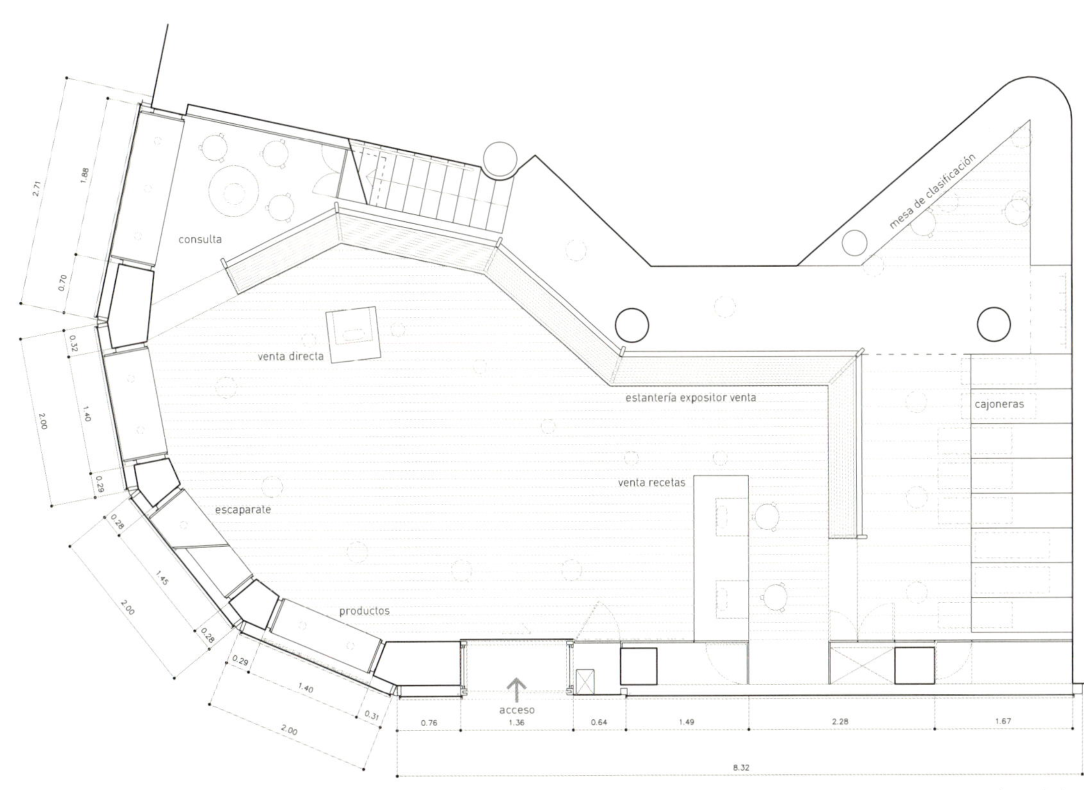
consulta
venta directa
escaparate
productos
acceso
estantería expositor venta
venta recetas
cajoneras
mesa de clasificación
2.71
1.88
0.70
0.32
2.00
1.40
0.29
0.28
1.45
2.00
0.28
0.29
1.40
2.00
0.31
0.76
1.36
0.64
1.49
2.28
1.67
8.32

farmacia

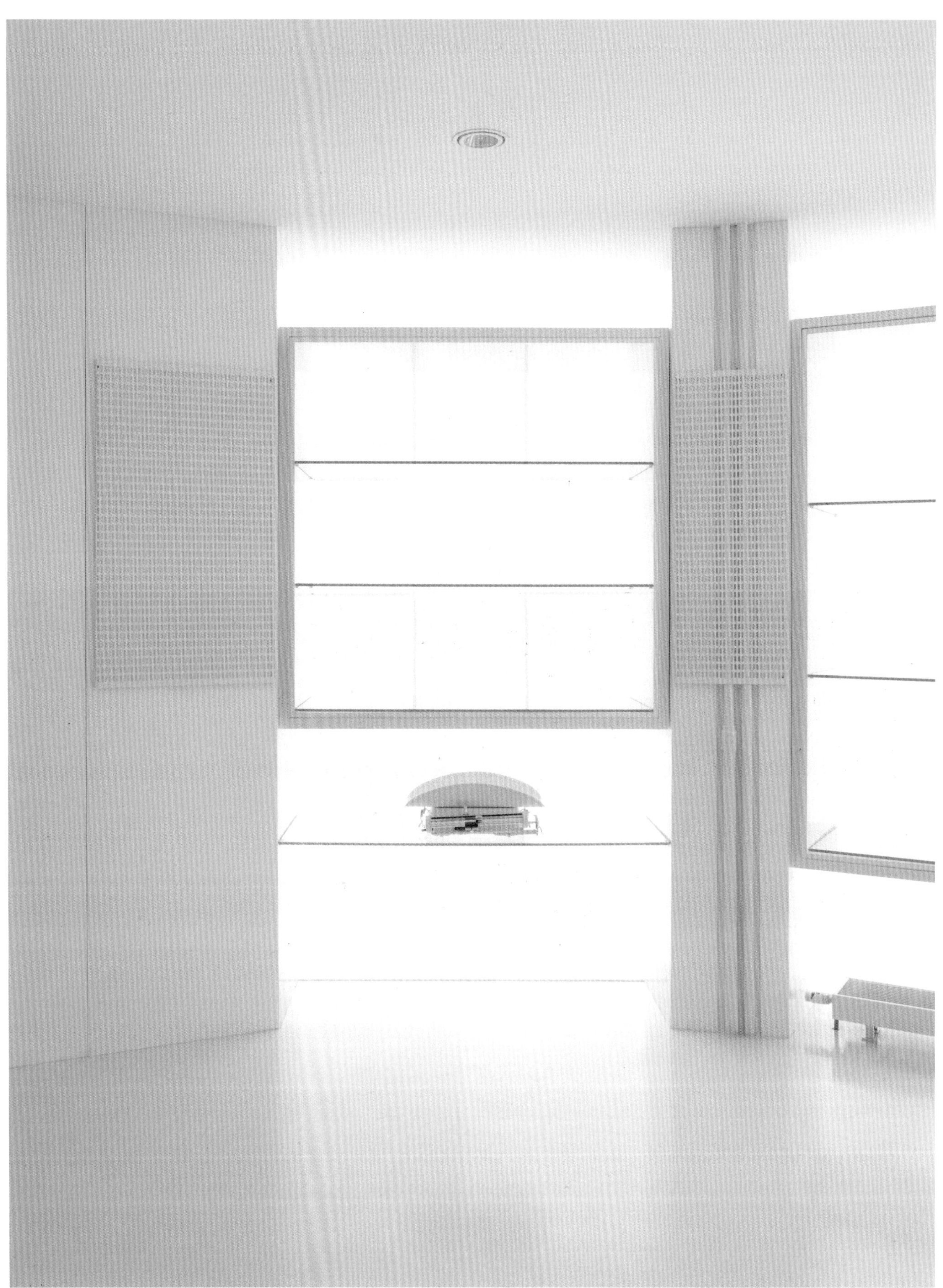

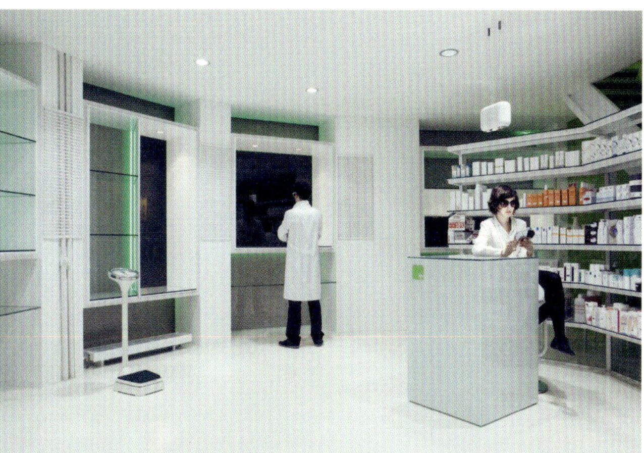

Floor:
Flooring in round space, printed leaves (Ginko Biloba) on outdoor paper, covered with transparent resin. (epoxy floor). Other spaces light green (Ral 6019) resin.
Wall:
Walls are mostly made up by the "furniture" which is the big round "cabinet" consisting of 522 drawers made of green perspex. The construction walls that are not covered by furniture, are plastered and painted white
Ceiling:
Round space: transparent white stretch ceiling. Workspace in the back has a stucco ceiling. Ceilings in other spaces which lead in and out of the round space are made out of plywood painted white, making them part of the big round cabinet.
Lighting:
Inside the round space i.e. inside the cabinet the ceiling which is transparent white functions as a light fitting lit trough from above. Inside the cabinet are 72 tube lights, with a green filter. Their light bounces off, of a white back wall that reflects the light trough the transparent green drawers. Lighting in the work space is provided by 3 large uplighters (ceiling washer from Erco 33210), other lighting, also in the entrance and "library" is provided by downlights (mini haloscan 20, Modular). In the entrance when the pharmacy is opened the large entrance-lightcase functions as a "lightwall", when the pharmacy is closed this wall, which is suspended from ceiling rails, is rolled towards the outside wall, completely closing of the entrance.
Furniture:
Entrance: Infowall, white plywood (betonplex) and 180 stainless steel booklet holders.
Round space: round cabinet: (36 partitions), white plywood (betonplex) sides,
522(altu glas) drawers, and aforementioned tubelights.
Counter: synthetic concrete on a steel frame suspended from steel beam (hidden by tree).
Seat: black leather covered wooden frame.
"Library": bookshelves: white plywood (betonplex).
Table: white plywood (betonplex) covered by Corian Seagrass green.
Back space: issue cupboard, green perspex (altuglas).
Tables and countertops covered by Corian Seagrass, drawers all white plywood (betonplex).

Company : *Concrete Architectural Associates*
Photographer : *Concrete Architectural Associates*
Client : *mevr. Marjan Terpstra*
Country : *the Netherlands*

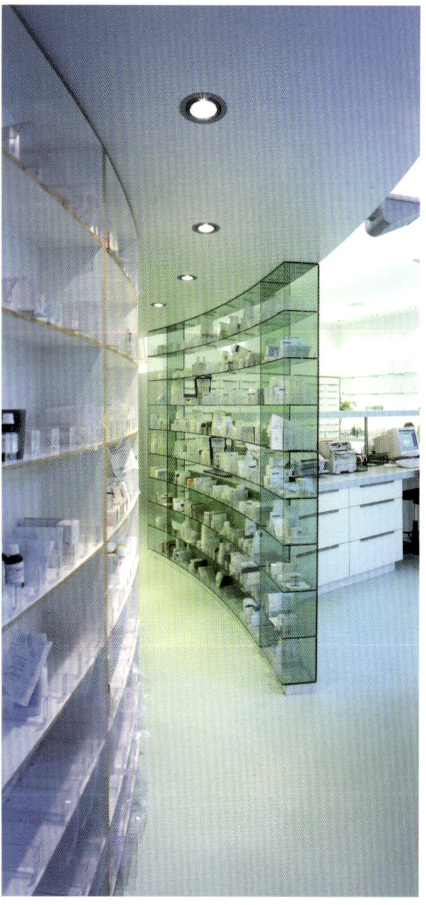

LINDEN APOTHEKE LUDWIGSBURG

The Linden Apotheke is an old-established pharmacy in Ludwigsburg. It has chosen to specialise in naturopathic products and natural cosmetics in response to the growing pressure of competition in the pharmacy market.

A rigorous reorganisation of the space resulted in a compact, high-ceilinged room, which is immediately ascertainable from both entrances. Continuous shelving units and the room's rounded corners support this impression. They establish a clear backdrop for the merchandise on display, which is well lit, both from behind and from the front. A spatial focal point is created by the new sales counter, attached to a central supporting column and projecting freely out to both sides. The unity of the room is further accentuated by a rounded transition from wall to ceiling, as well as by the continuity created by the white colouring. The granite cobblestone floor reflects the typical Baroque style, so evident in the town of Ludwigsburg, and creates a tantalising contrast to the otherwise demonstratively modern interior design. Three rotatable merchandise stands in the centre of the room offer an additional area for presenting and highlighting seasonal products.

With its clear, sweeping contours and monochrome colour palette, the room and furniture design direct the customer's eye towards an expansive ceiling motif. The motif is a fresco depicting eleven medicinal herbs, which was designed in cooperation with textile designer, Monica Trenkler. It is a modern interpretation of a traditional subject, executed in classic colours. The ceiling design acts as the new emblem of the pharmacy – both in a spatial and communicative sense. The interior design picks up on motifs from our collective memory: without indulging in wistful nostalgia, the vaulted ceiling, the fresco element and the granite cobblestones all hark back to an era when pharmacies had not yet become a part of a health industry. On the contrary, the design picks up on such traditions and translates them into a contemporary feel. The resonance of these images, however, is used to communicate unambiguous values such as personal welfare, sensitivity, dependability and of course the core focus of the pharmacy: the field of naturopathy. The modernity andclarity of the design on the other hand establish a connection to professionalism, precision and competence. The idea was to create an engaging, optimistic ambience in which all the worries of ill health can melt away for a moment. At the same time, the pleasure involved in cosseting body and soul with natural cosmetics or natural remedies such as herbal teas also finds expression. The ceiling motif also serves as a strong key visual, which underscores the pharmacy's positioning in order that its product range may be spread through word of mouth.

Designers : *Peter Ippolito, Gunter Fleitz,*
Sascha Kipferling, Tim Lessmann,
Fabian Greiner, Axel Knapp,
Sarah Meßelken
Photographer : *Zooey Braun*
Client : *Linden Apotheke*
Country : *Germany*

LINDEN APOTHEKE
LUDWIGSBURG

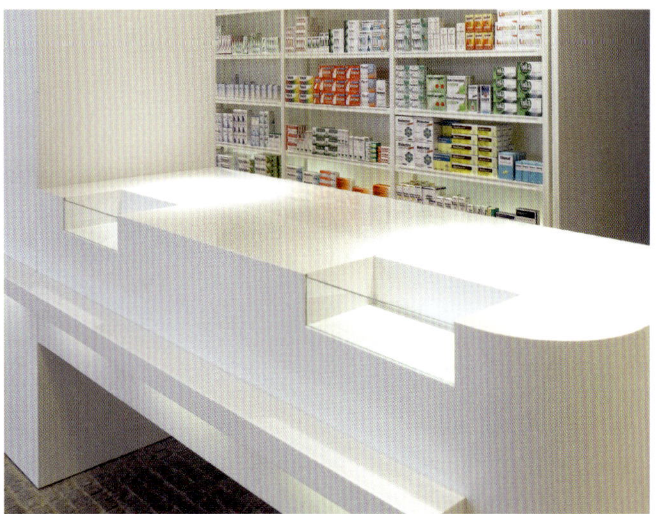

LINDEN APOTHEKE
LUDWIGSBURG

LINDEN APOTHEKE
LUDWIGSBURG

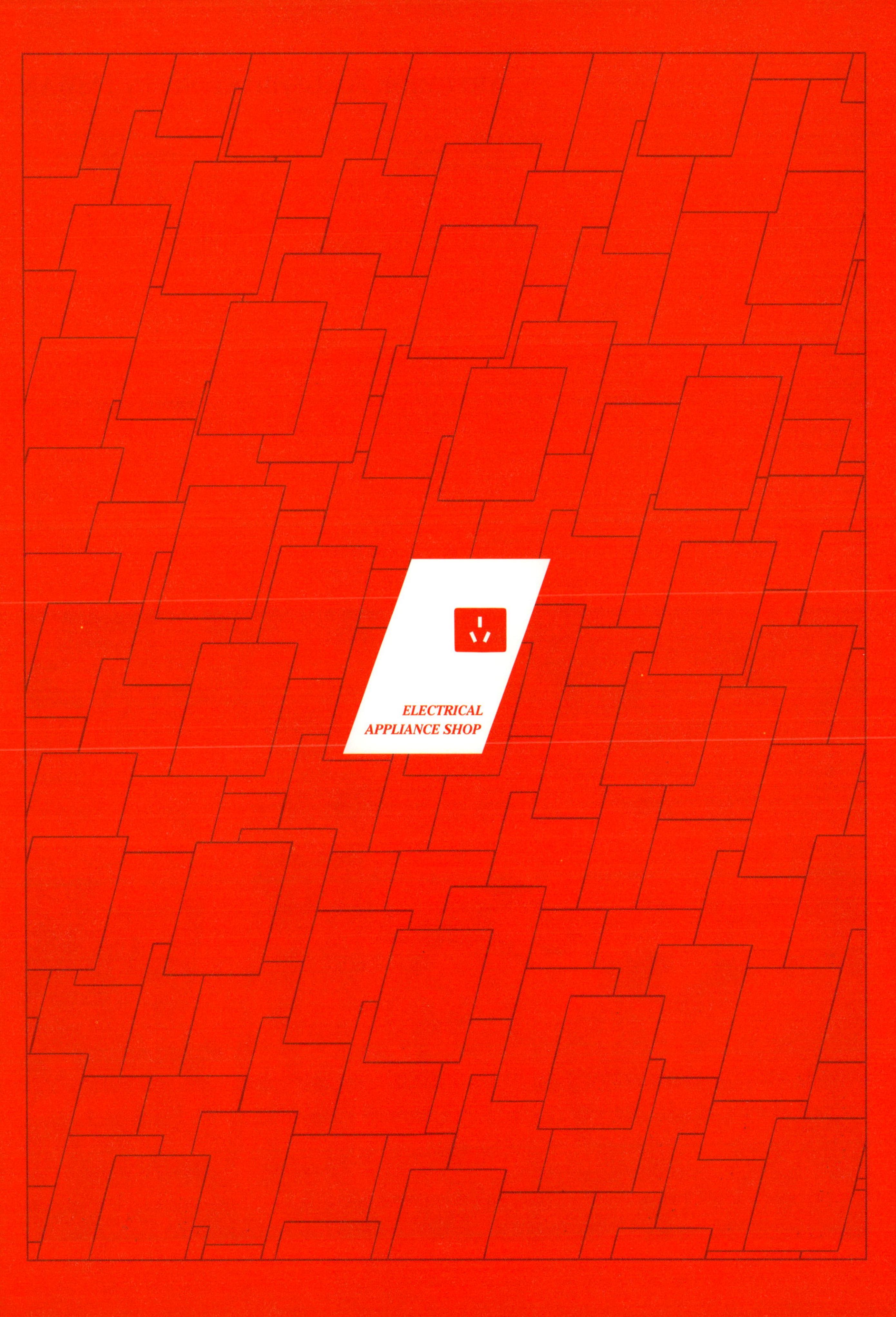
ELECTRICAL
APPLIANCE SHOP

Responding to Artemide's "Human Light" philosophy, lighting is a source of physical pleasure and mental comfort, Tsung-Jen Lin, Director of Crox International, beautifully embellishes the first Artemide Flagship Store in downtown Taipei – a store selling the emotional attachment besides the product.

To Tsung-Jen Lin, light is not just to brighten up a space; it implies a sense of warmth and care. With the concept of the brightness and the sense of hope, the store interprets the scene of sunlight breaks through the cloud making it stands as a landmark shining in the neighborhood.

With the full-height glass window on both sides, the corner store is completely open to the street and presents a welcome atmosphere that encourages people to come in. The floating cloud-like ceiling stretching outward to the sidewalk blurs the boundary of inside and outside. Together with careful arrangement of product display, a visual illusion of a large store space is created. The blue LED light above the extension ceiling dramatically increases the floating cloud scenario when viewed from the street, especially at night. The store successfully evokes the nearby neighborhood through the engaging reflection and curvilinear form.

To enhance the brand image, fiber-reinforced polymer (FRP), the commonly used material in aeronautic field, is selected to reflect the design approaches from one of Artemide founder Ernesto Glismondi who has the professional trainings in aeronautic engineer. The high strength yet light weight FRP makes the design realization possible. The one piece hanging freeform, extended from the ceiling to the wall and forming the counter desk, is carefully crafted and installed with skills workers. It covers the posts and beams perfectly to create the surreal atmosphere that enable an organic backdrop displaying strong-characteristics Artemide master pieces. Finished with glossy paint, reflection and shadow add on top of this unique sculptural composition presenting an interesting dialogue.

Behind the tassel is the stairway leads to the second floor where daylight glamour transforms into an evening calm with minimal decoration in black and white. The second floor is designed with the idea of gallery space to display the wide variety of lighting products in different styles. Black and white strong contrasting colors are applied to the wall in sections allowing exciting grouping to present products individually or in series.

If the entry floor is to draw attention and introduce the brand image of Artemide as forefront lighting design with balance in form and function by high craftsmanship, then the second floor is an elegant space to slow down and to appreciate the products. With concerns of both rational and emotional consumer experience, Tsung-Jen Lin delivers Artemide Flagship Store in Taiwan as the sensational palace of light.

Company : *Crox International Co., Ltd.*
Creative Director : *Tsung-Jen Lin*
Designers : *Zhuo-Wei Zou, Wei-Zhe Cai, Kuan Yu Chen*
Client : *Bravo Casa Co., Ltd.*
District : *Taiwan (P.R.C)*

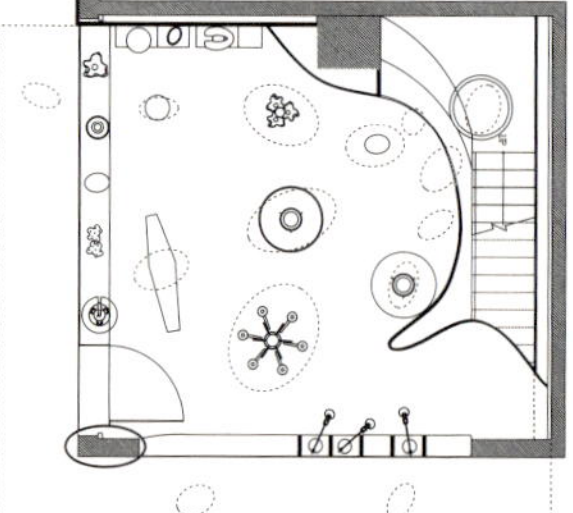

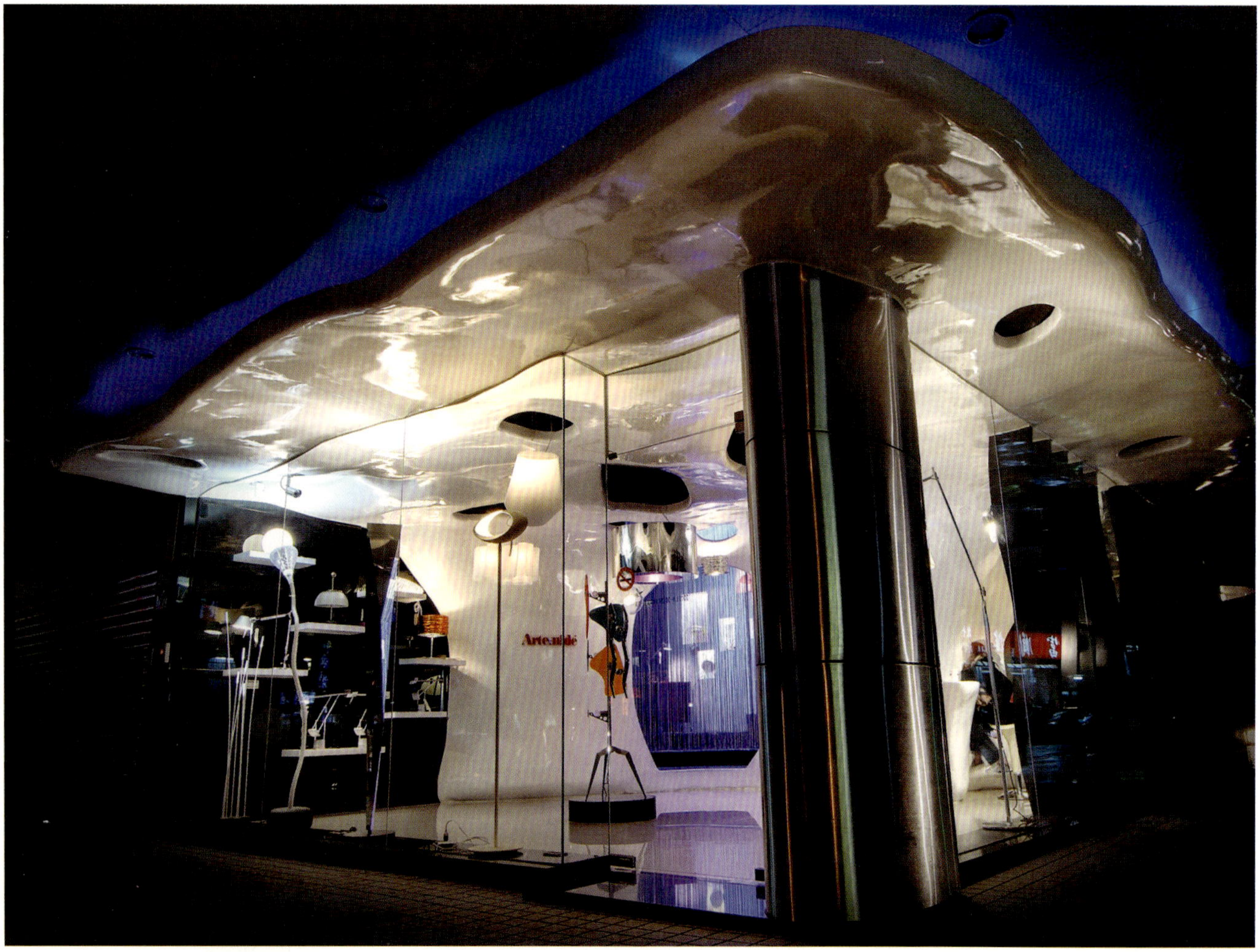

Artemide

COODOO APPLE PRODUCT RESELLER

Whole world the best electronic products. Therefore, when design Shenzhen Huaqiangbei Apple Products Flagship Store of Shenzhen COODOO Digital Co., Ltd. – one of Apple Company's top reseller in China, we will provide consumers the shopping experiences that match the Apple products:
Science and technology / conciseness / environmental protection and low consumption / functionalism
We plan to finish all works (from design to starting business) of the COODOO project which covers an area of 270 m^2 (first floor: 70m^2, second floor: 200m^2) from January 2008 to 8th March, 2008. The project budget is RMB 500,000.
The most important part of the entire shop design is the distribution of pedestrians flow, planning of multifunctional section, and lighting. We will choose the succinct and unified materials with high performance price ratio and high quality, such as artificial white crystal / outdoor ivory latex paint / oriented strand board sprayed with white paint coating. Partial properties will adopt backed varnish.

Company : *Hallucinate Interior Design Co., Ltd.*
Creative Director : *Leo Wang*
Designer : *Leo Wang*
Photographer : *Hallucinate*
Client : *Coodoo*
Country : *China*

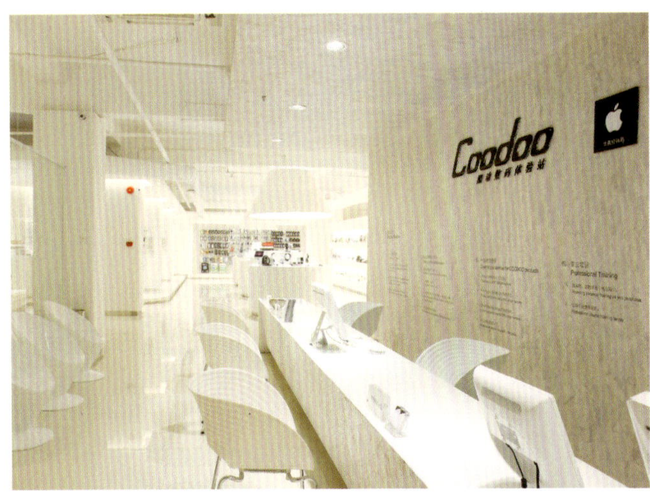

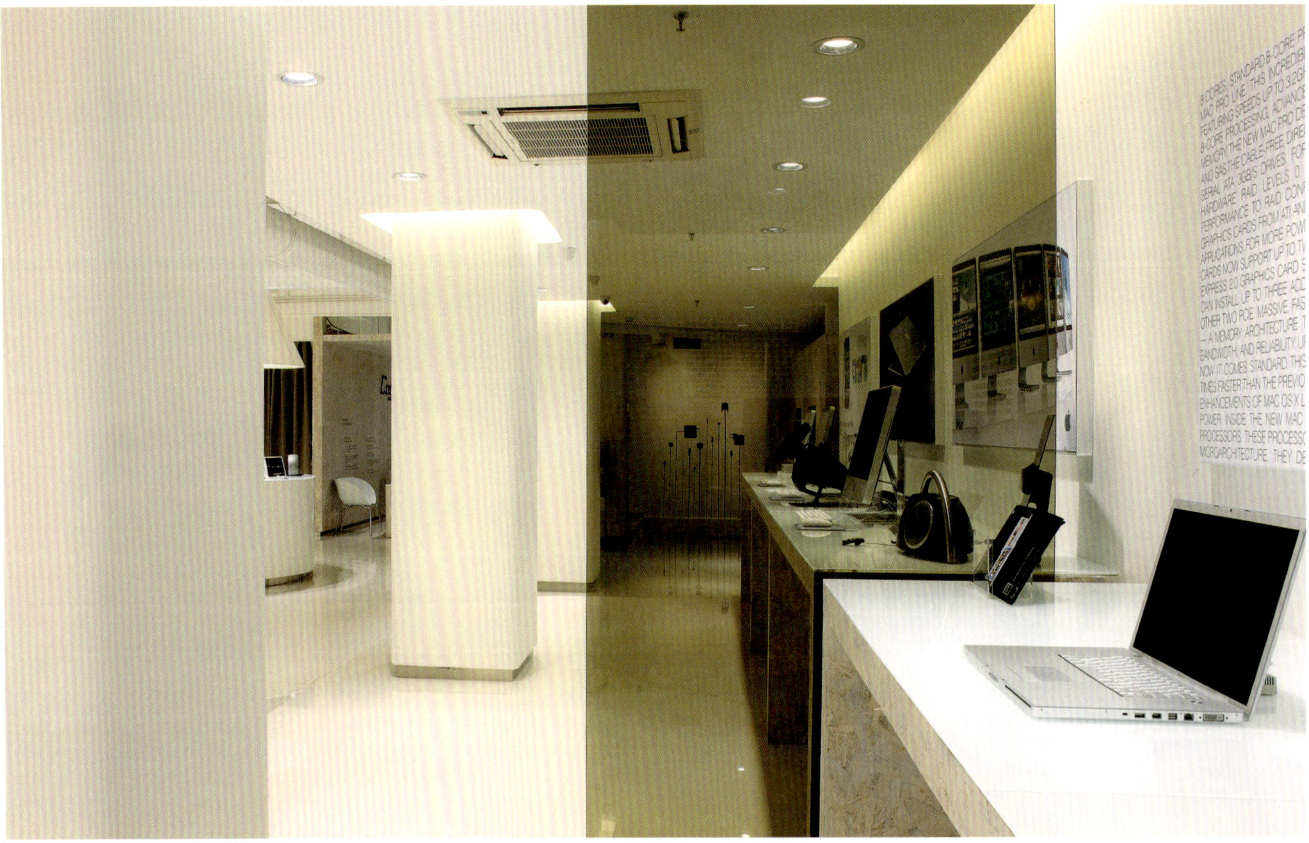

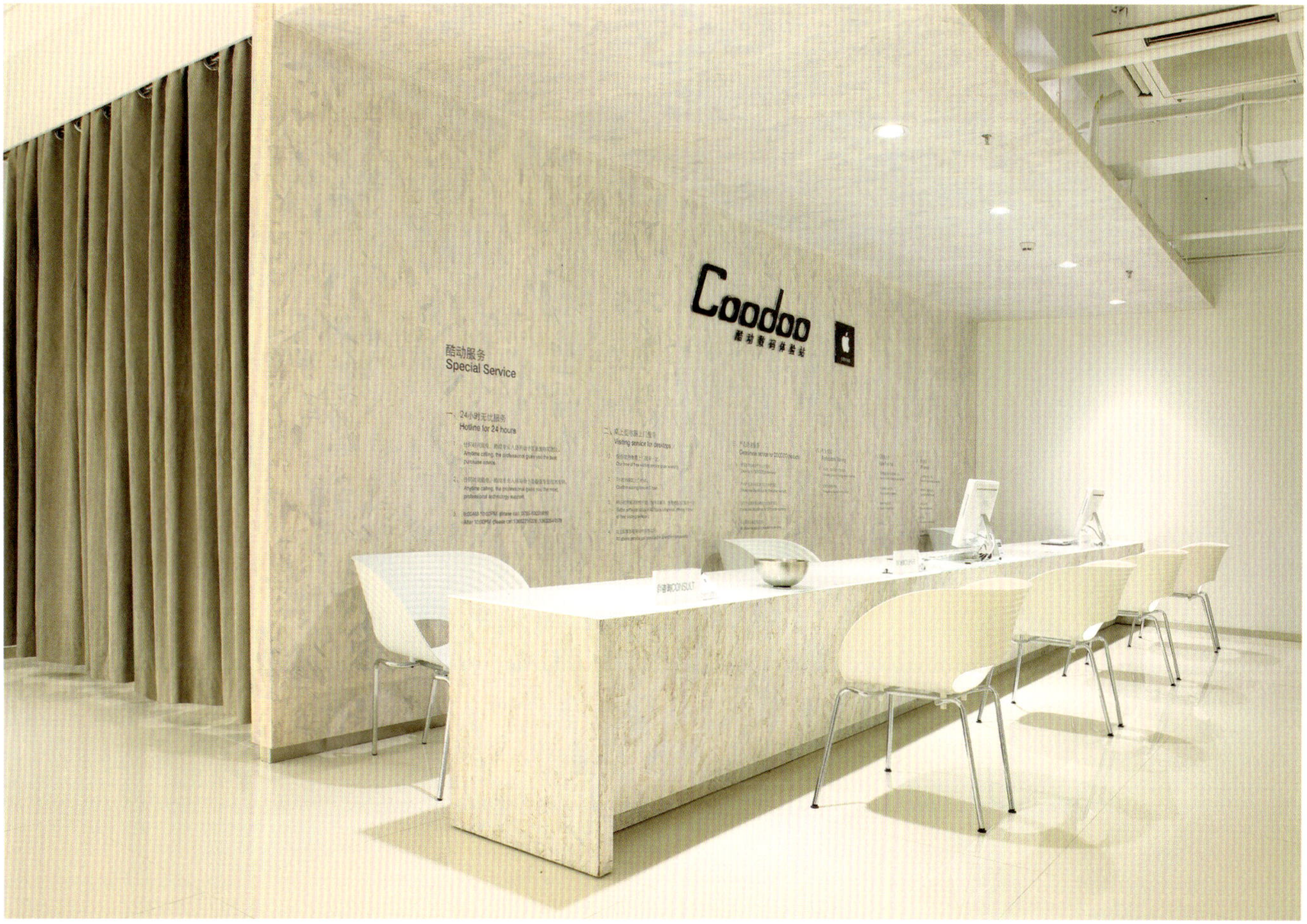
Coodoo
酷动数码体验站
酷动服务
Special Service
Hotline for 24 hours
Visiting service for desktops

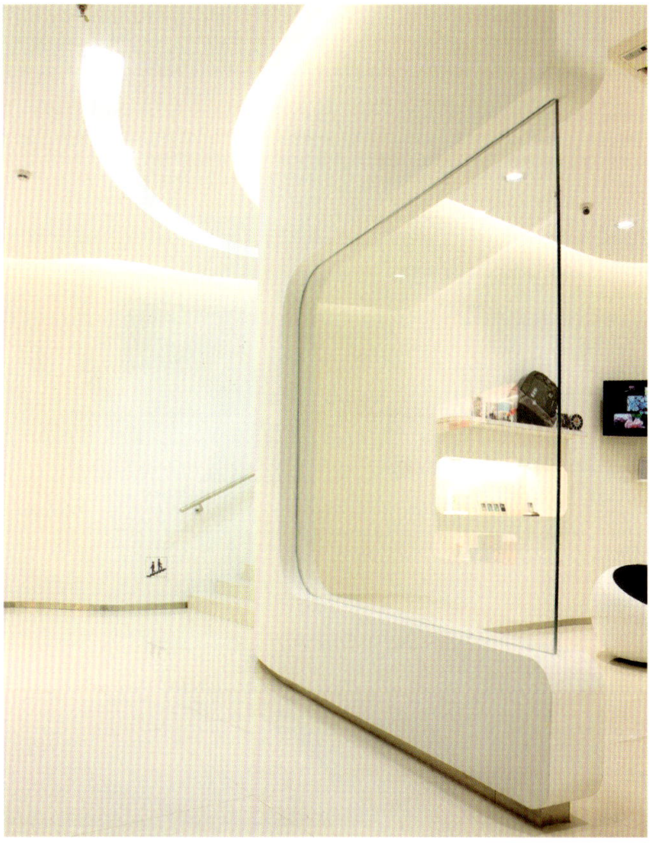

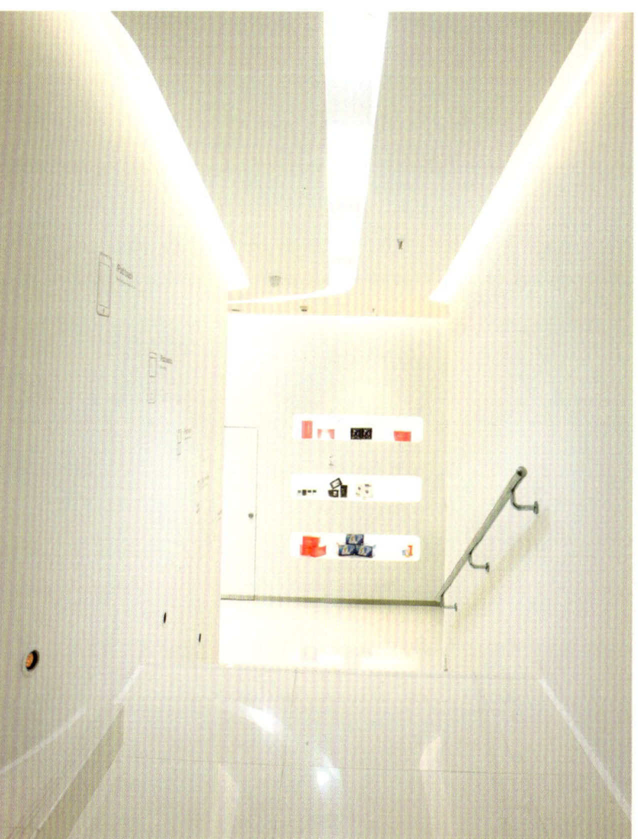

RESTAURANT

POCO A POCO

Inly products designed a cucina povera restaurant called "Poco a Poco" in Minami-senba , Osaka , Japan.
The project was subject to various limitations , such as budget , the small site that as an old folk house , and tight time frame.
We needed to understand those limitations and overcome them and need a radical change of standpoint.
In order to meet these limitations, at first, we restore the existing structure and reuse it. Second, we built on top of structural plywood. Third, we have planned collect dishes which was common materials and converted it into a menu board. With using 42 round dishes of various sizes we wanted to induce an uplifting feeling and novelty. And aimed at an effect to attract a visitor through the glass storefront.
About the second floor, we wanted to make full use of the characteristics of the existing old folk house. As the proverb says, "It's better to leave well enough alone".

Company : *Inly*
Designer : *Takahiro Fujii (Inly Products)*
Photographer : *Seiryo Studio*
Client : *Moai Co.,Ltd.*
Country : *Japan*

cucina
italiano

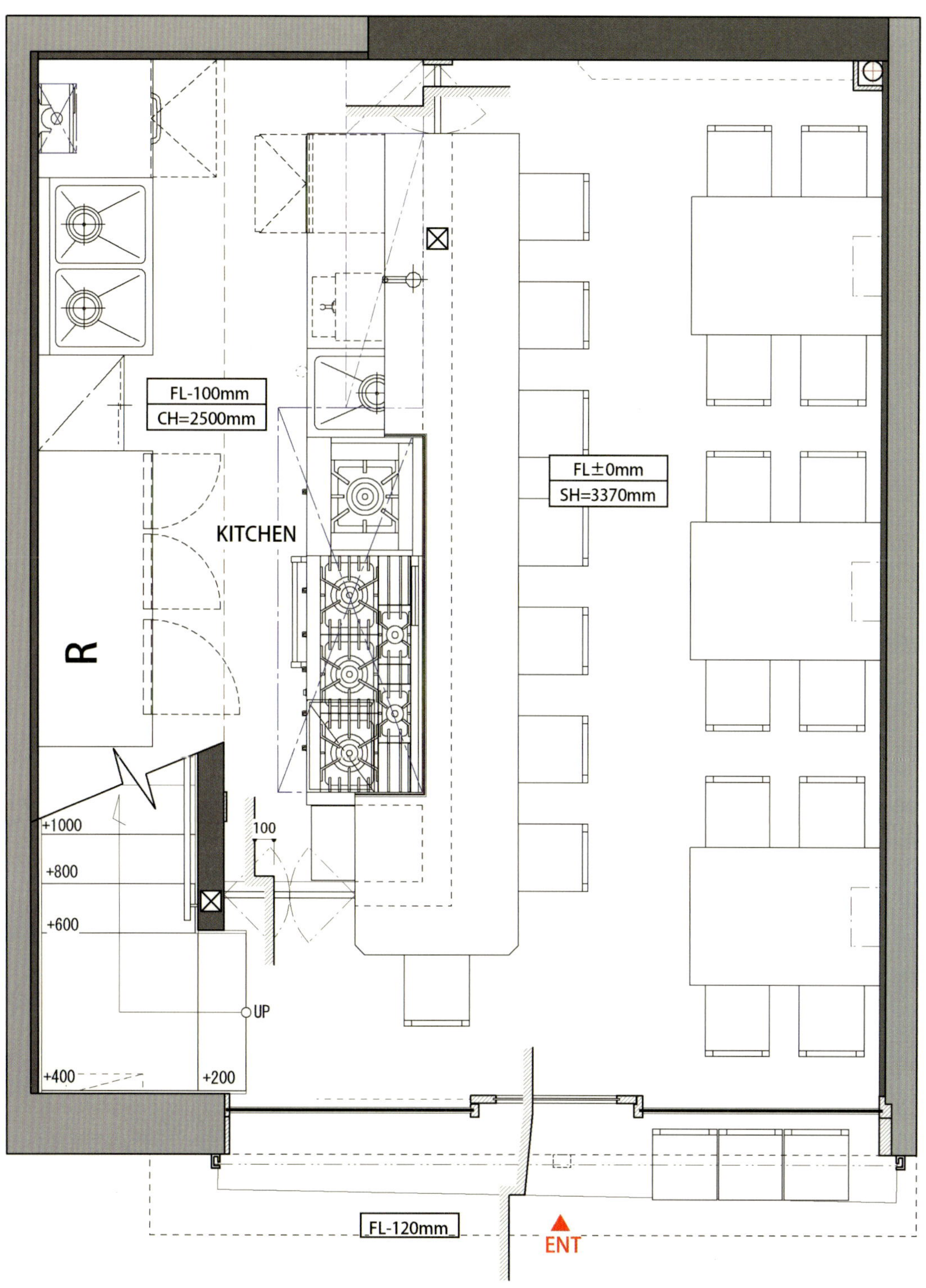

FL-100mm
CH=2500mm
FL±0mm
SH=3370mm
KITCHEN
R
+1000
+800
+600
+400
+200
100
UP
FL-120mm
ENT

OLIVOMARE is the last born belonging to the well known London brand OLIVO - by now an important presence in the aristocratic neighbourhood of Belgravia - and is a restaurant serving seafood. Apart from its name, such peculiarity is highlighted by the formal and decorative language adopted here to focus on its aspect using more or less clear references to the sea world and environment.

The most explicit among them undoubtedly is the wide wall that characterizes the main dining room, entirely covered by a large cladding featuring a pattern inspired by the works of the visionary artist Maurits Escher, in which each single portion of colour is laser cut out of a sheet of opaque laminated plastic and then juxtaposed on the vertical surface exactly as if it was a huge jigsaw puzzle. To counterpoint it, in this same room, from a channelling recessed in the fake ceiling drops down a linear sequence of tubular luminescent "tentacles", spirals and twists of tubular nylon mesh (lamps shades "Bigoli", By Innermost) evoking a stray shoal of jellyfishes or of sea anemones , while someone could vaguely recognize the meshes of fishers' nets in the wide lozengy glazed partition dividing this room from the entrance lobby. With regard to this space it should be said that it allows to access both the restaurant and the upper floors, and this through a huge panel split into smaller mobile and fix ones, integrating the necessary doors and taking up the colour scheme of the decorated cladding in the main dining room. In order to make appear this last one wider, the partition wall existing between it and the entrance lobby has been knocked down and replaced by a full height glazed partition supported by a rather thin frame (yet perfectly fire and smoke proof), which allows the best possible visual integration of these two spaces.

A sea of white colour has been used to enhance and link all these elements together, flooding all surrounding parts, from walls to ceiling, from the resin floor to the Corian made bar counter; a white sea working in this environment as an undifferentiated neutral background that intentionally disappoints any predictable expectation for blue colour.

The shopfront has been redesigned in order to match the existing one at the adjacent premises – where the delicatessen shop Olivino, that complements the restaurant, is located – and it has been painted aubergine colour, so that it can hold a dialogue either with the grey "pietra serena" slabs of the external pavement and with the colour scheme of the interiors' decoration.

Company : *Pierluigi Piu - Architetto*
Creative Director : *Pierluigi Piu*
Designer : *Pierluigi Piu*
Photographers : *Giorgio Dettori And Pierluigi Piu*
Client : *Olivo Restaurants And Shop*
Country : *Italy*

GIACOMO

Outstanding concepts in the food sector follow the same rules that prevail in the retail industry. Besides singularity and strong brand recognition, authenticity and emotional aspects are the most crucial factors. The giacomo gourmet fast food concept is not contradictory in itself. Rather it draws on the best of both worlds. Giacomo meets the yearning desire for quality and emotional authenticity in times where monotony abounds. In a world where time has become the greatest luxury and where work and leisure time tend to blend more and more, it is essential to provide the customer with fast and proper service. Therefore it is not inadequate to sell fast food, because for giacomo fast food does not equate to eating quickly but to be attended to quickly and exclusively.

All these values must be reflected in the design. How can this be attained? Giacomo reflects the ideas of an international design language, using appealing and fluid shapes of Asian architecture mixed with references of modernity and its proportions. These light and free flowing shapes can already be found in Asian residential architecture over a thousand years ago, where communication and the sense of community were most essential elements. Think of the circular gates to the typical Chinese courtyards. At giacomo the individual spaces flow into one another, underscored by the well-directed use of lighting. This subtle sensuality and the use of light, offset wall finishes imply a seemingly floating state, which cultivates glamour but also an easy-going setting for a business lunch. All finishes and colours are carefully tuned to the corporate design, resulting in an inherently consistent image with high brand recognition. The choice of the specific shade of gold as well as the accentuated use of other typical brand elements are all in tune with the space.

For Plajer & Franz studio it's always important that their projects do not preach uncompassionate architectural concepts, but always incorporate emotional aspects that speak to the customer. At giacomo part of the original wilhelmenian style ceiling has been exposed, playfully integrating this historic reference into the overall design. It's always the hot versus the cold, the rough next to the smooth that moves people, not the lukewarm. Despite the seemingly weightless material language, the design has been implemented with the most modern material technology and all functional aspects of a fast food chain to guarantee a smooth workflow behind the counter.

Company : *Plajer & Franz Studio*
Photographer : *Ken Schluchtmann*
Client : *Giacomo Natural Gmbh*
Country : *Germany*

GIACOMO
HEISSGETRÄNKE
KALTGETRÄNKE
FOOD

Company : *Slade Architecture*
Photographer : *Iwan Baan*
Client : *Mattel*
Country : *U.S.A*

Slade Architecture designed the Barbie Café and B-Bar on the sixth floor of the Barbie Flagship store in Shanghai, China as an immersive dining experience intended to expand on the overall Barbie Flagship store experience.

Mattel worked with Shanghai-based celebrity chef-restaurateur David Laris to conceive a place where European glamour meets classic American diner- expressing Barbie's international credentials and her American/Californian heritage.

By day the Barbie Café provides perfect place for a tasty lunch or an enchanting dinner. The sexy B Bar, a sculptural black bar under a hanging mobile of Barbie icon cut-outs rocks until 2am, serving an alluring menu of creative cocktails –BarbieTinis and Malibu Barbies – to real-life glamour girls and their attendant Kens.

To accommodate the different ages and atmospheres, Slade chose a simple and striking palette: black lacquer, white accents, pink upholstery and curtains. Slade designed the custom herringbone tile pattern on the floors and walls to recall the herringbone swimsuit that Barbie first wore when she debuted at the New York Toy Fair in 1959.

Furniture was also designed by Slade Architecture and included acrylic chairs printed with whimsical silhouette prints of iconic chairs: one Chinese antique, one European antique, one international modern. These silhouette prints create a literal blend of the café references. Table bases are flat cutout silhouettes of classic turned wood profiles continuing the play between two-dimensional flat silhouette and three-dimensional chair. This is a playful allusion to the Barbie Dreamhouse and other Barbie accessories which use flat graphics to represent realistic detail at toy scale. Continuing the reference to the number one Barbie, Slade conceived the signature plate as a circular array of the world famous doll in her timeless black and white dress.

HANSANG KOREAN REATAURANT

Stepping into Tomo Izakaya, you will feel like you've been transported straight to Japan. Such is the authenticity of this Japanese restaurant located in Clarke Quay. From the charismatic ceiling lamps to the intimate, low-lying cushions and tatami in the private dining room, every turn is a visual pleasure for the eye. The riveting factor lies with the feature wall, which doubles as magazine rack, and the dining tables that light up with brilliant effervescence from within. Tomo Izakaya is an exemplary display of easy charm with alfresco dining tastefully complemented with intimate, indoor dining areas.

Company : *ONG&ONG Pte Ltd*
Photographer : *See Chee Keong*
Client : *Hansang Korean*
Charcoal Grill
County : *Singapore*

Bella Italia is a wine store as well as a restaurant. The owner is a typical warmhearted Sicilian woman. While selling the products of her home country and offering a creative home-style cuisine on an upscale level she transfers the Italian spirit to Germany. "Bella Italia Weine" was run for many years in a small living-room-like place with a very personal atmosphere. To extend the sales area as well as the capacity of seats she decided to move to a new location.

The new restaurant is located in Stuttgart West, an urban district which is very popular as a housing area as well as a location for offices working in a creative field. The restaurant is situated in the ground floor of a freestanding multiple dwelling in a charming Wilhelminian style.

Our aim was to keep the familiar atmosphere of the first restaurant, highlighting the character as a wine store at the same time. The character of the room is determined by two elements: At the ceiling we have mounted over 90 different mirrors found on jumble sales. The second element is a kind of room in the room. With its large oval table, a large round mirror on a wall with textile covering, a carpet and a bunch of lamps hanging from the ceiling the space appears like a homelike sitting-room. Three large shelf elements allow an effective promotion of the products. A new corporate design completes the image of "Bella Italia Weine".

Company : *Ippolito fleitz group*
Designer : *Ippolito fleitz group*
Photographer : *Zooey Braun*
Client : *Bella Italia Weine*
Country : *Germany*

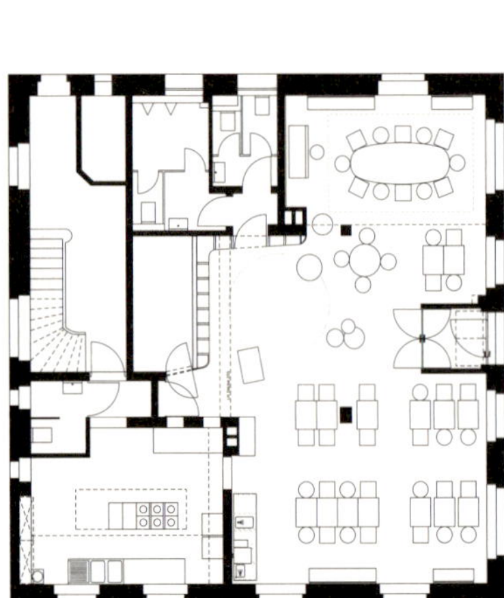

Heute
CARPACCIO
DI TONNO
SU FINOCCHIO
STROZZAPRETI
CON
RAGU CARNE
TAGLIATA
SU
RUCOLA
AL
BALSAMICO
CIOCCOLATO
FONDENTE

THE HOUSE CAFÉ KANYON

Latest branch of The House Café chain at the shopping mall Kanyon, is an integration of the mall's original architecture, The House Café brand identity and the Autoban design approach. A site-built structure made of steel and glass, which functions as a transparent box to house the café, is carefully planned and designed to fit the valley-like architecture of the mall and sat on a walnut platform to add warmth to the café's interior. Although an extension, the structure bears its own strong design identity while blending in with its surroundings.

Company : *Autoban*
Designers : *Seyhan Ozdemir, Sefer Caglar*
Photographer : *George Mitchell*
Client : *The House Café*
Country : *Turkey*

Autoban's first overseas project, 208 Duecento Otto restaurant has opened in Sheung Wan, Hong Kong. Inspired by the district surrounding 208 and the New York-style Italian menu, the design story was created to bring the authentic cuisine to HK. Art and design play a large part in the make-up of the restaurant's surroundings, creating a fresh Bohemian energy.

A striking rustic iron facade welcomes visitors along with the two Nest Chair, the latest item of the Autoban's collection. Two-storey restaurant seats up to 90 people, bar on the ground floor with a warm private dining room for up to 18 people, which leads up with an interior staircase to the dining room on the first floor. Blue and white ceramic tiles were used to decorate the interior walls which create the Chinese atmosphere while the leather bar stools express a rustic but at the same time an urban feeling of a New Yorker's evening. West's New Yorker and Italian style together with East's Chinese ambiance creates a fusion and offers its visitors a unique experience. The natural and true style of Autoban is featured throughout the restaurant, in steel pillars, marble table tops and solid walnut (as one the signature-material of Autoban), floors and ceiling.

What was a meat storage warehouse became this eye-catching Italian restaurant with a cosmopolitan modern feeling.

Company : *Autoban*
Designers : *Seyhan Ozdemir, Sefer Caglar*
Photographer : *George Mitchell*
Client : *Yenn Wong*
Country : *Turkety*

The founding concept for the Minibar was created by three Dutch friends, who were looking for a different way of having a drink in a relaxed environment. No more queuing, trying to catch the bartenders eye, or being ignored at the bar, but a comprehensive selection of drinks taken at your own pace, from your own personal minibar.

We translated this idea into an experience.

At the Minibar you'll be welcomed by a receptionist, checked in and given a key to your own personal minibar. There are beer bars, champagne bars or regular bars filled with combinations of drinks, allowing you to go straight, mix up a storm or try an exotic beer or two. Every bar has a list of the drinks and the prices, and if you're a little hungry there is a delicious selection of nuts, for something more, Sushi and Curry can be ordered and delivered.

After a good time with friends, clients or just having chilled with a magazine at the reading table, you can check out at reception and pay the bill.

The building in Prinsengracht, Amsterdam was a busy wood factory in the 1960's. Based on pictures found in the archives the 60's façade has been recreated, using 4 metre high wooden and glass panels to keep an open character. To preserve this feeling of space and history, but to keep the weather out when the doors are folded open, a glass façade has been placed about 1.5m further inside the building. These 4 metre high panels are ceiling high and constructed with a solid metal frame. The small area created between the doors and the façade is a perfect space for the smoking guests; smoking outside the bar while still being under cover and part of the party. Smokers have even been provided with a stylish refurbished 60's cigarette vending machine.

To create a distinguished and luxury feel for the central area of the Minibar, base colours and materials have been used to provide a clear and stylish contrast. A range of quality raw materials form the backbone. The custom made stainless steel, leather and oak furniture, in combination with the warm colours, add contrast and style to the raw base.

This emphasizes the concept of the Minibar:

placing the main ingredients, the custom made luxurious furniture into just any space in the world.

The contrast of raw and luxury is best experienced as a journey through the bar. Check in at the concrete reception desk with concrete floor and walls, get your minibar key and move into the oak woodblock floor, stainless steel fridges, and leather couch. Enjoy the digitally projected wallpaper adding vibrancy and an ever-changing world of animation across one wall.

Each of the 3 stainless steel fridges contain 15 minibars with their own number, lock and transparent door with individual colour coding. The warm colours from the fridge filters in combination with the golden accent of the 18 suspended lamps, the wooden floors and tables give the central area a warm atmosphere.

The fridges are all placed at an 83 angle from the walls, so as to allow the people walking by a great view of and into the 45 minibars. The 83 angle is carried through into the rest of the interior, with the wooden bar tables, the long custom made leather couch, the line of spots on the ceiling. To complete this picture, even the glass façade and the floor borders are set at the same 83 degrees.

At the rear of the building, further on from the luxury and comfort of the bar area the concrete motif/theme continues reflecting the reception area. A spacious reading table cast in solid concrete with an oak wood block top, sits on the returning theme of a raw concrete floor.

The back of house enables the staff to restock the fridges, as clients select their choices from the front. An indicator lights up when a fridge is opened, allowing the staff to check and refill the fridge from the rear as needed. Through a hand held computer, this information is relayed electronically to the reception, so the bill can be paid.

Company : *Concrete Architectural Assosiates*

Designer : *Concrete Architectural Assosiates*

Photographer : *Ewout Huibers*

Client : *Brewster Dubois-Reymond Macdonald B.V.*

Country : *the Netherlands*

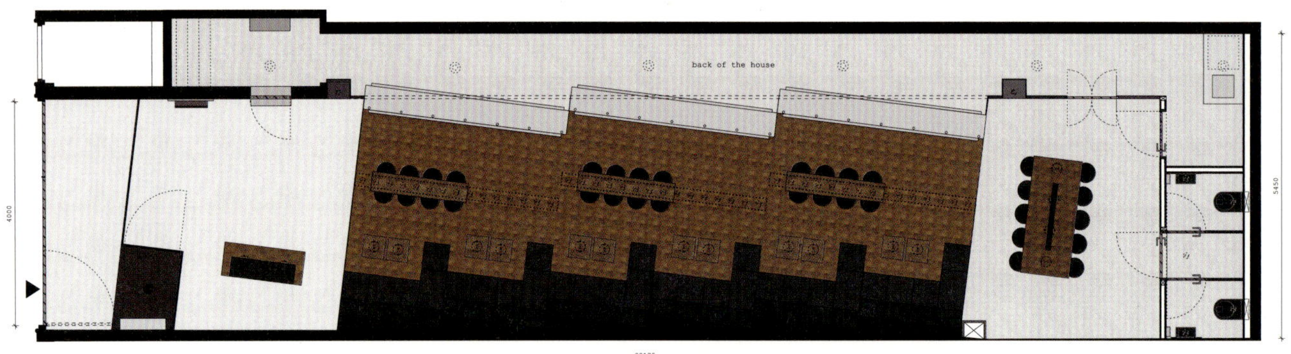

concrete architectural associates bv
rozengracht 133 III
1016 lv amsterdam
the netherlands

concrete reinforced
oudezijds achterburgwal 145
1012 dg amsterdam
the netherlands

t. +31(0)20 5 200 200
f. +31(0)20 5 200 201
info@concreteamsterdam.nl
www.concreteamsterdam.nl

alle maten in het werk te controleren
alle rechten voorbehouden
conform DNR 2005

datum: maart 2009
getekend door: charlotte van mill
contactpersoon: charlotte van mill

minibar
plattegrond

The Nautilus Project is located on the fourth floor of the ION shopping center, where opened recently on the Orchard Road, Singapore. The great strategy of the location has brought them lots of benefits as the floor composite of sales, drinks and food. Besides, the entrance of the restaurant is flanked on one side by an oyster bar and on the other side by displays of delectable dessert and trays of fresh crustaceans on ice. A certain concept of the design, chef, design and location have been prepared by the food consultant from the beginning had caused me difficulty in leading my own ideal interior design. However, the owner is the president of the cargo company and her beauty made me decide to reflect her sophisticate, elegant plus the tender characteristic to this restaurant project.

I stopped making a facade and designed the entrance where a common passageway for the restaurant in order to make visitor enter easily without any hesitation. Both are curved inward towards the middle to highlight the beginning of the passageway into the restaurant. This creates a non-intimidating welcome for passers-by to get a glimpse of what the restaurant has to offer, as well as sets the tone for the restaurant's focus on an interactive experience for the patrons.

Designer : *Yuhkichi Kawai*
Client : *AC2 International pte. ltd.*
Country : *Singapore*

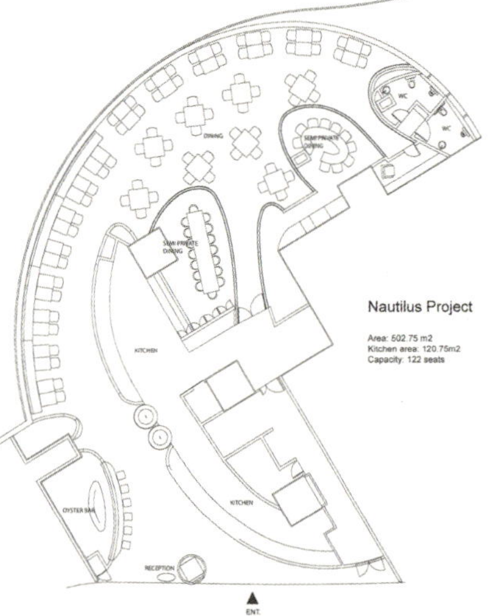

AG cafe is planned for gallery and cafe which aimed to offer the place can meet to art easily and to support artists at Osu Shopping street in the center of Nagoya City.

The owner requested a space which can enjoy the art at the space of cafe near place where picture is decorated in daily life, not at inorganic space in not daily life. Also he requested to harmonize two contrary factors, cafe's lively brisk and gallery's dignified atmosphere.

The space is composed of the design and the tone which feel warmth of cafe. Also added "quality" which necessary to gallery by stick to proportion and detail.

We designed abstraction pattern of birds' nest for feel warmth of design and placed everywhere. This pattern has part of frame and owner's desire that artists will bring up, flaps, and fly away from this cafe. This pattern had cut out by NC router's minimum radius 5 mm so it can realize beautiful detail.

Also we chose the furniture which becomes familiar to the pattern and expecting multiplier effect.

We made many models of each part of proportion and tried to create "quality".

The side of shopping street fitted with glass then people can see the inner part of cafe, therefore when the works display in the cafe, people who comes and goes in the shopping street attract to artists works naturally.

We wish many artists will flap and fly away from this space.

Company : *Kidosaki Architects Studio*

Creative Director : *Hirotaka Kidosaki*

Designer : *Hirotaka Kidsaki*

Photographer : *45g Photography Junji Kojima*

Country : *Japan*

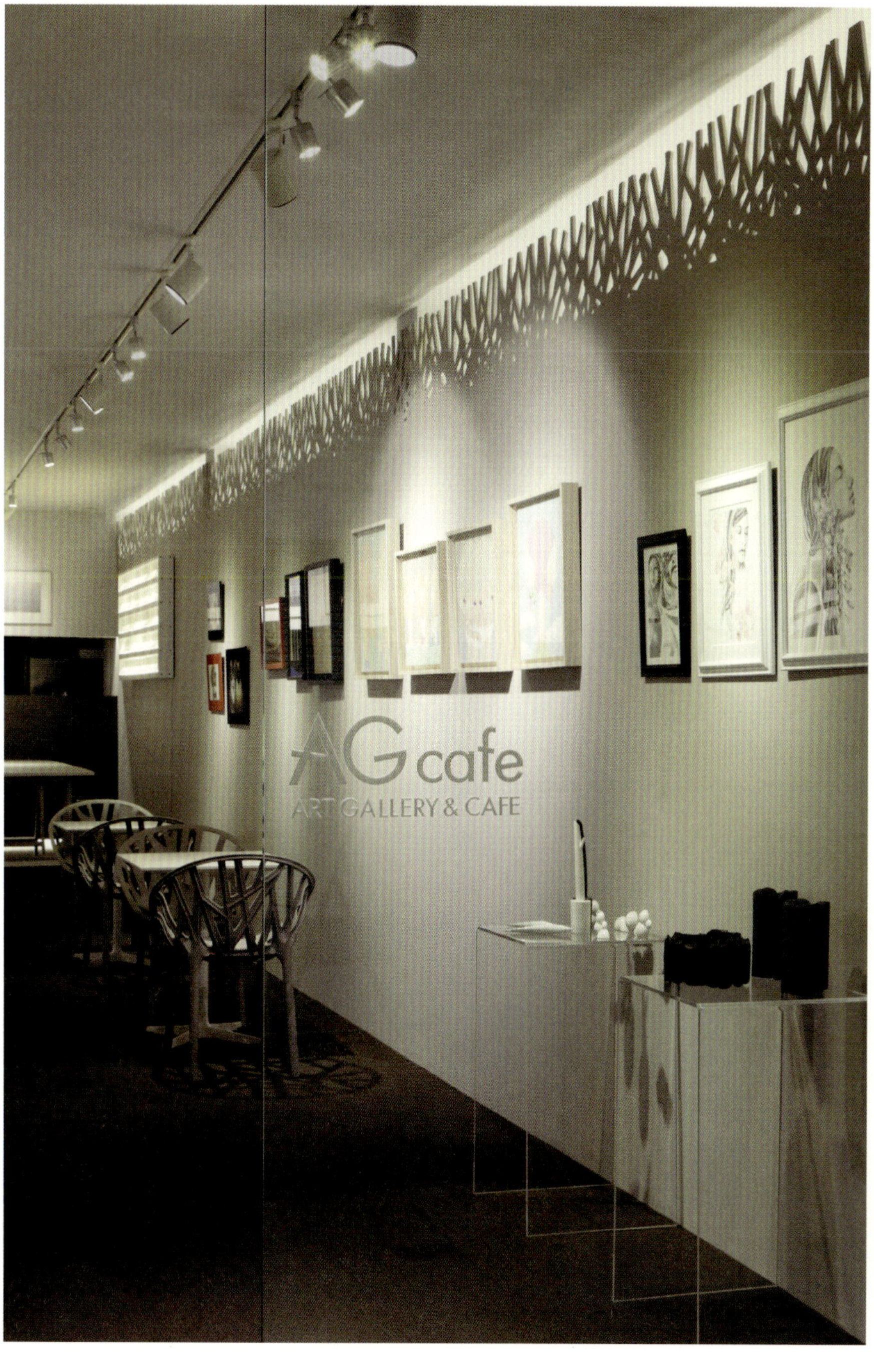
AG cafe
ART GALLERY & CAFE

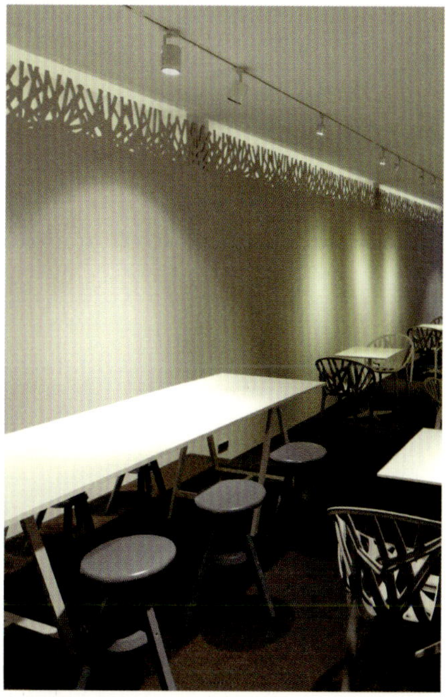

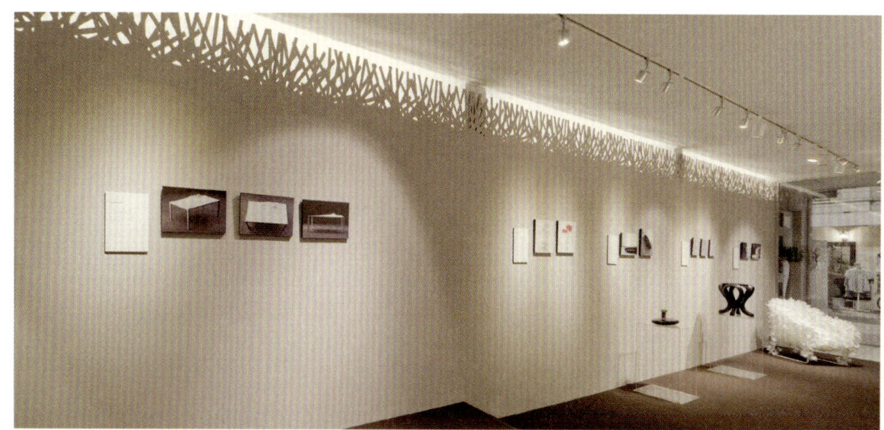

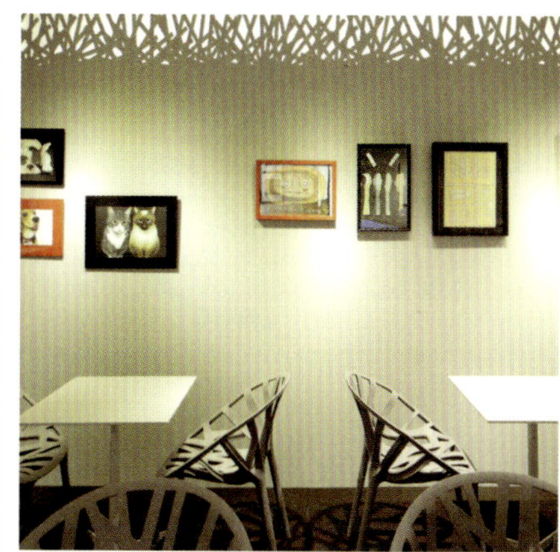

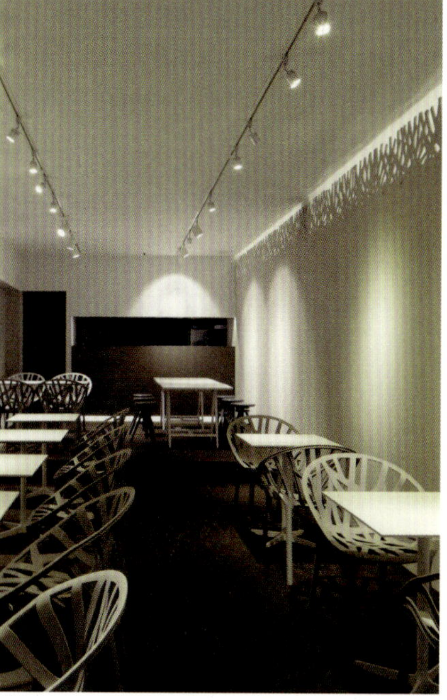

Growing shadow
C'fort is a deli style café bar which supplies different menu to various customers on time by time.
"Shadow" is naturally changing by time in this shop, therefore I designed interior with theme "Shadow design" throughout.
Firstly, tree branches, rebar, has spread out on ceiling which is to be worked for electric ducts.
Then, oval shaped sheets on ceiling lights create shadows which represent 木の葉 .
As the result, customers can feel sense of walking into the deep forest by creating deeper shadows by dimmer from day-time to night-time.
Customers naturally have experience of floating time through this intentionally created shadow.

Company : *Kamitopen Architecture-Design Office*
Designer : *Kamitopen Architecture- Design Office Masahiro Yoshida*
Photographer : *Keisuke Miyamoto*
Client : *C-Service Co.,Ltd.*
Country : *Japan*

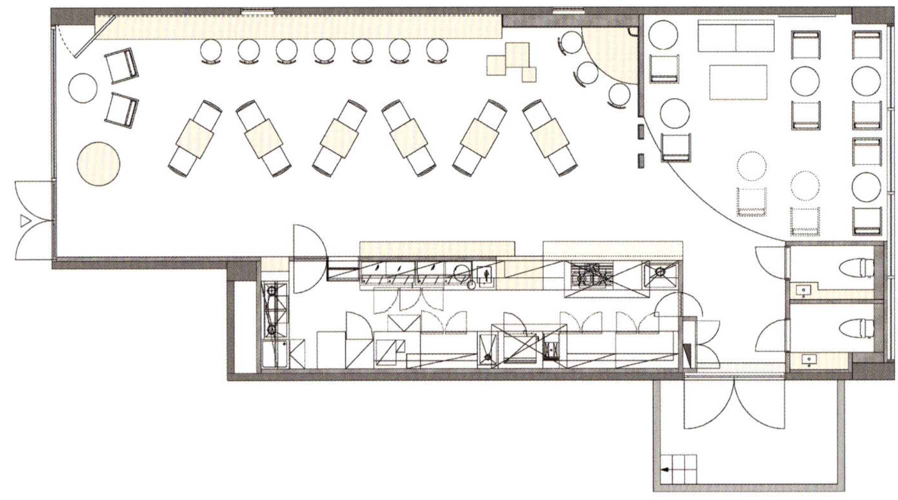

MAZZO AMSTERDAM

Mazzo, the eighth member of the IQ creative family in Amsterdam, is the Italian sister of Brasserie Witteveen – both in hospitality concept and in the interior there is an obvious connection. As with Witteveen the name and location of Mazzo share a history in the city of Amsterdam. Until six years ago Mazzo was a famous and notorious disco in the monumental building on the Rozengracht.

It's a typical Amsterdam building: narrow and very deep spaces fused together with different floor and ceiling levels, which automatically provides a natural positioning for the restaurant.

The first part, situated on the Rozengracht, has a five-meter high ceiling and faces directed outwards. The perfect area for a bar, where guests can order a fast espresso or have a drink at the high bar tables. Lighting from the Bestlite series by GUBI creates the intimacy in this space. The wall lights above the nine-meter chesterfield couch and the suspension lights above the bar and bar tables in XS and XL sizes create a living room ambiance.

The second part is obviously lower but twice as wide. A few original stone columns divide this part into two zones. The darkest part of the entire building is perfect to house the kitchen. The seating area of the restaurant is opposite to the kitchen with a simple but flexible, trattoria-like table arrangement. A variation of tables for two or eight are placed and every table has a great view of the chefs in the kitchen. Five Dear Ingo lights by MOOOI comfortably light up the seating area. Independent of the table arrangement, these modern chandeliers give a pleasant and intimate light. Four portraits of people in different age categories provide an Italian family-feeling of which the guests can be a part during dinner. For a real family dinner or a business meeting guests can use the boardroom. A cosy room with a TV screen and fireplace, next to the kitchen, which can be closed off if privacy is preferred.

The third part is orientated towards Bloemstraat. A narrowing in the building creates the small backroom where kids can play during the day under the watch of their parents. At night the toys can disappear in the cabinet behind a black-and-white blocked curtain and guests can retreat into the eleven-meter long chesterfield couch to enjoy a good glass of wine and have a nice conversation. Again the Bestlite wall lights by GUBI create a home-like feeling.

The diversity of the fused spaces and the natural restaurant layout need a connecting element: a huge wooden cupboard across the whole restaurant linking all the spaces to each other and organising them at the same time. The cupboard, created out of solid pine wood for storage and display of the products, becomes the stairs to the mezzanine floor, the back bar, point of distribution for the food, the transparent division between the boardroom and restaurant, the wardrobe, the access to the restrooms and the storage for the kids toys.

Five materials determine the ambiance of the raw and honest interior design: power floated concrete, chipped brickwork, stone, pinewood and raw steel. The first three materials are part of the shell of the building; all the new materials are steel and wood.

The window frames in the cupboard and the mezzanine floor in the front of the restaurant are completely made of raw steel. The steel beams and columns are exposed and the extra floor is provided with an untreated expanded metal mesh. The use of honest and simple materials doesn't distract the guests' eye and underlines the fact that the restaurant focuses on the food.

Embracing the past of the building and the name Mazzo by creating a logo that is a controversial part of the venue. The five letters are made of raw steel and filled with classic amusement lights, referring to the disco days of Mazzo. The light object crowns above the bar and will be noticed even in a flash by the cars and cyclists passing by.

Company : *Concrete Architectural Associates*
Designer : *Concrete Architectural Associates*
Photographer : *Ewout Huibers*
Country : *the Netherlands*

FIOR di RISO
Sanbittèr
SAPORI
FIORINO
GRANO DURO
PIZZA

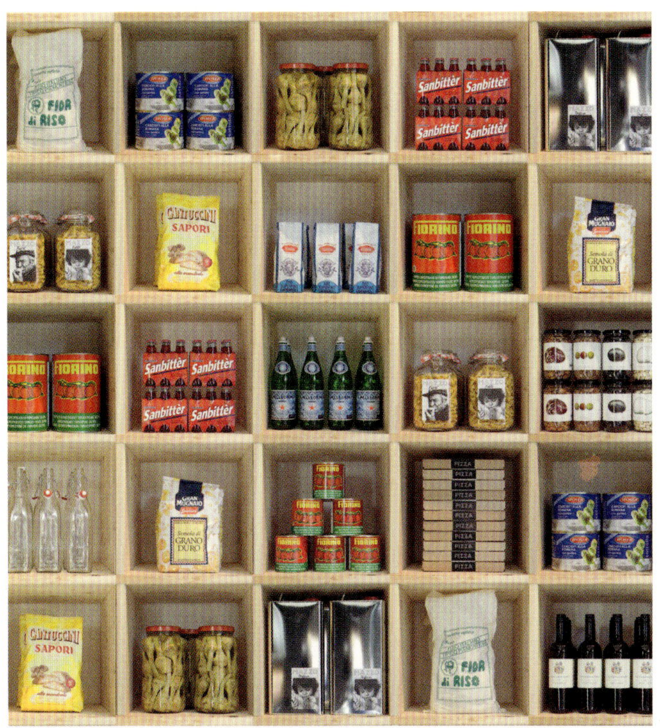

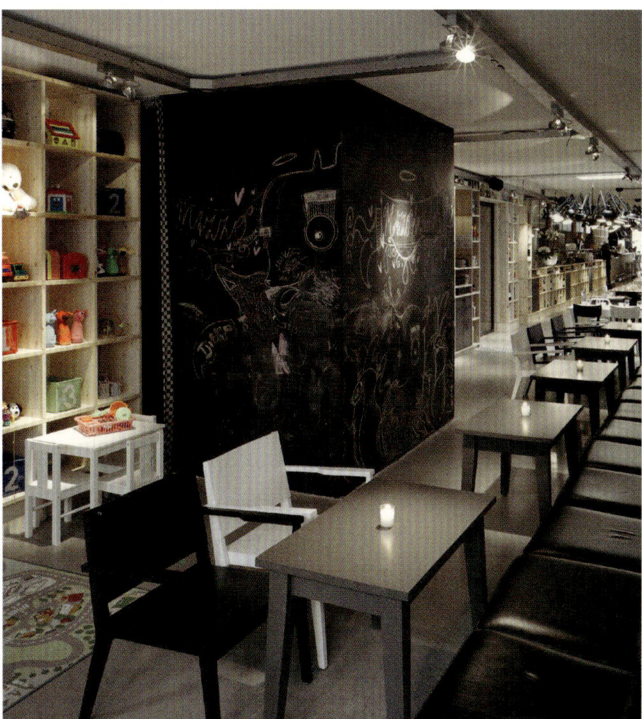

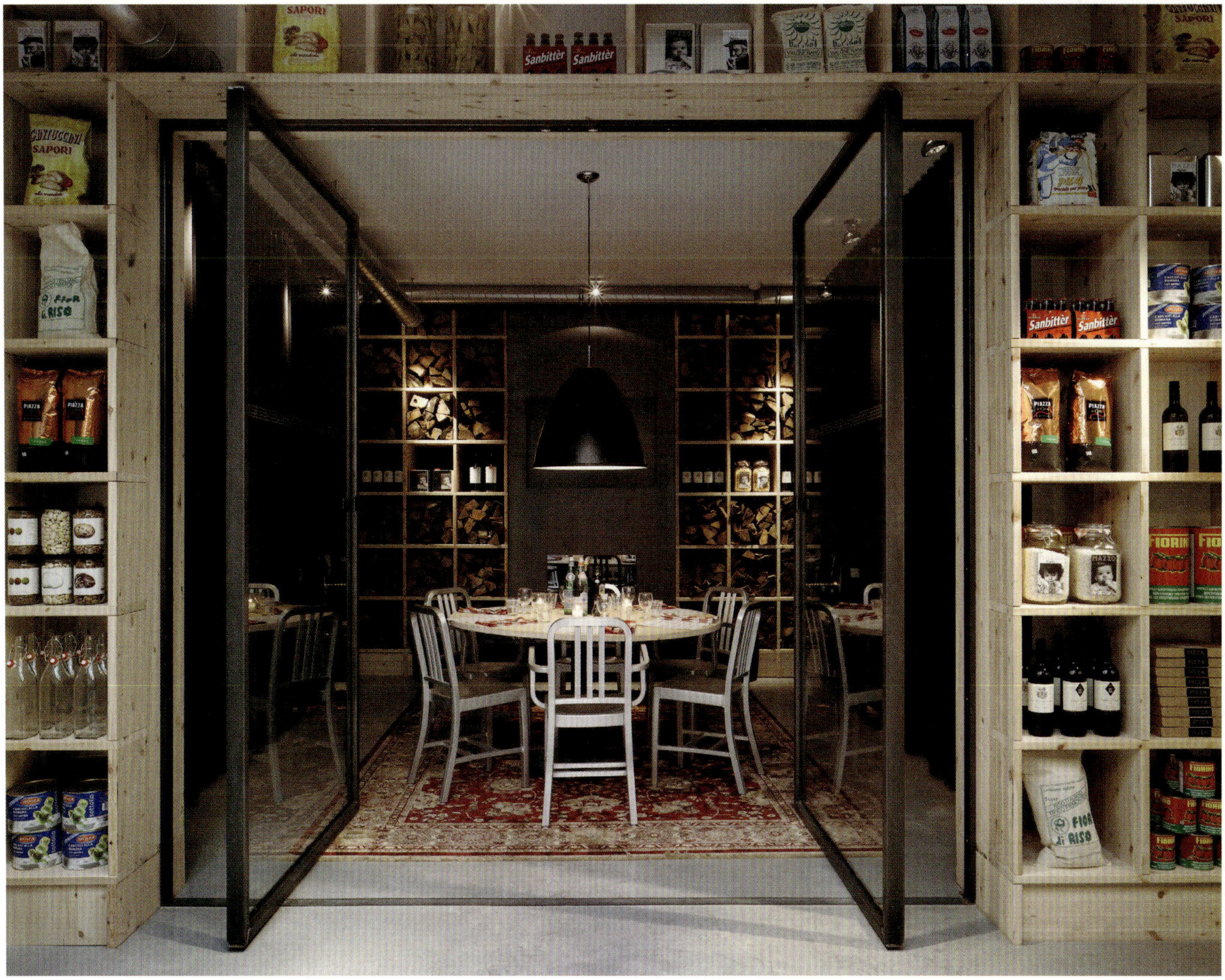
SAPORI
Sanbittèr
FIOR di RISO
PIZZA
FIORINO

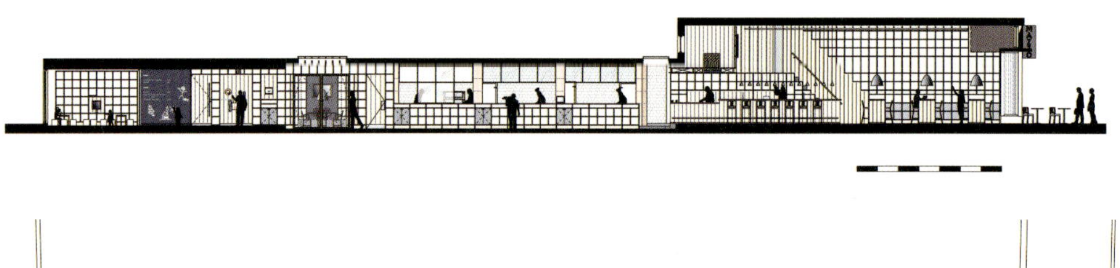

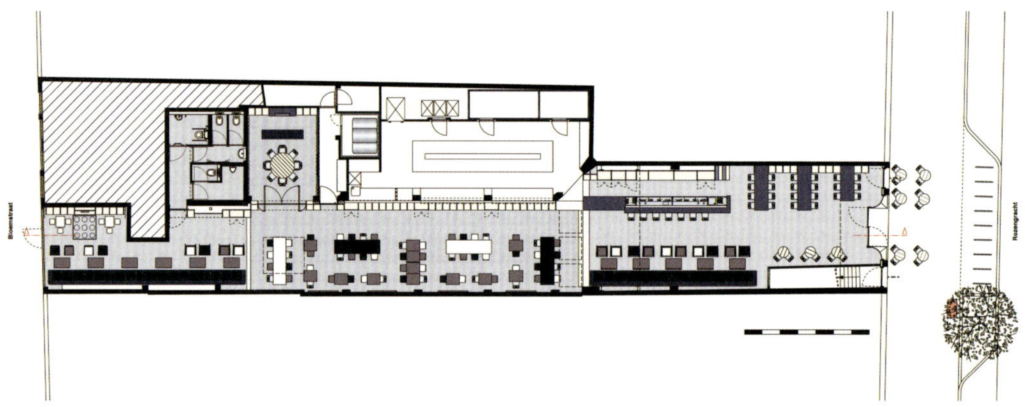

MAZZO

WIENERWALD – INTERIOR CONCEPT FOR RESTAURANTS

Friedrich Jahn's goal is now to build on the long tradition of the company, exploiting both the strength of the brand and the uniqueness of their gastronomic concept. Our studio was commissioned to develop new corporate architecture for the chain, which has already been rolled out in two Wienerwald branches in Munich.

The new interior design underscores the realignment of the brand, while translating the chain's traditional strengths of high quality, comfort and German cuisine into a contemporary design idiom. Materials and colours reflect the principles of freshness and naturalness, which find their expression in materials such as wood, leather and textiles, as well as in the dominant green tones that complement the fresh white. Gold is used as an accent colour, conjuring up associations of quality and the crisp, gold-coloured skin of the main product, the Wienerwald grilled chicken.

The space has been organised to ensure good visitor guidance, crucial in a self-service restaurant, as well as respecting the need for a differentiated selection of seating. Upon entering the restaurant, the guest is guided towards a frontally positioned counter, which presents itself as a clearly structured, monolithic unit. Menu boards suspended above the counter visualise the range of food on offer. The food itself is also visible: An indirectly lit niche in the rear wall of the service area presents a selection of salads adjacent to grilled chickens turning on a spit. The wall is covered in anthracite mosaic stones, into which frameless, stainless steel units have been precisely inserted, thereby underscoring the high standard of the products. A neon green arrow in the centre of the rear wall indicates a hatch to the kitchen where fried chicken dishes are prepared.

Order and payment terminals occupy the far ends of the white, solid surface counter. The chopping station is in the middle. After ordering, this is where salads are chopped, chicken is portioned and toppings are added from containers set into the counter under the guests' watchful eyes. In the wall adjacent to the payment terminal, a display refrigerator stocks drinks and desserts. The restaurant remains odourless thanks to a ventilation and extraction system integrated into the counter area.

In front of the service counter is a service station made of white solid surface, offering sauces, condiments and cutlery. It stands on golden chicken legs and looks expectantly towards the entrance. Green instructions and Wienerwald chickens set into the rustic wood floor show the customer how to navigate the ordering process.

The dining area offers a range of seating options catering toward different requirements. White solid surface high bar tables are available for guests with little time on their hands. These are supported by a single leg with a tapering cylinder at its foot, recalling the traditional turned table leg. Alternative seating is available in an elongated seating group upholstered in brown, artificial leather, a reflection of the traditional Wienerwald seating niches. Guests are really spirited away into the 'Wienerwald' (English: Vienna Woods) here. Overlapping, rough-sawn oak panels on the rear wall quote the forest theme. Round mirrors printed with the outlines of tree and forest motifs are set into this wall. Different-sized pendant luminaires at varying heights hang over the tables. These are sheathed in a roughly woven fabric in three shades of green and ensure a pleasant atmosphere. Forest images in different shades of green on wallpaper occupy one side wall, as well as transparencies on the windows. The view into the restaurant from the outside thus becomes a multi-faceted experience in which the individual elements on the mirror and glass surfaces reflect and overlap one another, making the brand world a truly holistic experience.

A display of dining plates on the wall is dedicated to the Wienerwald company and its long tradition, reminiscing on the history of the brand in 14 motifs. They pay tribute to Friedrich Jahn, the brand's founding father, and show a photograph of the first Wienerwald restaurant.

The new restaurant design repositions Wienerwald as a contemporary fast-food chain. Traditional elements of the brand have been incorporated and translated into modern spatial elements with an exciting twist.

Company : *Ippolito Fleitz Group –*
Identity Architects
Photographer : *Zooey Braun*
Client : *Wienerwald Franchise GmbH*
Country : *Germany*

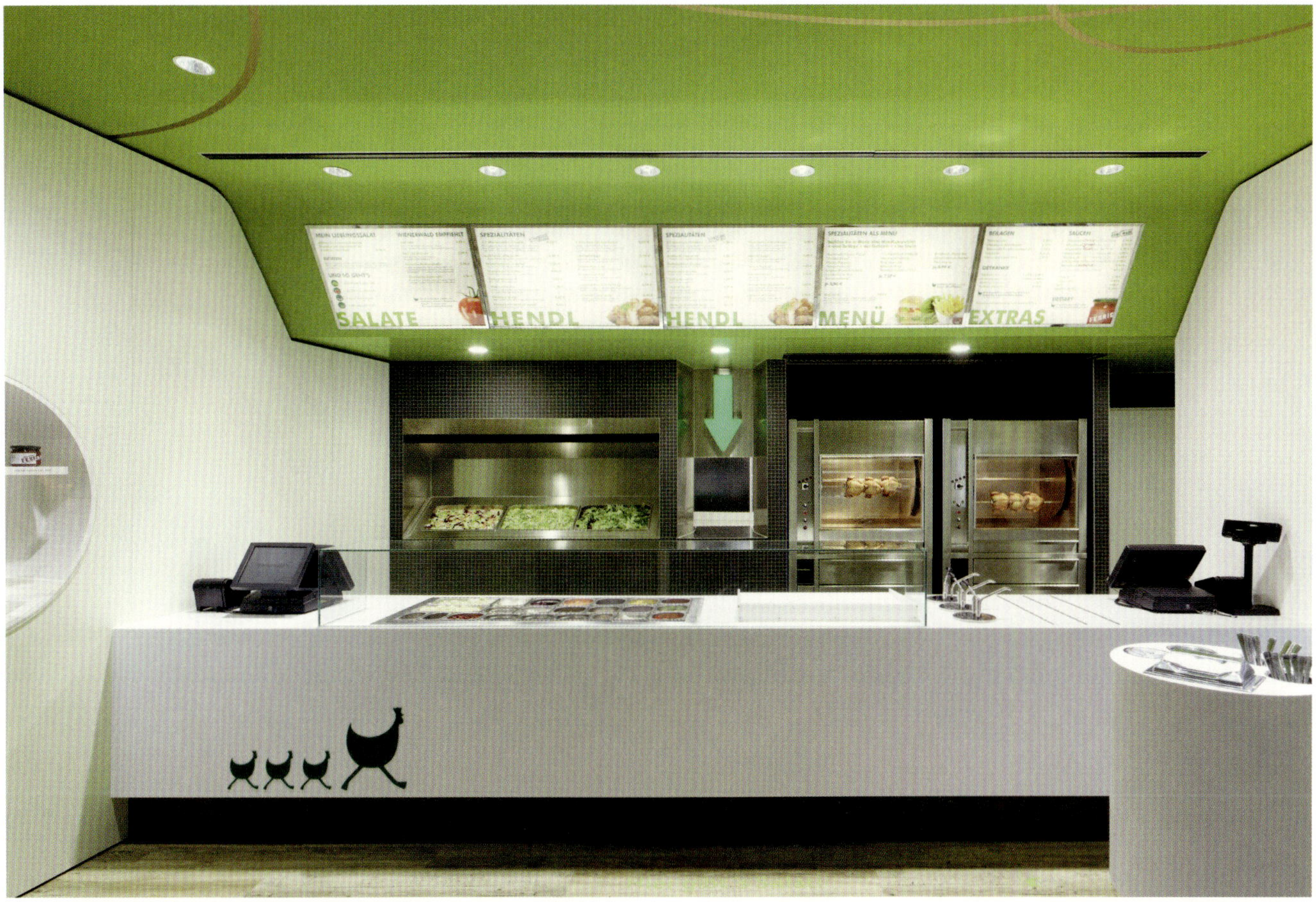
SALATE
HENDL
HENDL
MENÜ
EXTRAS

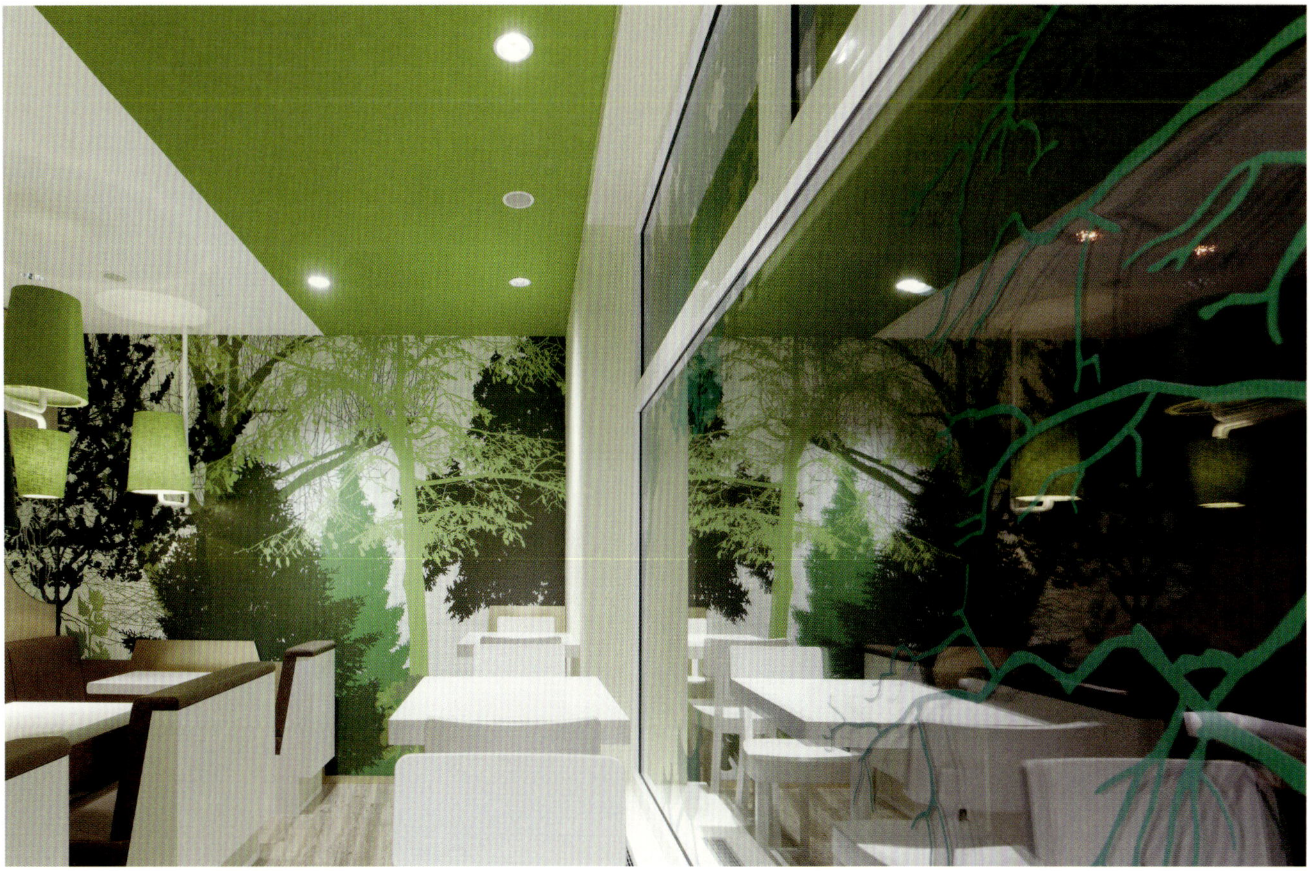

INDEX

Alberto Apostoli

Alberto Apostoli was born in Verona in 1968. Graduated in Industrial Electronics, degree in architecture in Venice in 1993 with a thesis about Economy. He opens in 1997, Apostoli & Associati Studio, characterized by a varied professional vocation consequence of its personal path. In 2006 opens its first personal exhibition at the headquarters of the European Parliament in Brussels by the title "contaminated architectures between communication and design", causing the attention of the European press. In the same year he opens a study in Guangzhou (China) and in 2007 a representative office in Casablanca. In 2010 Apostoli designs SaSHa (Sauna+Shower+Hammam) for Jacuzzi. Alberto Apostoli has design and marketing culture, that gives every project strong innovation. His projects are published all over the world. Takes conferences, courses and workshops in Italy and abroad on different areas of design.

Autoban

Email: info@autoban212.com

Established in 2003 by Seyhan Özdemir and Sefer Çaglar, Autoban is a design studio operating in the fields of interior design, architecture and product development.
The foundations of Autoban were laid in the Galata district of Istanbul, taking its name from the architectural landmark tower. Inspired by the chaos of the mega city, contrasts, contradictions and the co-existence of otherwise autonomous elements are all trademarks of Autoban projects and products. The Autoban studio is currently located in a grand late 19th century building in Galata's neighbouring Tünel district, a modern quarter rich with history.

Architecture EAT

Email: office@eatas.com.au

Established in 2000, Architecture EAT is a well recognized Australian architecture and interior practice now contributing significantly to the Melbourne design scene. With a new corporate identity created in 2006, EAT seeks to build on its unique brand and continue to offer our valued group of clients a creative, professional service.
With over 20 years of collective experience, out team of architects and interior designers has completed a body of work both here and overseas that demonstrates an ability to integrate an innovative and functional approach to projects.
We believe in the phenomenological dimension of design: architecture must be experienced intuitively first hand. This philosophical approach is based on the physical and haptic experience of building materials and their properties that pertain to the sense of touch, sound, sight, weight, patina and the interplay of natural light and shadows.
We approach our projects in logical, problem-solving sequences. By understanding the issues intrinsic to each project, a design basis is deliberated, evolving into a tangible reality that functions around the client's demands.
Our philosophy also takes account of what we term the "enrichment of lifestyle" and it is equally applicable to a restaurant, hotel, residence, institution or office. We place strong emphasis on context and demographics to achieve maximum interaction with the site and locality, but ultimately, the outcome must centre on strong design aesthetics and timeless experiences.

Antonio Gardoni Studio

Email: info@antoniogardoni.com

Antonio Gardoni. Architect and designer with international background of experiences, innovator in the design language for commercial and experiential projects. Collaboration with Ron Arad, cofounder of Jump studios and professor of industrial and interior design.

BUJ+COLÓN Arquitectos

Email: estudio@buj-colon.com

Raquel Buj García (Palencia) y Pedro Colón de Carvajal Salís (Gijón) son Arquitectos por la Escuela Técnica Superior de Arquitectura de Madrid y colaboran desde el año 2002 en el desarrollo de proyectos de urbanismo, paisaje, arquitectura y diseño. Actualmente desarrollan los estudios de Doctorado de Proyectos Arquitectónicos de la ETSAM. Sus obras se han publicado y expuesto en países como Estados Unidos, China, Rusia, Japón, Corea, Hungría, Alemania, Reino Unido, Italia, Francia y España.

Chrystalline Artchitect

Email: admin@chrystallineartchitect.com

People said we are uncompromisingly professional, that we provide solutions to their problem beyond expectations.
Actually, we just believe in ARTCHITECT. And do what we are good at. We call the process 'chrystallization'.

Crox International

Email: crox@crox.com.tw

Inspired by Rem Koolhaas, the world famous architectural theorist and his landmark publication S, M, L, XL, Crox International is a design firm established with the belief that the relationship between the users and the environment must reach the state of equilibriums in all space design projects. From metropolis plan, city landscape, interior decoration, exhibition design to scenery creation, Crox has successfully overcome the traditional space definition and presented a new experience of communication without boundaries.

Based in Taipei and Shanghai as one of the world's most dependable space design firms, Crox embraces every project type from all geographic regions and budget levels. With the enormous energy and insights from the global specialists, the team is committed to collaborating with clients and their ideas. Crox is continuously working in the productive team-cooperation system to deliver the inventive marketing conformity through design satisfaction.

Checkland Kindleysides

Email: claire@checklandkindleysides.com

Checkland Kindleysides founded in 1979, we are one of the largest design consultancies within the UK. We span a broad range of design disciplines including graphic communication, identity, retail, interior and interactive design. We work in partnership with both local and global brands across a diverse range of market sectors.Client's include Timberland, Levi's®, Sony Playstation, Boots, British Heart Foundation, Royal Bank of Scotland, Henri-Lloyd, George at Asda, Hammersons, Procter and Gamble, Ruby & Millie and WGSN.

Christian Ghion

Email : ghion@christianghion.com

1958 : Birth of Christian
1966 : Begins boarding school
1972 : Moves in with his grandmother
1976 : Begins Law school , five years
1982 : Intègre 1'ECM (Etude et Création de Mobilier), école d'architecture de Charenton.
1986 : Begins teaching at this same school
1987 : Grandmother passes away
Starts his own studio with Patrick Nadeau
1990 Is awarded the "Grand Prix de la Creation de la Ville de Paris "
1991 : Sucessfully seduces his wife, the unstoppable Claude Deloffre
1994 Meets Andree Putman , who will become his mentor and guardien angel
1995 : Travels to Japan, meets Kurosaki, the big boss of Idee who will later edit his furniture
1997 : Beginning of his relationship with Tarkett Sommer Meets Philippe Starck
1998 : Starts working solo
1999 : Exhibits his "inside out" collection of vases at the Galerie Neotu which is then edited (produced) by XO a few weeks later
2005 : Edited by Cappellini, Sawaya et Moroni, Driade.Designs Chantal Thomass' boutique, Jean-Charles de Castelbajac's concept store and Pierre Gagnaire's "restaurant elementaire "
2006 : Receives the "Ordre des Chevaliers des Arts et des Lettres " medal from the minister of cultural affairs
2008 : Designs Pierre Gagnaire's restaurants in Tokyo and Dubai
2010 : Presentation of the "Minister's desk" made of carbon fiber, manufactured by the Mobilier National

Cyrille Druart

Email: info@cyrilledruart.com

Born on 15th May 1980 in Paris.
General studies until earning a Baccalaureate specialised in Fine Arts.
Enters art school (Esag-Penninghen, Ecole Supérieur d'Arts Graphiques et d'Architecture Intérieur) in 1999 -Does several internships and notably works on the renovation of Karl Lagerfeld's fashion studio and the creation of villas.
Graduates from Esag-Penninghen in 2004 at the top of his class with a degree in Interior Architecture and Design.
Leaves for London.
Creation of "Cyrille Druart" company in 2007, based in Paris, for the development of Architectures, Interiors, furnitures and other products.
Opening of I-WAY in July 2008 Designer, Interior Architect, also passionate about Photography, Cyrille Druart excels in many fields. He grew up in an artistic environment, immersed in surrealism on his mother's side, which has had a profound influence on his work and interest in the imaginary. His father, an industrial designer, exposed him to the technical side of the profession. A creator at heart, he strives to design modern, non-decorative environments, but with an underlying language and sense of wonder. Architecture thus becomes a platform for introspection.

CASE-REAL

Email: futatsumata@casereal.com

CASE-REAL is a design farm based in Japan which is organized around Koichi Futatsumata and plans various designs such as spaces, constructions, furniture and products.

Concrete

Email: info@concreteamsterdam.nl

Concrete develops total concepts for businesses and institutions. The agency produces work which is commercially applied. This involves creating total identities for a company, a building or an area. The work extends from interior design to urban development integration and from the building to its accessories. Concrete, for example, also sets the perimeters for the graphic work and considers how the client can present itself in the market. This all happens from the 'one concept' philosophy. The designers of concrete create holistic plans and everything they design is used for the benefit of that total concept: that's where their strength – and thus the client's greatest advantage – lies. Concrete consists of 2 companies: concrete architectural associates and concrete reinforced. Concrete's entire team consists of about 30 professional people. Visual marketers, interior designers, product designers and architects work on the projects in multidisciplinary teams.

Cabinet Braun-Braën

Email: info@cabinetbb.com

A rebel and iconoclast, Bruno Braën describes himself as self taught. He learned his trade on construction sites, developing a signature style that can be called "structured creative improvisation."

More than the places, it is often the people, history, and spirit of sites that inspire him to create the unconventional originality found in each of his works, including Billy Kun, Porte, DNA, Club Chasse et Pêche, and Pullman, of which he is co-owner and for which he received the jury prize in the 2007 Créativité Montréal competition.

Chikara Ohno

Email: central@sinato.jp

Chikara Ohno, first class registered architect of Japan. Representative director of sinato inc. 1976 born in Osaka, Japan. 1999 graduated from the department of civil engineering, Kanazawa university.

2004   Established sinato.

[awards]

2007   NASHOP Lighting Awards, excellent prize
       WJCD Design Awards, winner

2008   Good Design Awards, winner
       JCD Design Awards, rookie award
       SDA Awards, encouragement prize
       Display Design Awards, winner

2009 DESIGN FOR ASIA, bronze award
       Gunma agricultural technology center

Design Competition, honorable mention
       Good Design Awards, winner
       JCD Design Awards, silver award
       SDA Awards, highest award
       Display Industry Awards, encouragement prize

       BEST STORE OF THE YEAR, excellent prize
       Display Design Awards, winner

2010   Mie Architecture Awards, winner
       BEST STORE OF THE YEAR, excellent prize

       JCD Design Award 2010, gold award
       Display Design Award 2010, encouragement prize

Dear design

Email: dear@deardesign.net

Dear design and architecture conceives design as a balance between both actual projects and innovative projects. The studio's philosophy is based on considering creativity as a whole.

Dear is composed of several multidisciplinary professionals, all of them mindful of research and innovation, willing to offer global solutions and sense to our customers' projects, by the creation of brand image, conceptualization and refurbishing spaces, industrial design and events creation.

Dear was founded in 2005 by Ignasi Llaurado and Eric Dufourd. They both met first in 2003 and quickly coincided on both design vision and inspirations.

Ignasi and Eric consider that design moves between functionality and pleasure. That is to say, that there's no border between art and technic.

Dastro Retailconcepts

Email: dastro@dastro.nl

In 2007 Rob Hoogendijk founded Dastro Retailconcepts , a Rotterdam design agency whose name clearly highlights the firm's core business: retail design. Dastro has gathered experience in various branches of the industry thanks to projects for fashion, shoe, perfume and jewellery stores; pharmacies; opticians; and spaces belonging to the automotive and telecom sectors.

Dalziel-Pow UK

Email: d.wright@dalziel-pow.co.uk

Our business was established in 1983, providing design services to a variety of clients. We have grown with our clients, to become a leading player in the creation of brands, branded environments and their communications.

We are a design consultancy with one aim: to create great customer experiences. We believe in the role of design to connect brands with their customers, stakeholders and staff. Design is a critical business tool and, when used effectively, it can deliver not only profitability, but also visibility, credibility and efficiency.

There is an irrefutable link between effective design and the financial performance of a business, no matter what size. It is hard to recall any successful business today that doesn't employ design as part of its strategy.

DesignSpirits

Email: designspirits@gmail.com

Establish since 1995. Design Spirits Sdn Bhd is a dynamic company that has always excelled in providing outstanding and innovative interior design services for many residential and commercial properties.

As a fast growing company, we are committed to offer the highest standard of our customers.

Eightsixthree

Email: info@eightsixthree.com

Eightsixthree is a design studio based in Hong Kong. Our work and our team are intentionally cross-disciplinary. A mixture that encourages fresh ways of exploring old problems, architects and project managers work with interior designers and urban planners, tackling projects as big as 600,000 sqm or as small as 45 sqm.

We are a small but flexible team, a strategy that allows appropriate talents to be assigned effectively to each project, be it architectural and interior design services, sophisticated CAD modeling and rendering, or project management. Our design approach is simple.

We have no house style. We create designs that are tailored to suit your needs and aspirations, and are sensitive to each project situation.

A clearly defined problem declares its own solution.

We begin this process by questioning, defining and researching the functional and technical issues contained within the client brief. Only after we are fully conversant with your needs do we commence the design.

With each project, the client collaborates with us by responding to our design proposals over a series of stages. The final design solution is reached with both parties – client and designer - understanding and endorsing all decisions.

We appreciate and encourage our clients to be demanding. You play a fundamental role in enriching our designs, goals, thoughts and working process.

Emmanuelle Moureaux

Email: contact@emmanuelle.jp

1971 Boren in France

1995 Graduated in Architecture, University of Bordeaux

1995 Received Architect's Diploma from the French Govement

1996 Moved to Tokyo

2001 Started working as a freelance designer

2003 Received the Japanese First Class Architecture's licence

2003 Established Emmanuelle Moureaux Architecture & Design, Tokyo

2009 Renamed to Emmanuelle moureaux architecture + design

Associate Professor, Tohoku University of Art & Design

Member of the 'Tokyo Society of Achitects"

PRIZES

1994 "First Prize" (Spazio Casa International Design Competition/Milan)

2005 "Best Installation Prize" (Design Tide/ Tokyo) Fresh Touch

2007 "Best Store of the Year-Excellent Prize":ABC Cooking/abc kids

2007 "40 Under 40" (Perspective magazine/Hong Kong)

2008 "Best Store of the Year-Excellent Prize": ABC ground/CS Design Center

2008 "15th CS Design Award-Special Jury Prize": touch the COLOR

Francesco Moncada

Email: mail@francescomoncada.com

Francesco Moncada received his M.Arch. from the University of Palermo, Italy in 2004. He has lived and worked in Spain, UK, Portugal, The Netherlands, Norway, and Dubai. His most notable experience comes from Foreign Office Architects in London, Vicente Guallart in Barcelona and OMA/Rem Koolhaas in Rotterdam. His independent work has been published in Frame, Interni, Case d'Abitare, Ottagono, Perspective Hong Kong, Dezeen, and in various books about interiors. Francesco Moncada is partner of ONOFFICE Architects from 2009 (www.onoffice.no).

Graft

Email: berlin@graftlab.com

GRAFT was established in 1998 in Los Angeles, opened the Berlin office in 2001, and opened its third office in Beijing in January 2005. GRAFT was conceived as a 'label' for architecture, design, and the "pursuit of happiness". Our collective professional experience encompasses a wide array of types, including urban planning and design, civic, governmental, institutional, industrial, residential, exhibition, hospitality, commercial, cultural, and product design.

With a worldwide staff over 100 professionals, Graft is currently executing award-winning projects around the globe. Gregor Hoheisel, Lars Krueckeberg, Alejandra Lillo, Thomas Willemeit and Wolfram Putz lead Graft as its partners. With a staff of talented architectural professionals and administrators, GRAFT has the resources and technology necessary to execute a project from programming and design, to the delivery of construction documents, governmental agency review and through construction administration. GRAFT continues to undertake an increasingly large role in master planning and urban design. Additionally, our firm maintains robustly successful relationships with associate architectural and engineering firms and other specialty consultants.

Gitta Gschwendtner

Email: mail@gittagschwendtner.com

Gitta Gschwendtner's design consultancy includes furniture, interior, exhibition design and public art for arts, cultural and corporate clients.

The studio specializes in a "tailor made" approach to design. Each project is carefully researched and every solution is an individual response to the project's particular needs. The designs have narrative at their heart and are derived from careful problem solving rather than styling.

Giles Miller UK

Email: studio@gilesmiller.com

Born in 1983 in the UK, Giles Miller studied Furniture Design at Loughborough University and formed the rebellious young British design collective in 2006. After going on to exhibit at the London Design Festival with Tent London, he showed both with his collective and solo in such shows as Maison et Objet in Paris, the Milan Furniture Fair, DMY Berlin and even as far as China with the British Council and [re]design amongst others. After a year of self-directed experimentation and continued exploitation of his signature material, corrugated cardboard, Giles began a master's degree at London's Royal College of Art on the Design Products course headed by Ron Arad.

Giles has continued to exploit unlikely materials, and demonstrated his wider spectrum upon graduation from the Royal College in summer of 2009. Following his graduation his "Hirsutio" Vase has gone into the collection of up and coming Fumi Gallery in London, and he now has work in production with Italian brands Dovetusai and newly-launched Italian furniture giant Skitsch. Giles culminated this work to date during the London Design Festival 2009 with his first solo-show "Giles Miller at Kingly Court". Since his graduation, he has been developing his product and surface material range and continuing with personal commissions.

Giles has won two Hidden Art awards for "Best International showcase" and "Most popular product" on the Hidden Art e-shop. He was shortlisted for the FX design award for "Breakthrough talent of the year 2009", Homes and Gardens "Classic Design Award" 2007 and the "New Designer of the Year" award 2006.

HUGE Company

Email: info@hugeshanghai.com

HUGE is an international partnership created in Sydney and Shanghai by Samuel Tsang and Victor Njo. The office has the skills, the knowledge and expertise of a large commercial firm combined with a more high-end and personalized boutique style approach in creating architecture. HUGE has a unique approach to problem solving. Our core focus is on practicing contemporary urbanism, architecture and interior design.

The colourful and diverse backgrounds of the HUGE partners created a platform which not only involves architecture, but amongst other things, creating events such as the Electrograss Stage at the JZ Music Festival and the 2009 NYE Lost Heaven Electrograss Music Festival in Shanghai. Additional activities of the company, such as Branding, Computer Graphics (CG) and Product Design are part of this unique HUGE mix of holistic and lateral approach to design. HUGE also has a reach to various other dimensions by collaborating with creative entities from the industries of fashion, graphic design, photography, advertising, music, video and arts.

Hallucinate

Email: hallucinate@126.com

Hallucinate Interior Design builds the complete image system with the high end brand, and provides the system design for commercial space, such as public environments, stores, clubs and offices, with the main design services in the architecture, interior, and commercial integration,

Found in 1993 by Mr. WANG Wenliang, HALLUCINATE covers various design services for commercial stores, headquarters, public environments, and clubs in Asia. Our mission is to build the complete image system with the high end brand, based on our international cooperation platform with European advanced design studio.

More than 20 designers and engineers from environmental, architectural, graphic, multimedia, and communication fields are gathered in HALLUCINATE. Meanwhile, a professional service process is established based on our experience to follow up the project with different professional teams of branding identity selection, style design, planning, project management, price assessing, and progress and cost control.

HEAD Architecture and Design Limited

Email: enquiries@headarchitecture.com

HEAD Architecture and Design Limited was established in Hong Kong by a group of Architects, designers and project managers who shared the common goal of the pursuit of excellence in architectural design. The scope of our experience broadly covers all aspects of building projects from inception and budget establishment, through brief development, conceptual and developed design on a wide range of architectural and interior projects.

During their careers Head Architecture and Design Limited staffs have been extensively involved in projects of varying size and complexity and in many regions throughout the world, including Europe, South East Asia, the Middle East, New Zealand, in addition to Hong Kong, Taiwan and the People's Republic of China. Our multi-disciplinary team enables a comprehensive design service from initial conceptual planning through to supervision and completion of project site works.

Ippolito fleitz group

Email: info@ifgroup.org

Ippolito fleitz group is a multidisciplinary, internationally operating design studio based in Stuttgart.

We are identity architects. We work in unison with our clients to develop architecture, products and communication that are part of a whole and yet distinctive in their own right. This is how we define identity. With meticulous analysis before we begin. With animated examination in the conceptional phase. With a clarity of argument in the act of persuasion. With a love of accuracy in the realisation. With a serious goal and a lot of fun along the way. Working together with our clients.

As architects of identity, we conceive and construct buildings, interiors and landscapes; we develop products and communication measures. We do not think in disciplines. We think in solutions. Solutions that help you become a purposeful part of a whole and yet distinctive in your own right. We architect your identity.

JGA

Email: info@jga.com

JGA has evolved to become one of the nation's leading retail design, brand strategy and architectural firms. Since 1971, JGA has built its reputation by helping retailers realize their visual marketing potential and attain leadership within their niche. JGA believes that bringing a creative idea into reality and achieving success requires the integration of strategic clarity, competitive and market awareness, conceptual innovation and a strong business sense.

As strategists and designers JGA's services are extensive. A team approach offers significant value over conventional firms. As part of the client's project team, JGA motivates the creative process of provoking ideas and solutions and facilitating the management process through strategic design, scheduling, budgets and implementation, resulting in increased consumer interaction and satisfaction.

JGA offers a diverse menu of services including market and design strategy, conceptual positioning, visual communication design and logo/brand identity, design and architectural development and implementation, retail tenant coordination, construction administration and fixturing/furniture and materials procurement.

As a company, JGA encourages a culture that empowers personal and professional growth to their fifty associates while providing expertise with the highest standard of service and design to our clients. Lead by chairman Kenneth Nisch, AIA, the firm has achieved success creating innovative and entertaining retail environments for a diverse roster of clients.

JGA's projects have been recognized by numerous design competitions and leading international publications, among them: The New York Times, USA Today, The Wall Street Journal, Chain Store Age, VMSD, Display & Design Ideas, Contract, Interiors and Sources and Women's Wear Daily. JGA recently published a book, 1,000 Retail Graphics, featuring global design solutions for in-store elements including signage, tags, ads, logos, and environments.

Jeffrey Hutchison & Associates

Email: info@jeffreyhutchison.com

Retail design is one of architecture's most demanding specialties. Every store, no matter how basic or elaborate, has to accommodate a diverse assortment of requirements: display space, dressing rooms, offices, storage, shipping and receiving, all the while romancing the merchandise and enticing the customer to make a purchase. It's a challenging task to be sure, multiplied tenfold when the client is a designer with a strong image. But for Jeffrey Hutchison - who has worked with such esteemed brands as Barneys New York, Donna Karan, Narciso Rodriguez, Ralph Lauren and over the course of his career - designing beautiful, functional stores is his professional calling.

"Retail architecture is equal parts creative expression and rational process," says Hutchinson. "That's a combination I've been drawn to all my life."

Since spring 2001, Jeffrey Hutchison & Associates has created the global retail image for the Theory stores, as well as numerous other projects worldwide for clients such as Barneys New York, Ann Taylor, Loewe, Nautica, Girbaud, Façonnable and many more.

Hutchison doesn't believe in forcing clients to adopt his personal vision, which is part of what makes him a success. As concerned as he is with the aesthetics of his projects, Hutchison is equally attuned to their function. "All of that plays into how successful the space will be. Design that's hand-in-hand with the company's philosophy and growth has a much greater chance of long-term success."

K1p3 Architects

Email: studio@k1p3architects.com

K1p3 Architects, established in 2000 by Karina Tollman, AA diploma, and Philipp Thomanek, AA diploma, is based in Tel Aviv, Israel. The studio has undertaken internationally projects in the commercial, cultural and residential sectors. As well as Art collaboration projects. K1p3 Architects provide full architectural, interior design and product and furniture design services. Since 2006 Karina Tollman also runs a design studio in 1st year studies at the Shenkar College of Engineering and Design.

KIDOSAKI ARCHITECTS STUDIO

Email: info@kidosaki.com

Hirotaka Kidosaki, Principal of the firm, worked for Kenzo Tange Associates for 13 years, and was a vice president during his later years there. After leaving the firm, he founded Architect Five with three other co-workers from Kenzo Tange Associates in 1993.

Kidosaki Architects Studio was established in 2000.

A number of our projects have been featured in Japanese architecture magazines, such as Global Architecture and Shin-Kenchiku. Moreover, several projects have been awarded prizes in the design field. Our Jakuseian project was granted Good Design Award in 2006. Essential aspects of our design work include having quality and dignity at the same time, creating architecture that matures as time passes and actualizing places where Japanese art, craft and architecture can meet and join together.

KAMITOPEN Architecture-Design Office Co., Ltd.

Email: yoshida@kamitopen.com

President MASAHIRO YOSHIDA

2007 Established KAMITOPEN Architecture-Design Office Co., Ltd.

2001 TAKARA SPACE DESIGN, Inc.

2001 Graduated from department of architecture, Kyoto Institute of Technology

1977 Born in Osaka, Japan

\>> AWARD

2010 JCD DESIGN AWARD2010"C-STYLE" Rookie of the year award

"NANA'S GREEN TEA KOBE" BEST100

"C's fort" BEST100

"Angelic" BEST100

The 16th CS DESIN AWARD

"C's fort" Excellent prize

The 14th SDA AWARD

"C's fort" Invitation judge prize

"NANA'S GREEN TEA KOBE" Selecting

"NANA'S GREEN TEA JIYUGAOKA" Selecting

"Angelic" Selecting

The 18th BEST STORE OF THE YEAR

"NANA'S GREEN TEA KOBE" Special prize

"NANA'S GREEN SHIKI" Excellent prize

2009 Town inside GOOD DESIGN AWARD 2009

"TIARA" SHOP DESIGN AWARD

JCD DESIGN AWARD2009

"PRODUCE NARUSE" BEST100

"NANA'S GREEN TEA URAWA" BEST100

DIPLAY Industrial prize2009

"TIARA" Selecting

The 13th SDA AWARD

"PRODUCE NARUSE" Selecting

"NANA'S GREEN TEA URAWA" Selecting

DDA AWARD 2009

"PRODUCE NARUSE" Selecting

"NANA'S GREEN TEA URAWA" Selecting

"NANAHA ODAKYU" Selecting

2008 AICA SHOP DESIGN AWARD

"PRODUCE NARUSE" Excellent prize

JCD DESIGN AWARD2008

"PRODUCA HASHIMOTO" Selecting

2007 Nashop Lighiting AWARD

"PRODUCA HASHIMOTO" Selecting

LOLA

Email: infi@lola-architecture.com

LOLA was created by Rute Brazão, Sandra Carito Ribeiro and Riccardo Cavaciocchi. The three partners, after work experiences at architecture firms in Holland, Italy and Spain opened their first base of work and research in 2002 in Barcelona (Spain), thein in Lecce (Italy) and Lisbon (Portugal). LOLA is a platform focused on multi-disciplinary architecture and contemporary design. It expresses itself through the production of spaces with a responsible approach to mass and life issues, the nature of places and their materiality as a form of organized and spontaneous expression. Collaboration and ongoing dialogue with studios and professionals from different areas enables LOLA to create a flexible and diverse background. LOLA, lays the foundations of critical, positive and pluralist thinking, followed by the development of projects in various sectors, from design to the interior, from the conversion and renovation of buildings to retail design in Spain, Italy, Portugal, Saudi Arabia, Brazil and USA.

MINKUS Architects

Email: mail@minkus.eu

After working in Vienna, Leipzig, London and Tokyo on a wide variety of projects (including a fit-out of the Onassis Theaters in Athens), the German-Japanese architects Felix and Noriko Minkus established Minkus Architects in 2009. While the work is deeply specific to persons and place, budget and constraints, our making of architecture aims for a poetic quality. The practice motivates all elements for a sensual experience, bringing them into dense relations and creating a meaningful space.

Miss Led

Email: mail@missled.co.uk

Award winning live painter and illustrator both in London and Europe, Joanna Henly is barely in her 2nd year of working under the guise of Miss Led. In this time she has managed to amass a lucrative body of work with a high profile clientele. From painting live, a window for Selfridges and large-scale illustration work for Reebok and Diesel to painting bespoke interior pieces for celebrities and Brompton Rd boutiques. Led has created her distinctively playful, flirtatious and diverse styles on many surfaces in a plethora of mediums. Her illustrations have been commissioned; her artwork featured and published in magazines and newspapers nationwide. With a string of group shows under her belt she plans for a solo exhibition next year.

Monki

Email: joel@joeldegermark.com

Electric Dreams is a Stockholm-based architecture/design studio formed by Joel Degermark and Catharina Frankander in 2006. Degermark is a product designer trained at the Royal College of Art, London, Beckmans School of Design, Stockholm, and Danmarks Designskole, Denmark. Frankander is an architect trained at the Architectural Association, London, Royal College of Fine Arts, Sweden, and Royal Institute of Technology, Sweden. We specialize in brand environments and products. Our designs are much about story-telling and themes, a fascination of playful exaggeration... We like things that are too colourful, too weird, too beautiful, too dark, too many... Our design becomes surreal because it is a lot about shifting scales, bringing two familiar things together to create the unfamiliar, and playing with visual effects.

Moomoo architects

Email: info@moomoo.pl

Founded in 2008 by Jakub Majewski and Lukasz Pastuszka. In 2009 Wallpaper Magazine selected MOOMOO as one of the best 30 young offices in the world. Our works has been previously shown on exhibitions in London, Shanghai, Rotterdam and Brussels.*

Norm Architects

Email: info@normcph.com

NORM is a multidisciplinary design studio focusing on residential architecture, commercial interiors and industrial design. NORM was founded in 2008 by architects Kasper Rønn and Jonas Bjerre-Poulsen by their vocation to create timeless architecture and meaningful design products.

ONG&ONG Pte Ltd

Email: info@ong-ong.com

ONG&ONG offers a complete 360º solution – i.e. a parceled cross-discipline integrated solution, encompassing all aspects of the construction business. This three-pronged solution encompasses design (architecture, urban planning, landscape, graphics and interior design), engineering (civil, structural, electrical and mechanical) and management (development, project, construction and place). We are an ISO14001 certified practice with offices in Singapore, China, Vietnam, India, Malaysia and the USA. In-depth knowledge of the local context, culture and regulations allow us to better understand our clients' needs to enable us to meet and exceed their expectations.

Plajer & Franz Studio

Email: studio@plajer-franz.de

Plajer & Franz studio is an international and interdisciplinary team of 45 architects, interior architects and graphic designers based in Berlin. All project stages – from concept to design as well as roll-out supervision – are carried out in-house. Special project-based teams work on overall interior and building construction projects and on communication and graphic design.
The company's client list includes galeries lafayette, s.oliver, bmw, mini, timberland, pierre cardin, kunert, hudson, burlington and salewa. Plajer & Franz studio has also established itself in the premium sector of luxury residential projects and hotels in both Europe and Asia; these include a recently completed hotel in Porto, a five star resort in Croatia and 50,000 sqm premium apartments on the portuguese coast, both in development. several other major projects, for example luxurious villas in Thailand and Kazakhstan are also currently in the design phase.

Pierluigi Piu

Email: info@pierluigipiu.it

Pierluigi Piu was born in Cagliari (Sardinia, Italy) in 1954. He later pursued his studies at the University of Architecture in Florence, in which city he lived until 1989. Here he also establishes and carries out - between 1982 and 1985 – the design practice and production company "Atelier Proconsolo", under the auspices of which he participates in various exhibitions and trade fairs, both in Italy and abroad. Since 1985 he works as an associate consultant (for Product and Interiors Design) at the firm ACME Consultants (Association pour la Création et les Méthodes d'Evolution), based in Paris, taking part in the development of products for firms such as Gaz de France, Essilor (a leader in the world of spectacles), Fiat-Iveco and Paris Airports, amongst others. In 1990 there followed a collaboration with the Belgian architect Pierre Lallemand, at his architectural practice "Art & Build" in Bruxelles. In the course of 1991 he carried out, under his own auspices, his first assignments in England, before returning to Cagliari , his birthplace, where he opened his own office and began working in the field of interior design and architecture. In 1995 he undertook a new project in London. Then, from 1996 until 1998, he was back in Bruxelles, where he had been summoned by the architect Steven Beckers to collaborate on a project for the reconstruction and refurbishment of the Berlaymont Palace, the historic seat of the Council of Ministers of the European Community, and so undertook - working together with a specially formed international equipe - the supervision and coordination of the aesthetic and formal language for the interior design of the entire building. In 2006/2007 he carried out the design of two new commercial projects in London, for which he was assigned the "Russian International Architectural Award 2007" in Moscow, the "International Design Award 2008" in Los Angeles and the "Archi-Bau Design Award 2009" in Munich, Germany. Since 2009 he is one of professional commentators of the British dedicated web site restaurantandbardesign. com and is a member of Italian "Accademia del

Pensiero a Colori". Mainly based and working in Cagliari, he continues his professional career most particularly in the fields of private residences and of commercial space as well as working on overseas projects. His designs and works have been reported in several specialist books in Italy, Europe, Asia and the United States and in some of the most important national and international trade magazines.

Ruscio Studio Inc.

Email: info@rusciostudio.com

Ruscio Studio Inc. now in its 8th year, and as a result of much hard work and dedication to his clients, Robert has successfully grown his interior retail design firm to one that is recognized both nationally and internationally by retailers and malls alike.

reMiks

Email: maja@remiks.eu

reMiks is a Belgrade based design studio providing service in the field of design (interior, architecture, graphic/web, package an dindustrial) as well as branding.
reMiks together with its sister organization Mikser is one of the organizers of Belgrade Design Week and many design promotions (Rem Koolhaas, Karim Rashid, Mirko Ilic...)
Clients are from Serbia, US, Japan, Sweden Spain...

Rajmund rajchel

Email: rajmund_r@go2.pl

I graduated from The Department of Graphic Design on Academy of Fine Arts in Warsaw. I have been writing my diploma in Graphics Publishing Workshop under professor Lech Majewski guidance, annex from photography in Photography Workshop under professor Rosław Szaybo guidance.

I'm interested in the broad sense of graphic design and photography.

My works was presenting on exhibitions like: Galeria Obok ZPAF, Warsaw (2010), The 7th International Poster Triennial in Toyama (2003), 18th International Poster Biennale, Warsaw (2002), Galerie Anatome, Paris (2001).

My works was published in Gazeta Wyborcza, Przekrój and Polish Design Quarterly 2+3D as well.

As a designer I was cooperating with: Nordea Polska, TVP, Commercial Union, Centertel, Gutek Film, Polish Association for Persons with Mental Handicap and Galeria Obok ZPAF.

Nowadays I'm employed as a designer in architectural company Kuryłowicz & Associates Sp. z o. o., where I see about public image of that company.

Last time my project „ANTONIONI DVD box" has got Grand Prix in the contest for the best packaging of the year - ART OF PACKAGING 2009 and bronze medal in the contest European Design Awards in the category CD/DVD packaging.

Rafael de Cárdenas

Email: enquiry@architectureatlarge.com

Rafael de Cárdenas received his B.A. from The Rhode Island School of Design and, following graduation, took a job at Calvin Klein, working for three years as a designer for the men's collection. In 1999, he began pursuing an architecture degree at Columbia University, later transferring to UCLA where he received his Masters in architecture in 2002. His first project following graduation was working with the architect Greg Lynn on the redesign of the World Trade Center site. Their submission, a series of five buildings interconnected to create a cathedral-like space, was one of the six final entries. De Cárdenas then began work in the New York offices of special effects production house Imaginary Forces. As a creative director working on experience design projects, he oversaw a range of innovative concepts including the BMW Experience at their headquarters in Munich, and the HBO store in New York. In 2005, de Cárdenas opened his own design firm out of an office in New York's Chinatown. His interest in creating environments with moods, as opposed to any specific style, has allowed him to work with an array of clients. Using color, light, and pattern, de Cárdenas has created artful, imaginative interiors for boutiques, restaurants and private residences in London, Rome, Athens, Chicago, Miami, New York, and The Hamptons.

Romi Khosla Design Studios

Email: admin@rk-ds.com

Romi Khosla Design Studios is a Lead consultancy led by architects Romi Khosla and Martand Khosla. Both graduated at the Architectural Association, U.K. They are well known international consultants on Urban Planning, Tourism planning and Educational issues.

Their Design Studio engages in creative contemporary designs ranging from large Industrial projects to small interiors. It was formed to combine the lifetime international experience of Romi Khosla and the contemporary design initiatives of younger designers who have excelled. Amongst their varied projects are the 600 acre SEZ for Suzlon in Udupi, National Gallery of Modern Art, Bombay, the School for Spastic children in New Delhi, the Corporate Office of United Breweries in Bangalore, the 200 acre campus of the Assam valley School as well as a number of recreation buildings, including the Luxury Merridian Golf Resort and Spa in Kathmandu. Current work includes the Eicher-Volvo Head Quarters in Gurgaon, the Indian Embassy in Uzbekistan, and Apeejay Corporate office in Kolkata.

RKDS is the winner of Five World Architecture Awards. One of the best buildings of the 21st century has been designed by RKDS, as judged and published by Phaidon in the United Kingdom. Over the last 4 years, RKDS works have appeared in nearly 30 International Publications and Several National Publications. In 2010, RKDS came first in the International design competition "Reclaiming the streets" in Rotterdam, the Netherlands.

Rockwell group

With a desire to create immersive environments, Rockwell Group takes a cross-disciplinary approach to its inventive array of projects. Based in downtown New York with a satellite office in Madrid, our innovative, internationally acclaimed architecture and design firm specialized in hospitality, cultural, healthcare, educational, product, theater and film design. Crafting a unique and individual narrative concept for each project is fundamental to Rockwell Group's successful design approach. From the big picture to the last detail, the story informs and drives the design. The seamless synergy of technology, craftsmanship and design is reflected in environments that combine high-end video technology, handmade objects, special effects and custom fixtures and furniture.

SAKO Architects

Email: info@sako.co.jp

2004 to 2005 Visiting Scholar at Columbia University.

2004 to 2005 Overseas artist dispatched by Agency for Cultural Affairs.

2004 to 2002 Established SAKO Architects.

2004 to 2005 Jointly presided over Asian Architects Associates.

1996 to 2004 Worked with Riken Yamamoto & Field Shop.

1996 to 2002 Obtained a Masters Degree from the Tokyo Institute of Technology.

1994 to 2002 Graduated from Tokyo Institute of Technology.

1970 to 2002 Born in Fukuoka, Japan.

Sergio Mannino Studio

Email: info@sergiomannino.com

Sergio Mannino Studio is located in Brooklyn's progressive art community of DUMBO. It is a collection of forward thinking architects, graphic/interior/product designers, who bring disparate ideas and materials together to create bi- and tri-dimensional projects that delight, enlighten and inspire.

The Studio has several years of experience in the retail and design industry and can provide services from brand strategy and identity to interior design, graphic and architecture. Through an extensive close network of consultants and partners, projects can be taken from preliminary brainstorming to built form virtually anywhere around the world.

This team has worked on several commercial and residential projects for renowned companies such as Vince Camuto, Jessica Simpson, Miss Sixty, Energie, Kensiegirl, Morellato, Breil and several others.

Sergio Mannino graduated in Architecture in Florence, Italy with a thesis developed under the direction of Ettore Sottsass Jr in 1999. In the same year he registered in Italy as a licensed Architect. In 2002 he presented "100 Storie", his first furniture show at the internationally acclaimed Memphis-Postdesign Gallery in Milan. The exhibition, developed again under Sottsass' guidance, consisted in 100 watercolors and 9 limited edition pieces.

A collaboration with Dutch designer Jan Habraken has produced the ooo! Lamp, presented in 2008 and awarded product of the week by I.D. Magazine and best pick of the ICFF by Metropolis.

Serie Architects

Email: info@serie.co.uk

Serie Architects is an international practice based in London, Mumbai and Beijing. Serie works in the diverse field of architecture, urbanism and design.

The practice is fascinated by the evolution and mutation of building types in today's cities and the projection of these forms of intelligence into spatial solutions. Working typologically, or in our terms, thinking and exploring in series - harnessing the cumulative intelligence of building types - is key to the work of Serie.

The practice consistently pushes the boundaries of architectural and masterplanning projects worldwide and provides full architecture and masterplanning services for private and public sectors.

The work of our practice is closely linked to the research conducted in the renowned Architectural Association School of Architecture, London where the practice's principle, Christopher Lee holds the position of Diploma Unit Master since 2002.

He is also a visiting critic to various universities including the Berlage Institute, University College London and Cambridge University.

Kapil Gupta, principal of Serie India, is also director at the Urban Design Research Institute in Mumbai, which is leading several research projects on the City.

Studio metrico

Email: mail@studiometrico.com

Studiometrico was born in Milan in 2004 from the collaboration between Lorenzo Bini and Francesca Murialdo and is the place where some people conceive and develop architectural projects and researches on interior and outdoor spaces, on both existing buildings and new constructions. The practice works for private clients in Milan, in Italy and abroad, designing, transforming and building places for living, working and traveling. Studiometrico's roots are in Milan, but its branches are articulated and scattered over an international network of collaborations, links and physical places.

Studiounodesign

Email: giemoney@hotmail.com

Uno Design Studio is a professional Web design company based in Manila, Philippines. We specialize in best-in-class custom wordpress design, Flash multimedia, corporate identity and print graphics. Uno Design Studio features an integrated team of web consultants, creative designers, writers, programmers and SEO.

Our business-driven approach differentiates us from typical web design companies. For the past few years we have built up an outstanding reputation for creating a positive return on investment for our clients. If you are serious about your web design success, just tell us, we can get you there.

If you are looking for strategic thinking, high quality designers, supports, competitive prices, company success – We can take you there.

Sybarite-Tara Robertson

Email: studio@syb.co.uk

Sybarite is an architecture and design practice drawing its passion and inspiration from organic forms in nature as well we technologies transferred from other industries, creating a distinctive style both fluid and timeless. The word "Sybarite" encapsulates the philosophy—voluptuous, luxurious and pleasurable.

The practice has a large portfolio of completed work, having executed over 300 projects in diverse locations worldwide since forming in 2002. We have a growing reputation as experts in the field of retail architecture, from one-off destination boutiques to large department stores, and focus on service has ensured that much of our work comes from repeat clients.

At the same time, we are strive to continually innovate and experiment with design and materials. Striking a balance between realized and conceptual projects have been crucial in keeping us at the top of our game.

As a chartered RIBA practice, Sybarite has a wealth of expertise in construction and a demonstrated ability to deliver both local and international projects. With 95% of our clients based outside of the UK, we have extensive experience putting together teams in a multitude of locations worldwide.

Snarkitecture

Email: info@snarkitecture.com

Snarkitecture is a collaborative practice between an artist and an architect. Rather than make buildings, the interest of Snarkitecture lies in working on designs within existing spaces or collaborating with other architects and artists on existing projects. The firm's work involves investigation of the structure and materials within a space and how they might be manipulated in order to serve new and imaginative purposes. Searching for sites within architecture with a possibility for confusion or misuse, Snarkitecture aims to reconfigure these existing elements to make architecture do things that it is not supposed to do.

Snarkitecture was established by Daniel Arsham and Alex Mustonen.

Slade architecture

Email: info@sladearch.com

SLADE ARCHITECTURE is a New York City based architecture and design firm founded in 2002 by James and Hayes Slade. The firm has completed a diverse range of domestic and international projects. Their work has been exhibited and published widely in over 200 publications. The Architecture League of New York selected Slade Architecture for the 2010 Emerging Voices Lecture Series held in the New Museum.

Among Slade Architecture's awards are a national AIA Small Projects Award, multiple NY AIA Merit Awards, Association of Retail Environments Store of the Year Award, Chain Store Age Best in Show Award, Fast Company Masters of Design issue, multiple Best of Year awards from Interior Design Magazine, Contract Magazine and Businessweek/Architectural Record. Slade Architecture's work has been exhibited at the AIA Center for Architecture in New York, the Venice Biennale, Florida International University, the German Architecture Museum in Frankfurt and many other exhibits in Europe, Asia and the United States.